Colección Támesis

SERIE A: MONOGRAFÍAS, 182

PLAYING THE KING

LOPE DE VEGA AND THE LIMITS OF CONFORMITY

MELVEENA McKENDRICK

PLAYING THE KING

LOPE DE VEGA AND THE LIMITS OF CONFORMITY

TAMESIS

First published 2000 by Tamesis, London

ISBN 1 85566 069 5

Tamesis is an imprint of Boydell & Brewer Ltd
PO Box 9, Woodbridge, Suffolk IP12 3DF, UK
and of Boydell & Brewer Inc.
PO Box 41026, Rochester, NY 14604–4126, USA
website: http://www.boydell.co.uk

A catalogue record for this book is available
from the British Library

Library of Congress Cataloging-in-Publication Data
McKendrick, Melveena.
Playing the king: Lope de Vega and the limits of conformity / Melveena McKendrick.
p. cm. – (Colección Támesis. Serie A, Monografías : 182)
Includes biographical references and index.
ISBN 1–85566–069–5 (alk. paper)
1. Vega, Lope de, 1562–1635 – Criticism and interpretation. 2. Monarchy in literature. 3. Politics in literature. 4. Politics and literature – Spain. I. Title.
PQ6490.H5M3 2000
862'.3 – dc21 99–41910

This publication is printed on acid-free paper

Printed in Great Britain by
Antony Rowe Ltd, Chippenham, Wiltshire

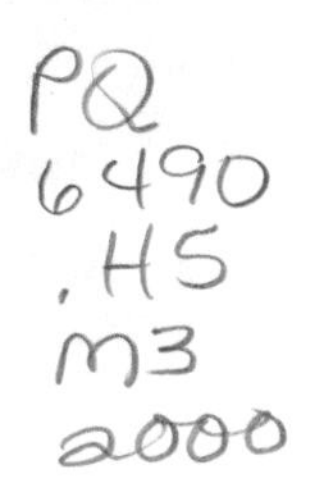

CONTENTS

For Neil

ACKNOWLEDGEMENTS

This book has been a long time in the making. I have been reading, teaching and writing about Lope and the *comedia* all my professional life and I realized from fairly early on that I would at some stage have to write this book or something very much like it. What was at first conceived as a chapter in the book mushroomed into the book itself as the sheer scope and weight of an engagement with Renaissance kingship struck home. A major part of the research was made possible by a two-year British Academy Readership in 1990–92, for which I am extremely grateful, although I have in part paid my dues since then by serving for two years on the British Academy's Humanities Research Board and a further year with the Arts and Humanities Research Board. Along with a major, four-year exercise in civic virtue within my own university, this commitment contributed to the book's delayed completion. In the event the delay turned to advantage, as I ended up travelling in productive directions I had not at all envisaged when I first set out. Along the way earlier versions of several chapters were given as papers or lectures in places as widespread as London, Warwick, Columbia Missouri and Victoria BC, and benefited from the helpful comments of colleagues, including Henry Sullivan, Peter Dunn and the late Louise Fothergill-Payne, who listened to what I had to say. At a later stage Frederick de Armas and Henry Sullivan had occasion to read the complete text and I am very conscious of the value of their suggestions. The enterprise in its entirety has gained from the wisdom and scholarship of Robert Pring-Mill and the late John Varey, to whom I owe a great debt of gratitude for their generous interest and support. My greatest indebtness is as usual to Neil McKendrick, who read every draft, subjected the argument to a professional historian's rigorous scrutiny, and never for a moment doubted that I was engaged in an enterprise of major importance. Needless to say, the book's shortcomings are all my own.

Los reyes son como nieve,
que, tratados, se deshacen.
Para ser mirados nacen:
nadie a tocarlos se atreve.
Conservar esta blancura
conviene a la majestad.

El Duque de Viseo, Act I

1

RECONSIDERATIONS

Since the publication in the 1970s of two influential works on the seventeenth-century Spanish theatre by first J.A. Maravall and then J.Mª Díez Borque,[1] it has become received wisdom amongst Spanish historians and theatre critics that the seventeenth-century Spanish theatre was an instrument of state and that its playwrights were the conscious propagandists of an aristocratic élite,[2] a view that has much in common with the Foucault-inspired argument of New Historicists that Renaissance theatre in general represented an extension of authority.[3] And the orthodoxy has spread: the author of an edition of one of Lope de Vega's saints' plays, published in the late 1980s, takes it for granted that the role of *all* the arts in seventeenth-century Spain was to reassure and reinforce the people's traditional view of their social and religious structures.[4] Such a claim scarcely seems tenable in the light of much seventeenth-century Spanish verse and of recent work on the picaresque novel – but the view that that opiate of the seventeenth-century Spanish masses, the theatre, flourished because it gave the authorities and the public no more and no less than they wanted may seem a more acceptable proposition. Such a view, however, overlooks the fact that the Spanish drama of the day had a dual, not a single, identity: it was indeed a national institution, but it was also the artistic expression of the vision of individual playwrights. To come to terms with it, we must remember that it was the servant of many masters – theatre directors, actors, conditions in the playhouses, moralists, literary theorists, censors, municipal and central authorities, and, by no means least, its own public. The *corral* was a micro-

1 J.A. Maravall, *Teatro y literatura en la sociedad barroca* (Madrid: Benzal, 1972), particularly 105–35; J.Mª Díez Borque, *Sociología de la comedia española del siglo XVII* (Madrid: Cátedra, 1976), 163–80.

2 Outside Spain there have been a few sporadic attempts to question this view, for example Charlotte Stern, 'Lope de Vega Propagandist?' *Bulletin of the Comediantes* 34, I (1982), 1–36.

3 See Walter Cohen, 'Political Criticism of Shakespeare', in *Shakespeare Reproduced: The Text in History and Ideology*, ed. Jean E. Howard and Marion F. O'Connor (London: Methuen, 1987), 18–46.

4 Diego Bastianutti, *La niñez del Padre Rojas: By Lope de Vega*, American University Studies. Series II: Romance Languages and Literature 54 (New York/Bern/Frankfurt am Main/Paris: Peter Lang, 1988), 66.

cosm of the society that produced it, its audience encompassing a social and economic range from labourers, tradesmen and artisans, through young bucks, scribes, academics, priests, prelates and nobles, to the king himself. A significant proportion of the audience was female. It necessarily worked, therefore, at more than one level, and the result was a highly popular, commercial theatre which succeeded in becoming, at its best, great art. It achieved this extraordinary fusion only by being a triumph of accommodation, a balance of external pressures and artistic conscience made possible by the production of richly nuanced texts. The true identity of a play obviously lies not in the plot alone but in the inter-relationship of plot, characters and language, of text, context and subtext. And close reading of the Spanish plays themselves suggests not an ideologically monolithic and complacent drama, but one which is multivalent and which potentiates ambiguities and subversive readings. E.M.W. Tillyard's enormously influential *The Elizabethan World Picture*,[5] that picture into which much thinking about the Spanish drama has been so snugly fitted, is now seen by cultural historians to offer only a very partial picture of a world that was in fact ideologically very layered and complex, ignoring the differences and divisions that moved beneath the set of beliefs and assumptions that held quasi-official sway during the sixteenth century.[6] In reality in the late sixteenth and early seventeenth centuries, in Lawrence Stone's blunt words, 'The almost hysterical demand for order at all costs was caused by a collapse of most of the props of the medieval world picture.'[7] The legacy can be seen in the drama of Calderón, where the intense need for patterns of order and meaning reflected structurally and linguistically in Calderón's highly stylized dramatic discourse is in fact generated by a cosmic vision composed of patterns of chaos and disruption. Keith Thomas's *Religion and the Decline of Magic* reveals that in Early Modern Europe the props and patterns of the medieval world not only toppled under pressure from new discoveries and ways of thinking but were anyway still hedged around by older, less orthodox practices and affiliations.[8] In Spain's traditionally multi-racial society, cultural difference, for all the measures taken to annihilate it, was not obliterated overnight or instantly assimilated into an officially Catholic-Christian state. Neither of course were the heterodox beliefs of Spain's sixteenth-century Erasmians and dissenters. Superficially, the Inquisition, instituted to deal with difference, with that per-

[5] London: Chatto and Windus, 1943.

[6] For a discussion of the layered nature of culture see Raymond Williams, *Marxism and Literature* (Oxford: Oxford University Press, 1977), 121–27. An application of this idea to the Early Modern period may be found in *Political Shakespeare: Essays in Cultural Materialism*, ed. Jonathan Dollimore and Alan Sinfield (Manchester: Manchester University Press, 1994; first edition 1985), 6.

[7] *The Family, Sex and Marriage in England, 1500–1800* (London: Weidenfeld and Nicolson, 1977), 653.

[8] London: Weidenfeld and Nicolson, 1971.

ceived to be alien and therefore dangerous, did its work and did it extremely effectively, but the official uniformity it imposed rested upon an experience of diversity that could only have been slow to dissolve. Henry Kamen has disputed the view that sixteenth-century Spain was a monolithic society, and has identified a number of elements of dissent present in Spanish society. He argues that

> the excesses of the time were always, within Spain, opposed by a body of opinion so substantial and influential that we must reckon it to be not a negligible movement but a major alternative tradition – not necessarily 'liberal' but simply alternative – that was no less representative of the Spanish attitude of mind than the persecuting mentality which frequently prevailed (4),[9]

and he concludes that the presumption that Spain was a wholly conformist society is difficult to sustain seriously (22). His judgement is that Spain at the time, while neither a radical nor a liberal society, has to be seen as a society of conservative dissent. It was the very real spectre of difference and dissent, religious and secular, that made the desire for orthodoxy, political, social and religious, so pressing in authoritarian seventeenth-century societies. The health, indeed the very life, of the state was seen to depend on the compliance and order generated by the convenient certainties, hierarchical and patriarchal in nature, with which every aspect of public and private life, superficially at least, was clothed. There was certainly little room in this vision for the troublesome individuality which Jacob Burckhardt identified as being a major outcome of Renaissance thinking.

J.H. Elliott, however, has warned against the tendency to overestimate the passivity of seventeenth-century societies, including Spain, and to exaggerate the capacity of those in authority to manipulate those societies for their own ideological ends.[10] He points out that the most recent historical writing 'has been less impressed by the effectiveness of monarchical power in Early Modern Europe than by its limitations'.[11] The views on tyrannicide propounded in 1599 by the Jesuit political philosopher and historian Juan de Mariana (which were censored) and those on the equitable distribution of wealth published in 1627 by the magistrate and political theorist Mateo López Bravo (which were not censored) show that there were independent

9 'Toleration and Dissent in Sixteenth-Century Spain: The Alternative Tradition', *Crisis and Change in Early Modern Spain* (Aldershot: Variorum, 1993), first published in *The Sixteenth-Century Journal* 19 (Spring 1988), 3–23.

10 In his review of J.A. Maravall's *The Culture of the Baroque*, *New York Review of Books*, 9 April, 1987. Maravall's writings, of course, have been largely responsible for the view of the Golden-Age theatre as the willing instrument of a monolithic orthodoxy.

11 'Power and Propaganda in the Spain of Philip IV', *Spain and its World 1500–1700* (New Haven / London: Yale University Press, 1989), 162–88, p.162.

minds in late sixteenth- and seventeenth-century Spain.[12] And the covert assimilation of Machiavellian theory, albeit in somewhat modified form, in the forty-five years between Rivadeneyra's fiercely anti-Machiavellian tract of 1595, *Tratado del príncipe cristiano*, and the *aprobación* written by Fray Pedro de Cuenca y Cárdenas for Saavedra Fajardo's *Idea de un príncipe político-cristiano* of 1640, which praises the erudition with which 'la razón de estado se adorna' in the treatise, is a vivid indication that even in Spain entrenched thinking moved on; indeed the difference in the very titles of the two works says it all. One has only to read Elliott's monumental work on the Count-Duke of Olivares,[13] or Ruth Lee Kennedy's book on relations between Tirso de Molina and his contemporaries in the 1620s,[14] to realise that the view that the Spanish establishment, let alone the whole of Spanish society, thought with one mind and spoke with one voice is patently absurd. The large body of political satire produced during the seventeenth century, particularly during the reigns of Philip IV and Charles II, is evidence of severe disaffection with the government and the Crown, even amongst the nobility.[15] The huge body of hard-hitting comment on and analysis of Spain's economic problems is evidence of widespread and very vocal concern with the way the country was being governed; Quevedo's hatred of *arbitristas* (or 'projectors' as their equivalents in England were called) was aroused largely by the nuisance value of these devisers of expedients, sometimes serious and intelligent, sometimes eccentric and impractical, devised to cope with the nation's ills. Controversy over contemporary issues did not come to an end in Spain with the Counter-Reformation as is sometimes the impression given. On the contrary, debate of a wide range of social, political, economic and literary concerns – the state of Spain, kingship, absolutism, Machiavellianism, Tacitism, reason of state, rule by favourite, racial purity, social mobility, honour, the social and professional standing of painting, the rival merits of popular and classicizing literary traditions, the legitimacy of the theatre, over which the Church itself was divided, to name but a handful – was extremely

[12] For a convenient survey of Spanish thinkers and theorists during this period, see José Luis Abellán, *Historia crítica del pensamiento español*, vol.2, *La Edad de Oro (Siglo XVI)*, and vol.3, *Del Barroco a la Ilustración (Siglos XVII y XVIII)* (Madrid: Espasa-Calpe, 1979 and 1988).

[13] *The Count-Duke of Olivares: The Statesman in an Age of Decline* (New Haven / London: Yale University Press, 1986).

[14] *Studies in Tirso de Molina I. The Dramatist and His Competitors 1620–26* (Chapel Hill: North Carolina Studies in the Romance Languages and Literatures, U.N.C. Department of Romance Languages, 1974); see also her 'La perspectiva política de Tirso en *Provar contra su gusto* y la de sus comedias posteriores', *Homenaje a Tirso* (Madrid: Revista Estudios, 1981), 199–238.

[15] See Teófanes Egido, *Sátiras políticas de la España moderna* (Madrid: Alianza Editorial, 1973); and Mercedes Etreros, *La sátira política en el siglo XV* (Madrid: Fundación Universitaria Española, 1983).

lively, often heated, in this so-called monolithic society. Even the possibility of religious freedom within the state was given an airing. To read through the arguments for and against the theatre collected together in Cotarelo y Mori's *Bibliografía de las controversias sobre la licitud del teatro en España*[16] is to be impressed by the number of eminently reasonable, tolerant ecclesiastics and professional men prepared to make themselves heard. And we can be fairly sure that what some were writing for public consumption on all these issues many were saying in the confines of social and professional gatherings, and many more were thinking in the privacy of their own consciences. López Bravo's analysis of the connection between poverty, absentee landlords and rural depopulation only articulated what thousands of Spaniards observed and experienced:

> La abundancia de uno sume a muchos en la miseria y la opulencia de unos pocos supone calamidades para la masa. La consecuencia es o la sedición o la despoblación. Es muy nociva la miseria derivada de la mala distribución de las riquezas: el poder, la desvergüenza y la haraganería por parte de los que tienen, y la miseria, la servidumbre y la desesperación para los que nada tienen. El resultado (como ya he dicho) es la sedición o el abandono de los pueblos, tanto por estar los bienes en manos de unos pocos como por el hecho de que tanto los que tienen como los que no tienen abandonan los pueblos y aldeas dirigiéndose bien pronto a la ciudad adonde confluyen todos los bienes y males; éstos como seguidores y criados, aquéllos para poder entregarse con mayor desenfreno al lujo y al placer.[17]

To claim that the theatre as a whole, not just the court theatre, was directly harnessed to the purposes of government and class is seriously to underestimate the complexity of the relationship between the Spanish theatre of the day and the society that produced it.[18] It seems to be based on two very dubious assumptions. First, it implies, in Marxist vein, that Spanish society at large did not share the social and cultural values of its masters and had to be persuaded to do so. What the evidence in fact points to is considerable diver-

16 Madrid: Revista de Archivos, Bibliotecas y Museos, 1904, reissued 1933.

17 *De rege et regendi ratione*, from the translation by Antonio Pérez Rodríguez, *Del rey y de la raçón de governar*, in Henry Mechoulan, *Mateo López Bravo: Un socialista español del siglo XVII* (Madrid: Editora Nacional, 1977), 285–86. The first two parts of López Bravo's treatise, *Del rey* and *De la raçón de governar*, were published in 1616; the promised third section, *Del arte de gobernar o Sobre la abundancia de bienes*, appeared in the second edition of 1627.

18 J. Leeds Barroll has similarly argued that there is no historical justification whatsoever for the attempt of New Historicists to implicate the English theatre wholesale in the policies and theories of the reign of James I. See 'A New History for Shakespeare and his Time', *Shakespeare Quarterly* 39 (1988), 441–64. The same line is taken by Brian Vickers, *Appropriating Shakespeare: Contemporary Critical Quarrels* (New Haven / London: Yale University Press, 1993).

sity within a broad pattern of agreement concerning those matters accorded the highest claim on people's loyalty and obedience – faith, king and country – despite the fact that two of those were not above serious criticism and concern. Seventeenth-century Spaniards could harbour doubts about a king's ability to rule without wavering in their commitment to monarchy, which was for contemporary Spanish theorists the logical and most effective form of government in the face of the mutability that characterized all human existence. For all the existence of subordinate and marginal cultures and for all the ample range of opinion that existed, the values within the dominant culture outwardly admired and aspired to by Spaniards as a whole were to a large extent and through a process of percolation the values of Spain's élite.[19] Such a generalization necessarily comes couched in unspoken qualifications: the values of a swineherd in remote Extremadura, of a mercury miner in Almadén, and of an urban Castilian gentleman would not have been identical. But in so far as any society can be said to share a common culture, that of seventeenth-century Spain enshrined the values of the upper classes. This was particularly true of the capital, characterized as it was by its dependence on the court and its obsession with social status and advancement. The theatre's immense popularity was due precisely to the fact that, at the level of plot and stage business at least, it was a product of the collective will. It gave its very varied audience exactly what it wanted to see. It certainly was not feeding it an uncongenial diet composed of alien values, although it almost equally certainly played a part in the consolidation, even the propagation in one or two cases, of familiar values. Seventeenth-century attitudes to honour, for example, were undoubtedly influenced, positively and negatively, by dramatic formulations of honour's thornier problems.[20] But what was at work here was a spontaneous symbiosis between theatre and audience – all literature feeds off and nourishes, reflects and affects, simultaneously – not a conscious attempt to indoctrinate. It was a process of natural propagation, not propaganda, and this is a vital distinction which has to be made.

Secondly, to present the theatre as an instrument of government assumes – or at least one assumes it assumes, for the process by which the influence of the theatre is supposed to have been officially harnessed is never identified – that a systematized, organized or at least concerted campaign to promote particular ideas or practices could be achieved and sustained for almost a century

[19] Cf. Louis Dumont's general analysis of social and cultural patterns in *Homo hierarchicus: The Caste System and its Implications*, translated from the French by Mark Sainsbury, Louis Dumont and Basia Gulati (Chicago: University of Chicago Press, 1980).

[20] The theatre was also fully capable of ruthlessly sending up its own themes and conventions, including honour and Spain's national heroes, historical and legendary. See Salvador Crespo de Matellán, *La parodia dramática en la literatura española* (Salamanca: Ediciones Universidad de Salamanca, 1979), where reference is made, for example, to a play (author unknown) titled *No hay vida como la honra o No hay vida como la olla* (33).

in a theatre of prodigious size, fed by a succession of playwrights of very different temperaments, interests and backgrounds. This is just not credible; the concept of state propaganda as elaborated by twentieth-century repressive régimes is simply not applicable to any seventeenth-century society. Alfredo Hermenegildo has categorically stated that 'Lope de Vega, poniendo su arte al servicio de la ideología dominante, consiguió un público. Y en este momento el Estado se apoderó de la máquina teatral y llevó a cabo una auténtica nacionalización de tan eficaz medio de propaganda del sistema vigente.'[21] What, one wonders, are such claims actually supposed to mean in practical terms? They hardly square with the Consejo de Castilla's perpetual readiness to introduce legislation to inhibit the theatre's activities, or even to close the theatres down, whenever the anti-theatre lobby pressed hard enough. The pressures which allowed the theatre to survive, since it helped fund municipal charities, were predominantly financial, not political; when a minority resolution of the Consejo de Castilla did adduce a political argument in 1648 for its recommendation that the theatres should be reopened after four years' closure, it was the very practical one that far from promoting public order and improving public morals, the closures had deprived Spaniards of a favourite form of recreation and had actually promoted anti-government feeling: 'No se han visto en muchos años tales conmociones y inquietudes de pueblo; horror a los ministros, que antes solían ser respetados, y tenidos porque entienden que por su consejo se les prohibe un solo entretenimiento que hallaron introducido desde que nacieron, a que favorece la costumbre tan antigua.'[22] Even so the majority, in another resolution, argued strongly against reinstatement, and the king in the face of the disagreement took no official action – although a blind eye was increasingly turned in the next two years to the performances that that inaction encouraged.

There can be no doubt that the theatre's opponents saw it as being the very reverse of an arm of the establishment. P. Ignacio de Camargo, writing in 1689 after a century of theatrical activity, in his *Discurso theológico sobre los theatros y comedias deste siglo* expressed the views of moralists throughout the entire period that the *comedia* reviled traditional values:

> El descaro y disolución de un mozo escandaloso y perdido es ardimiento noble de la sangre, y la compostura y modestia pusilanimidad reprehensible. La temeridad es valor, y cobardía la prudencia. El duelo, el punto, el desafío, la defensa del pundonor mundano, la estimación de la honra vana sobre el alma y sobre Dios, el desprecio de la vida y de los riesgos, el andar

21 'Cristóbal de Virués y los signos teatrales del horror', *Horror y Tragedia en el Teatro del Siglo de Oro, Actas del IV Coloquio G.E.S.T.E., Toulouse 1983*, *Criticón*, 23 (1983), 93.

22 Cotarelo, *Controversias*, 166.

siempre con la espada en la mano vengando los pensamientos mismos, es el crédito y distintivo de la nobleza, y todo lo contrario a esto es la vileza.[23]

It is obvious from this typical ecclesiastical denunciation of the theatre for exploiting the conventions of honour (one establishment value) at the expense of Christian values (another establishment value) that, far from setting out to provide propaganda for all major aspects of some official *status quo*, as Maravall and Díez Borque maintain, the theatre obeyed its own imperatives. These imperatives were variously inscribed or imposed by the culture of which the theatre was an integral part, a culture which itself embraced and tolerated such contradictions – even in seventeenth-century Spain secular and religious values could be uneasy bedfellows. The trouble with the establishment-propaganda theory is that it is extremely difficult to locate either in seventeenth-century Spain or in seventeenth-century Spanish drama a monolithic set of entirely complementary establishment values – within the immovable boundaries of Catholic devotion itself doctrinal differences and ecclesiastical and other rivalries were openly acknowledged. How, therefore, could the theatre implement some comprehensive ideological brief that did not exist? To propound such a theory merely on the basis that the theatre in principle supported God, king and country is, in the context of seventeenth-century Europe let alone seventeenth-century Spain, to propound very little at all. It is obvious from Camargo's diatribe, however, that the *comedia*'s severest critics found it difficult in their indignation even to acknowledge this. Lest it be thought that the Jesuit father's was a voice too obviously partisan, eighteenth-century lay critics of the *comedia* saw it, significantly, in much the same light. Blas Antonio Navarre, in the prologue to his 1749 edition of the plays of Cervantes, accused Calderón of encouraging immorality with his plays, and the writer and theatre director, José Clavijo y Fajardo, a few years later in 1763 in his *Discursos críticos sobre todos los asuntos que comprende la sociedad civil* went as far as to accuse the *comedia* of teaching anarchy and revolution: 'el desprecio de la autoridad, de las leyes de Dios y de la patria. Aquí se aprende el falso pundonor, a anteponer su antojo a cuanto se representa; a hollar la humanidad y todas las reglas y deberes de la vida civil; a ser intratables y querer llevarlo todo a punta de espada.' The *comedia*, he concludes, creates a picture which would give Turkey or Hindustan a bizarre impression of Spain.[24] To the eighteenth-century, francophile eye the *comedia* was the very antithesis of orthodoxy and respectabilty and offered a supremely unreal view of Spanish society – indeed the *comedia*'s unreality was a major moral and aesthetic objection. Spanish neo-classicism, like the seventeenth-century Church, obviously had partisan reasons of its own for disapproving of the *comedia*, but it has to be

23 Cotarelo, *Controversias*, 126.

24 'Pensamiento LXV', Cotarelo, *Controversias*, 154–5

significant that its seventeenth and eighteenth-century critics alike perceived it as socially and politically as well as morally subversive.

It is all the more significant in view of the fact that the theatre's defenders did not use the contrary arguments in a way that suggests it was seen as an instrument of government or the establishment. They stressed, as they needed to, its function of holding up a mirror to life (the Horatian adage continually quoted but never explored), its morality and exemplarity, its provision of models of virtuous and reprehensible behaviour, and its capacity for moral and political instruction; vice, they pointed out, is punished and virtue rewarded, love affairs end properly in marriage, saints' plays incite the people to devotion. Even the Council of Castile's minority resolution of 1648, in a difficult decade of military defeat abroad and unrest at home when such an argument might well have been considered appropriate, made no attempt to present the theatre as a prop to the aims of government or state except negatively in so far that as entertainment it provided a little opium for the people. In the debate over the theatre's legitimacy its political role was never conceived in other than general terms – the setting of examples, the issuing of warnings, the illustration of the mutability of earthly matters and the need for *desengaño*, all of which were concerns and motifs common to European literature. If the theatre was indeed regarded by the state as a tool of government – for can a state possess a supremely effective propaganda machine without being aware of the fact? – one wonders why there is not the glimmer of such a purpose even in a confidential memorandum written to justify the theatre's existence to the monarch himself at a time when things were going badly for the country.

The *comedia*'s identity as a popular, national theatre in a particular society at a particular time in history inevitably helped shape it, and undoubtedly placed constraints of various kinds upon it, but to present it as an instrument of state propaganda or aristocratic elitism is not only a misuse of such terms but is reductive and misleading in the extreme. No one, I think, would deny that the *spectacle* of theatre at court played a political role, above all under Philip IV when the court theatre played a significant ceremonial part in the conscious theatricalization of power that characterized his reign; aesthetically it was an attempt to achieve the sublime in the service of the state, its political purpose to celebrate the splendour of monarchy and promote belief in the greatness and prosperity of Spain. Plays commissioned to celebrate national events and victories did what was required of them, and patriotism guaranteed the concurrence of their authors in the mood of celebration. It would have been very odd, in Spain's embattled position, if such works did not reflect government policy in their portrayal of international affairs: it is highly likely that the emphasis in Lope de Vega's *El Brasil restituido* (1625) on Spanish–Portuguese co-operation and on the need for clemency to go hand in hand with victory does indeed reflect the Count-Duke of Olivares's own promotion of these policies – they are in any event unexceptionable goals.[25] But even the court plays, which were subsequently performed before the public, often have a multiple identity and represent a skilful compromise between the demands of art and conscience and a specific consumer audience. As literary texts, as opposed to court spectacles, they function as propaganda only in the widest sense that they endorse such generally accepted values of the time as reason, order, harmony, self-denial, duty and responsibility, in order to contest the divisive, destructive realities of seventeenth-century existence. And even so, their recommendations are directed as much at the monarch himself as at his subjects. Distinctions appropriate to the time, the culture and the circumstances concerned have to be made in any meaningful discussion of the issues involved.

Where religion was concerned, there can be no doubt that the Spanish dramatists thought and wrote within the legitimate boundaries of faith and theological debate, though even here they sometimes unwittingly got things wrong, or occasionally even took a deliberate risk. In 1662, Calderón had a set-to with the Inquisition over his treatment of the doctrine of the Immaculate Conception in his sacramental *auto Las órdenes militares* (*Las pruebas del segundo Adán*) and chose to withdraw the play rather than compromise his artistic integrity.[26] However, their social and to a large extent their political consciences were free. The theatre superficially promotes one fictionalized reality (an ordered, stable society, conformity of values and attitudes, the tyranny of honour, the equivalence of nobility with honour and racial purity) but mirrors another reality (social mobility and social climbing, insecurity, class prejudices, an obsession with racial origins), and these tensions force their way through. A considerable number of plays seem to have been written from a position at variance with the ideologies of the day or are at least ideologically ambiguous. It is a drama preoccupied with rebellion – social, political, generational and sexual – and with conflict – between society and individual, duty and conscience, social prescription and Christian morality. Many plays have conclusions which continue to resist any complacent expectation of justice done, order restored or happiness guaranteed ever after, and in many others with seemingly conformist endings the enduring spirit of the work as a whole is the very reverse of conformist. It is not irrelevant, it seems to me, that the national theatre was born in controversy, flouting as it did the neo-classical literary theories of the day, that it continued to be surrounded by literary controversy for almost thirty years, and that it was dogged by moral controversy and opposition from Church and government throughout

25 See Robert M. Shannon, *Visions of the New World in the Drama of Lope de Vega*, American University Studies, Series II: Romance Languages and Literature, vol.67 (New York/Bern/Frankfurt am Main/Paris: Peter Lang, 1989), 163–84.

26 For further details see E. Cotarelo y Mori, *Ensayo sobre la vida y obras de don Pedro Calderón de la Barca* (Madrid: Revista de Archivos, Bibliotecas y Museos, 1924), 302–03.

most of the seventeenth century. The theatre itself, therefore, in its assumptions and procedures essentially anti-elitist and anti-aristocratic, can be seen as a paradigm for rebellion in the challenge its very existence and identity offered to the literary, aesthetic and moral orthodoxies of the day,[27] and its readiness to ignore many of the legislative efforts made to control its activities indicates that it was by no means reluctant to adopt an oppositional stance. Indeed the theatre's success in this respect should in itself make us wary of making unrealistic claims for the extent and conviction of government and even Church control, continually failing as these did in the face of two greater pressures – public demand and financial advantage. On 29 May 1623, for example, when the actor–manager concerned appeared on stage at the Corral de la Cruz to announce that the performance about to take place of *La primera parte del Emperador Carlos Quinto* had been banned by the authorities, the riot that ensued ensured that the ban was repealed a few days later and the play was performed to a packed house.[28] The very controversies the theatre provoked reveal that radically different views existed within the ecclesiastical, administrative and literary establishments, and the fact that priests and churchmen regularly patronized the playhouses, indeed had their own designated boxes, in spite of the fact that the Church forbade them to attend, offers a glimpse at once into the very special place the theatre occupied in Spanish society and into the complex nature of seventeenth-century authoritarianism.

The theatre's answer to the influence necessarily exerted upon it by the forces of social orthodoxy and popular taste – as Lope de Vega said, 'Paga el público' – was to exploit the capacity of drama, with its dialectic and its multiple perspectives, for dealing 'innocently' with received values and ideologies, so that it could be made to support and subvert simultaneously. It is not just that in great art one reading perhaps necessarily suggests a contrary one; what I believe we often see at work in the Spanish theatre is an application of the contemporary political theorist Saavedra Fajardo's principle that an appearance of accommodation can be an instrument of liberty; Borges was presumably thinking along similar lines when he called censorship the mother of metaphor. Since the *comedia* creates alternative worlds that both replicate and differ from the real world, simplistic equivalences between what characters say or do and what the playwrights think or believe are

27 Suárez de Figueroa in *El pasajero* said of the *comedia nueva*, 'Allí, como gozques, guiñen por envidia, ladran por odio y muerden por venganza' (Alivio III), ed. Mª López Bascuñana (Barcelona: Promociones y Publicaciones Universitarias, S.A., 1988), 215.

28 See *Noticias de Madrid, 1621–27*, ed. A. González Palencia (Madrid: Ayuntamiento de Madrid, 1942), 59–60. The account gives no reason for the ban, but the motive was presumably political. If the play was a revival or *refundición* of Lope's *Carlos V en Francia* (1604) then the reason is clear, for that play, written when relations with France were good, presents a very flattering portrayal of François I whereas by 1623 the two states had returned to their normal state of hostility.

inadequate to cope with the enormously complex procedures at work. The fact that art works not didactically but in a more all-embracing way is as necessary to a reading of the Spanish plays as it is to a reading of Shakespeare. Both dramas are complex, oblique and often puzzling, as the critical controversies over the 'meaning' of many Spanish plays show. The Spanish theatre requires not so much readings against the grain as an investigation of a complicated identity screened for good reasons behind conventional plots.[29] The drama's potential for speaking with more than one voice was in fact acknowledged in the late seventeenth century by the playwright and theorist Bances Candamo, who referred to plays written for kings as 'decir sin decir' – saying without saying.[30] Before then the political need to cultivate the art of truthful prudence in speaking to kings had already been articulated by Calderón, a master of the skill, in the words used by Alejandro in *Darlo todo y no dar nada*, to explain his choice of Apeles's portrait of him in accurate, but not fully revealing, half-profile:

> . . . para que quede al mundo
> este político ejemplo
> de que ha de buscarse modo
> de hablar a un rey con tal tiento,
> que ni disuene la voz,
> no lisonjee el silencio; (Act I, 1027–8)[31]

My aim in what follows is not to appropriate Lope de Vega for a particular ideology or critical theory but to open up his (pseudo) historical and political plays to fresh inquiry after a period during which they have virtually been closed off to anything other than the view of him as a lackey of the system, a jobbing genius who tamely sold his soul to his political masters, uncritically swallowing all the ideological platitudes of the day. This revisionist enterprise was prompted by the discrepancy between what the texts themselves seemed to me to be doing and saying and the received wisdom which still dominates discussion of them. The book sets out to offer an argument which reads the plays as at once politically anxious and probing and which identifies, partly by drawing on the insights of linguistic theory, techniques and stratagems utilized by Lope to negotiate a path of prudence between the acceptable and the unacceptable in political commentary in the commercial theatre. I do not believe that the argument distorts the plays as they were

[29] Cf. Bruce W. Wardropper: 'Una importante función de la comedia del Siglo de Oro sería – sugiero – ésta: proporcionar una salida legítima a pensamientos y aspiraciones ilegítimos.' *La comedia española del Siglo de Oro* (Madrid: Ariel, 1978), 232.

[30] *Theatro de los theatros de los passados y presentes siglos*, segunda versión, ed. Duncan W. Moir (London: Tamesis, 1970), 57.

[31] His two rivals paint the king full-face, one emphasizing his injured eye, the other ignoring the disfigurement altogether.

experienced by contemporary audiences watching the plays performed in the *corrales* – indeed one of my guiding principles has been to try to understand the plays as historical products on their own terms. They are texts-in-history, directed at a physically present audience of considerable social reach. In writing them their author was working within a shared horizon of expectations (albeit a horizon that gradually expanded in response to the theatre's own skilful initiatives) and it is important to always bear always in mind the interchange between the plays and their spectators – what they would have brought to the occasion and what they might have taken away. Playwright, plays and audiences were all contributors to a continuing political dialectic between the historical and fictional worlds of the stage on the one hand and contemporary reality on the other. Lope no more wrote 'innocently' within some sealed bubble called 'literature' than his audiences innocently watched and listened to what he wrote, weaving no connections and spinning no thoughts that strayed beyond the confines of the play.[32] The plays are also of course texts-through-history, since different ages and societies inevitably read and reconstruct them in the light of their own concerns and expectations. But it is the play-texts within the particular context of their production that I am concerned with here. And this context necessarily includes the circumstances of Lope's own life and career and his relationship to the system within which he lived, a relationship determined in turn by personality, experience and ambitions. The appeal to history, like the appeal to language theory in chapter four, is intended to promote debate not to end it in any sort of authoritative way sanctioned by history (or theory) itself. At the same time I hope that examining Lope's handling of kingship with its related issues, and determining inductively whether any patterns emerge, brings his theatrical engagement with the nature, remit, limits and problems of political power into clearer and fairer focus, and even to some extent recovers him for the reputation for daring and iconoclasm that he enjoyed in his own day. The concern with kingship might now seem historically very specific, but kingship is merely a particular manifestation of political and social governance, which in all ages and societies centres on the same issues – the right of those who govern to govern and the suitability of those who govern to govern. Hereditary monarchy combines the two issues in a peculiarly problematic way, but the concern with the exactness of the match between man and role, private individual and public image, is one that runs through post-war Western politics. The impact upon the conduct of kingship of the *comedia*'s continuing interrogation of monarchical theory and practice is impossible to

[32] No British theatre or cinema audience in 1994/5 watched *The Madness of King George* without their thoughts straying to contemporary royal life. Their monarch was not mad – far from it – but there was much in the play and its film which drew on contemporary concerns, and audiences were quick to read the clues in the way intended by the playwright and scriptwriter, Alan Bennett.

determine, not least because the message of the plays reinforced the messages of history, political philosophers and church teaching alike, but its contributory role in the dissemination and circulation of political ideas was undoubtedly considerable. The theatre was part of the historical situation it scrutinized, and meaning in the theatre was determined largely by the historical moment. At the same time its enactments of political situations not only exposed and elucidated but actually helped construct and shape contemporary issues and anxieties; it was an agent of the social process and not merely a recorder of it. In this way theatrical practice contributed to meaning and thence to politics and political history.

2

MONARCHY AND THE THEATRE

In an age deeply preoccupied with theories of state and the nature of kingship, Spaniards had more reason than most in Europe from the late sixteenth century on to be concerned about their monarchs. An unwieldy, far-flung empire, a self-appointed role as defender of the Catholic faith in a Europe rent by religious schism and threatened by Islam, and a failing economy made the burden of kingship in Spain seem a heavy one indeed. Little wonder that in 1598 Philip II contemplated the imminent reign of his vapid, ineffectual son with considerable misgiving: 'God who has given me so many kingdoms, has denied me a son capable of governing them.' His remark to his secretary, don Cristóbal de Moura, a few days before he died, 'I fear they will rule him',[1] proved prophetic: both Philip III and Philip IV chose to hand over power to favourite ministers and, in the second half of the seventeenth century, the wretched Charles II was incapable of ruling even had he wanted to.[2] The ideal of personal monarchy still so strongly held at the end of the sixteenth century in Spain was to be sadly betrayed. This ideal and the grave misgivings that lurked behind it in the minds of intelligent men in the late 1590s can be seen at work together in the guides for princes written by two Jesuits – Pedro de Rivadeneyra's *Tratado del príncipe cristiano* of 1595[3] and Juan de Mariana's *De Rege et Regis Institutione* of 1599.[4] In spite of a diplomatic disclaimer from Rivadeneyra, both works were clearly written with Philip II's young heir in mind and on publication both were dedicated to him, Mariana's shortly after his accession. Philip II, it is said, urged his son to make Rivadeneyra's *Tratado* the basis of his future conduct. Although the two works assume an innocent face, therefore, Rivadeneyra's being in large part a critique of Machiavelli (whose works had appeared on the Index of

1 This and the previous remark are quoted in Modesto Lafuente, *Historia general de España* (30 vols, Madrid, 1850–67), vol.11, 77–8; and again in John Lynch, *Spain Under the Habsburgs*, 2 vols, II, *Spain and America 1598–1700* (Oxford: Basil Blackwell, 1969), 14.

2 For an account of the rise of political favouritism in seventeenth-century Spain see John Lynch, *Spain under the Habsburgs*, vol.II, *Spain and America 1598–1700*, 23–30.

3 Reference is to *Obras escogidas del Padre Pedro de Rivadeneyra*, Biblioteca de Autores Españoles, 60 (Madrid: M. Rivadeneyra, 1868).

4 I have used here the Spanish translation of Book I by E. Barriobero y Herrán, *Del rey y de la institución de la dignidad real* (Madrid: Mundo Latino, 1930).

1559) and reason of state, Mariana's a disquisition on tyranny, they have a complicitous subtext; writers *and* readers know that the covert issue is a real-life prince's capacity to rule. It is no coincidence that two other major Spanish treatises on kingship appeared during the early years of the next reign – Quevedo's *Política de Dios y gobierno de Cristo* in 1625 and Juan Pablo Mártir Rizo's *Norte de príncipes* of 1626.

Such treatises of course had a long ancestry going back to the Middle Ages – Saint Thomas Aquinas's *De regimine principum* being the most famous. The nature and role of the prince was an important element of Renaissance thought, and the idea of the Christian prince continued to be the keystone of political theory during the Counter-Reformation – indeed the theory of state was inseparable from the figure of the prince. The controlling preoccupation was the relation between the princely role and virtue, and the education of the prince was therefore seen to be a factor of paramount importance. Tracts *de regimine principum* abounded in the sixteenth and seventeenth centuries as contemporary events sharpened concern about the nature of monarchical rule. Following Machiavelli, European theorists began to take the view that virtue in a prince, although essential, was not enough. Modern politics demanded of the prince not just moral exemplariness in personal terms but political acumen and skills, that personal conscience should in certain circumstances and for the sake of the state come second to political expediency. The Counter-Reformation rejected the argument of reason of state and returned the theoretical emphasis to the personal worth of the monarch: political considerations must stem from and be subordinate to Christian virtues and principles. In practice, however, Early Modern Spain was severely exercised by the inescapable fact that even when virtue was present it did not in itself meet the requirements of modern government. The ethical dilemma is encapsulated in Philip II's handling of the thicket of political intrigue, involving both the government of the Netherlands and the Portuguese succession, that surrounded him in the 1570s. Morally austere and generally politically adept, in 1578 he reluctantly allowed his treacherous secretary Antonio Pérez to persuade him that the death of Juan de Escobedo, secretary to his illegitimate son Don John of Austria, was necessary on grounds of reason of state. When, after months of agonizing over the decision, he discovered the depth and extent of the deception, he rounded implacably on Pérez and, in spite of his own complicity, had him and the Princess of Eboli, another intriguer, arrested. Opponents of the reason of state philosophy had seen their worst fears realized, and many of those complacent about the ideal of the Christian prince, which Philip was considered to represent, had had their confidence severely dented. In the face of his successors, much less than ideal kings, this complacency finally crumbled. In the reign of Philip III the *privanza* system that followed the rise to power of the Marquis of Denia, soon Duke of Lerma, whereby government was effectively handed over to a succession of favoured ministers, paradoxically represented a recognition of the reality that monarchs did not necessarily make the best rulers and, at the same time, a way of preserving inviolate the idea of exemplary majesty by separating practical governance from it. And seventeenth-century political theorists increasingly recognized the fact, while never shaking off their concern with the dangers inherent in delegated rule.[5] At the end of the sixteenth century Mariana with prophetic insight saw *privanza* as a historical phenomenon that might well become again a troubling reality; by 1640 it was for Saavedra a long-established fact of political life.

The idea of exemplariness, of the prince as a mirror in which his subjects could then see themselves reflected, died hard in Europe, for to lack virtue was obviously to lack divine and popular approval and therefore to lack power. According to Rivadeneyra, princely example was more effective than laws: 'Más puede el buen ejemplo del Príncipe para persuadir a los otros la virtud, que todas las leyes y diligencias que sin él se usan' (550). But even in Spain Christian conviction was forced to yield to the pressure of political realities, and by 1640 the Christian ideal of the prince had become a political–Christian ideal, as the title of Saavedra Fajardo's *Idea de un príncipe político-cristiano* shows. In this, the best-known political work of seventeenth-century Spain, an erudite, cultured, widely travelled and admirably reasonable diplomat set out views which, grounded as they are in historical example and personal observation and experience, encapsulate the Tacitism which permitted Spanish intellectuals to reconcile Machiavellian theory with Christian principle: political imperatives, it maintained, must be held in balance with ethical considerations.[6] Saavedra's analysis masks, just as do the treatises of Mariana and Rivadeneyra, a covert critique of Spain's contemporary situation, but the true nature of the discourse was no less legible here than it was in these other tracts, or for that matter in the plays about kings that audiences saw performed in the *corrales*. Present, sensitive realities did not have to be directly invoked when utopian and fictional discourses could be safely employed to achieve the same purpose.

The seventeenth-century Spanish consensus on the virtues that should be expected of the prince privileged the traditional qualities of prudence, liberality and justice, justice being a concept that comprehended the equality of all

5 As well as those of Mateo López Bravo, Quevedo, Mártir Rizo and Saavedra Fajardo, seventeenth-century treatises on kingship include Diego Gurrea's *Arte de enseñar hijos de príncipes y señores* (1627), Jerónimo Fernández de Otero's *El maestro del príncipe* (1633) and P. Andrés Mendo's *Príncipe perfecto y Ministros ajustados* (1662).

6 See Abellán, *Historia crítica del pensamiento español*, vol.3, 83. Abellán defines *tacitismo* as a 'reconocimiento de la política como una esfera autónoma que tiene sus propias normas y técnicas, pero intentando hacerles compatibles con la moral cristiana'. See also André Joucla-Ruau, *Le Tacitisme de Saavedra Fajardo* (Paris: Editions Hispaniques, 1977); and Francisco Sanmartín Boncompte, *Tácito en España* (Barcelona: Consejo Superior de Investigaciones Científicas, 1951). See Chapter 6 for a more extended consideration of Tacitism in Spain.

men, including the king, before the law, and embraced both distributive and commutative justice; these governed respectively relations between the state and its parts (justice in the distribution of rewards and punishments) and those between parts of the state (equality in the distribution of rewards and punishments). The false pretence, lies and deceit which Spain associated with Machiavelli and false reason of state were unequivocally proscribed, but their place was taken by the convenient notion of dissimulation, which was considered entirely suited to the awe-inspiring remoteness of majesty cultivated by the seventeenth-century Spanish Crown. A largely new, key factor of seventeenth-century political thought, however, was the idea of reputation – the idea that the image of a monarch or a country is important, not only to an appearance of strength, but to a nation's actual strength and health.[7] In the reign of Philip IV the prestige and image of the monarchy occupied the very heart of Olivares's vision of empire.[8] Saavedra Fajardo puts it with his usual clarity and common sense:

> . . .los imperios se conservan con su misma autoridad y reputación. En empezando a perderla, empiezan a caer, sin que baste el poder a sustentallos; antes apresura la caída su misma grandeza. Nadie se atreve a una coluna derecha; en declinando, el más débil intenta derriballa; porque la misma inclinación convida al impulso; y, en cayendo, no hay brazos que basten a levantalle. Un acto sólo derriba la reputación, y muchos no la pueden restaurar; porque no hay mancha que se limpie sin dejar señales, ni opinión que se borre enteramente. Las infamias, aunque se curen, dejan cicatrices en el rostro; y así, en no estando la corona fija sobre esta coluna derecha de la reputación, dará en tierra.[9]

How familiar such sentiments are to those acquainted with the seventeenth-century Spanish theatre. They saturate the very air its characters breath, as they saturated the self-perception and thinking of a real-life nation remorselessly losing confidence in itself, for all the hectic attempts of some contemporary commentators to propagate messianic political theories.[10] In practice, of course, there could be little real separation between the image and the reality behind it; the strong prince may be well served by a reputation for strength but a weak prince and his reputation for strength are soon parted. Not for

[7] See Abellán, *Historia crítica del pensamiento español*, vol.3, 86–7; also J.A. Maravall, *La teoría española del estado en el siglo XVII* (Madrid: Instituto de Estudios Políticos, 1944); and 'Maquiavelo y maquiavelismo en España', *Estudios de historia del pensamiento español: Siglo XVII* (Madrid: Ediciones Cultura Hispánica, 1975).

[8] See J.H. Elliott, 'A Question of Reputation: Spanish Foreign Policy in the Seventeenth Century', *Journal of Modern History* 55 (1983), 475–83.

[9] *Idea de un príncipe político-cristiano, Empresa* XXXI. *Obras de Don Diego Saavedra Fajardo*, Biblioteca de Autores Españoles, 25 (Madrid: Atlas, 1947), 81.

[10] See E. Tierno Galván, 'El tacitismo en las doctrinas políticas del Siglo de Oro español', *Escritos 1950–1960* (Madrid: Editorial Tecnos, 1971).

nothing did the prince's relationship with a favoured vassal come to dominate discussion of kingship in the seventeenth century as the sixteenth-century preoccupation with the origins and legitimacy of monarchical power gave way to a passionate interest in its exercise. Spanish political thought at the time offered no exact parallel either terminologically or conceptually to the king's 'two bodies', the body natural and the body politic which transcended the body natural and was effectively absolved of its human defects, but it certainly perceived the king in dualistic terms, as human by nature and suprahuman by role, and writers, including playwrights, became obsessed with the tension between the two.

For the *ancien régime*, of course, the prospect of inadequate kings raised questions that went beyond practical considerations of successful government. Monarchy was the only available viable model of social and political organization, authorized by the natural order where all things were seen to be part of a necessary and inevitable hierarchy. It was one of a set of shared structures of belief, of common assumptions made by high and low alike across the spheres of politics, religion, natural history and social issues. The Spanish conceptualization of royalty had traditionally possessed little mystical or charismatic content – Spanish monarchs eschewed crowns, coronations and sacramental oil and favoured the soberest of dress[11] – and sixteenth-century political philosophers in Spain, with the exception of the jurist Vitoria, did not accept the view that dominion was founded upon grace.[12] Juan Luis Vives, writing in the 1520s, had been firm about the humanity of princes: '¿Qué otra cosa es al fin de cuentas un príncipe sino un hombre sabio, investado de poder público?'[13] And Spanish political thought later in the Early Modern period never quite lost sight of that principle, for all that the reign of Philip IV brought a conscious attempt to create a truly charismatic monarchy and a full-blown ideology of kingship that embraced not just the kingly virtues but such elements as magnificence, display as a symbol of power, distance, formality, even a semi-divine presence. In spite of one or two rhetorical flourishes, Mariana was surprisingly reticent when it came even to linking kingship with the divine, and firmly located royal authority in

11 J.A. Maravall, *Estado moderno y mentalidad social: Siglos XV a XVII*, 2 vols (Madrid: Revista de Occidente, 1972), vol.2, 333. As Maravall points out, in the seventeenth century the use of the idea of the crown as a depersonalized symbol of royalty fulfils much the same function as the notion of the monarch's transcendental identity, his body politic.

12 Maravall, *Estado moderno*, vol.2, 262; see also Maravall, 'Moral de acomodación y carácter conflictivo de la libertad (notas sobre Saavedra Fajardo)', *Cuadernos Hispanoamericanos*, nos. 257–8 (1971), 682.

13 *De Concordia et Discordia in Humano Genere*, book 4, trans. as *Concordia y discordia* by Laureano Sánchez Gallego (Mexico D.F.: Editorial Séneca, 1940), 418.

the consent of the republic. Rivadeneyra's views were more representative: the king's authority comes from God and he reigns in his name,

> Siendo el Rey y príncipe soberano como el ánima de su reino y como otro sol, que con su luz y movimiento da vida y salud al mundo, y como un retrato de Dios en la tierra, debe con grandísimo cuidado considerar las obligaciones precisas que le corren, para representar dignamente. . .a Dios en su gobierno y para dar vida a toda la república (518).

While it is apparent from both Rivadeneyra and Mariana that the Spanish concept of kingship stopped short of any notion of divine right – they were supporters of parliament, believed that kings were subject at least to the directive force of law if not the coercive,[14] and that their subjects had inalienable rights – the belief that the king was God's representative on earth and possessed therefore of an *aura*, at least, of the divine, was deeply entrenched. Mariana's nicely judged assessment was that the ideal king by virtue of his outstanding qualities *appeared to his subjects to be* 'un hombre casi bajado del cielo y superior a la condición humana' (chap. III, 63). However, Spanish writers of the time did like to make a crucial distinction between divine and royal authority, and although the plays of the day often use the rhetoric of kingship, the metaphorical language of royal absolutism with its divine allusions, they do so more as a technique of identification and definition or as a way of communicating purposes of their own rather than as an expression of fundamental conviction. The business of the plays proceeds in accordance with very different assumptions, establishing an image of kingship which is scarcely divine. As R.A. Stradling has pointed out, the arguments for royal absolutism as propounded by Bodin were rejected in Spain at the end of the sixteenth century along with the practice of reason of state, and the assertions of the divine right of kings made in England by the Scots William Barclay and James Vl would have struck Spanish thinkers as both barbarous and blasphemous. He goes on, 'Their objections were clear: to cynicism they opposed ethical idealism and to absolutism, a constitutional legalism. Surprising as it may be for the English mentality to discover such round Whig principles with deep roots in Spanish thought, they were in fact the fundamental assumptions of political philosophy under the Philips.'[15] Gregorio López Madera in his *Excelencias de la monarquía y reino de España* (1625) went so far as to equate tyranny with nothing more than the exercise of the king's own will, 'no consiste en otra cosa la propia tiranía que en hacer los príncipes su propia

[14] Other sixteenth-century writers who expressed comparable views were Luis de Molina, Domingo de Soto, Francisco Suárez and Francisco de Vitoria. See Bernice Hamilton, *Political Thought in Sixteenth-Century Spain* (Oxford: Clarendon Press, 1963).

[15] *Philip IV and the Government of Spain, 1621–1665* (Cambridge: Cambridge University Press, 1988), 14.

voluntad, sin sujetarse a la razón y derecho'; in other words, it is tyranny for a prince to act as if he were independent of and above the state.[16]

It was in the interests of the Crown for tractarians such as Juan de Salazar (in his *Política española* of 1619) to claim that Spain was heir to the great empires of the past and God's chosen country, and to insist that the Christian religion was the very basis of the Spanish monarchy. While providentialism naturally provided the underpinning for hereditary and absolute monarchy and – in the view of some European theorists and their princes at the time – for divine right, in Spain it was used to explain and justify the Hapsburg's self-appointed messianic role as defender of the faith in Europe and beyond and their teleological understanding of Spain's medieval past.[17] This assumed, however, that monarchy served the faith and not the faith monarchy, and this fundamental position survived the strategic attempts, during the rule of Olivares, at quasi-deification of Philip IV in his apotheosis as the Planet King. Philip himself deliberately cultivated his suprahuman status through the theatrical use of court ritual and protocol to enhance his separateness from other beings,[18] but in confessional vein in a letter to his confidante the nun Sor María de Ágreda he shrugs off the cloak of divinity and concedes that he is a man as other men who has painstakingly to instruct himself in the ways of rectitude and truth, philosophy and moderation:

> Y porque quede anticipadamente prevenida la malicia, he tenido por conveniente advertir aquí que todo lo que diré de mí. . .está tan lejos de ser presunción, que antes se puede argüir por sobrada modestia cuanto digo, confesando faltas de noticias y modos de adquirirlas (aunque decentes) casi comunes a todos los otros hombres: humanidad de que hasta las mismas leyes nos excusan, presumiéndonos sabios de lo más escondido por sola la dignidad y carácter real. No llegando a decir que sé, sino que voy sabiendo, desnudándome de la divinidad por afectar más la filosofía y moderación y sobre todo la rectitud y verdad.[19]

16 Madrid 1625, fol.17, quoted in Abellán, *Historia crítica del pensamiento español*, 67.

17 Machiavelli and his followers interrogated, even rejected, providentialist explanations of events – for them politics was not governed by the workings of Providence.

18 See Jonathan Brown and J.H. Elliott, *A Palace for a King: The Buen Retiro and the Court of Philip IV* (New Haven/London: Yale University Press, 1980), 31–2; also J.H. Elliott, 'The Court of the Spanish Habsburgs: a Peculiar Institution?', *Spain and its World 1500–1700*, 142–61.

19 'Autosemblanza de Felipe IV', *Cartas de Sor María de Jesús de Ágreda y de Felipe IV*, ed. Carlos Seco Serrano, Biblioteca de Autores Españoles 109 (Madrid: Atlas, 1958), 231–6, p.231. The 'Autosemblanza' was written by the king to explain why he had undertaken the translation of books eight and nine of Guicciardini's *Historia de Italia*.

The phrasing is revealing: divinity is not something intrinsic, not an attribute, but a costume that comes with the role, to be assumed or discarded at will. Political realities in any case made many realize that such providential rhetoric as Salazar's was neither truthful nor helpful. Religious problems and preoccupations faded in the face of more urgent threats – hence the growing acceptance of the theory of reason of state once it had shaken off its association with Machiavelli. The pressures of government in a changed world placed heavy strains upon the very notions of kingship which that world had elaborated to suit the new sovereign state. Spain might have rejected the idea of *rex legibus solutus*, but even there the monarch, if not in any sense himself divine, was firmly perceived as an image of the divine on earth, a reflection that, ideally, replicated itself in turn in his subjects; Saavedra Fajardo conveys the prince's delegated role with striking elegance, 'La mayor potestad desciende de Dios. Antes que en la tierra, se coronaron los reyes en su eterna mente' (*Empresa* XVIII, 49). The idea of the prince as God's representative in the secular domain was the very linchpin of orderly Christian government. Hand in hand with this view, therefore, went the vision, found in Rivadeneyra, Mariana and most other theorists, of a just, prudent, active and accessible prince who sought the counsel of the wise but without ever relinquishing government; in whom, in the words of Saavedra Fajardo, 'son convenientes aquellas virtudes heroicas propias del imperio, no aquellas monásticas y encogidas que le hacen. . .más atento a ciertas perfecciones propias que al gobierno universal' (*Empresa* XVIII, 51). That severely upright political moralist, López Bravo, put his view of the need for active authority more uncompromisingly, 'Esclavo es, no señor, el que, ageno del propio, siempre está sujeto a ageno albedrío; más noble y generoso spíritu se desea en el Rey' (*Del rey*, 99). Real-life royal inadequacies were therefore a shattering contradiction, setting up strains and tensions that reached far beyond secret confidences at court or the pages of treatises written so that princes might be educated into the capacities expected of them. Francisco de Quevedo in his *Política de Dios* expressed views on kingship which barely concealed his contempt for Philip III, and Philip is implicated, too, in a little satirical poem addressed to his favourite and first minister the Duke of Lerma:

> Uceda, Lerma y el rey
> que procede de los dos,
> trinidad, mas no de Dios,
> antes de diversa ley;
> porque del hijo cruel
> el padre, echado el cielo,
> padece no por el suelo,
> antes el suelo por él.[20]

20 See Teófanes Egido, *Sátiras políticas*, 83.

In *Memorial a S.M. el rey don Felipe Cuarto*, which targets both the king and Lerma, Philip IV was likened to a hole:

> Grande sois Filipo, a manera de hoyo;
> ved esto que digo, en razón de apoyo:
> quien más quita al hoyo más grande le hace
> mirad quien lo ordena, veréis a quien place.

While *El 'padre nuestro' glosado. Décimas* bade the king wake up and rule for himself:

> Filipo, que el mundo aclama
> rey del infiel tan temido,
> despierta, que, por dormido,
> nadie te teme ni te ama,
> despierta, rey, que la fama
> por todo el orbe pregona
> que es de león tu corona
> y tu dormir de lirón;
> mira que la adulación
> te llama, con fin siniestro,
> padre nuestro.[21]

In the reigns of Philip IV and Charles II political satirists openly, though of course always anonymously, targeted the king himself.

The largest and most democratic forum for the expression of concern on the subject of kingship was a perhaps unexpected one – the public theatre, as Stradling recognizes: 'There is certainly no reason to doubt that in the now-settled and burgeoning capital – approaching 150,000 souls by the end of Philip III's reign – political debate and speculation was as much at home in the theatre and the tavern as it was in the court and the Cortes.'[22] The *comedia nueva* from the beginning made ample use of Spanish history and legend to entertain contemporary Spanish audiences, and was therefore not merely confronted in the very process of going about its business by the dilemmas of monarchy, but simultaneously given the means whereby those dilemmas could be discreetly explored. With the arrival on the political centre-stage of Lerma these dilemmas acquired extra urgency and bite, and such was the market for plays about government that in the years that followed hundreds of plays overtly or covertly weighed into the debate. It was of no consequence that the plots were historical, quasi-historical or fictional, for to think that audiences then would watch kings on stage and not draw parallels between what they saw and heard and the contemporary political situa-

21 Both in Egido, *Sátiras políticas*, 115.
22 Stradling, *Philip IV and the Government of Spain*, 13.

tion, is as unrealistic as to believe that fictional portrayals of, or references to, prime ministers or presidents now always inevitably take place in some dimension entirely separate from real-life circumstances. At times when problems concerning Crown and government existed, playwrights composed and audiences listened in a different way, or rather with a heightened sense of relevance and appropriateness. Playwrights could not but have been sensitive to this and proceeded accordingly. We may therefore assume that any perceived relevance was wilful, otherwise it would have been carefully avoided, for all that there was no sustained repression of political critics during the Lerma régime.[23] Kingship was a live issue and all theatrical kings led from and back to it. The costumes were contemporary, the metaphors were familiar, the customs identical, the circumstances often topical. In Lope's novelesque courtly play *El rey por semejanza* we see the King of Assyria fighting the Moors, and grandees being allowed to keep their hats on in the royal presence. References to sun kings and divine majesties are standard. Indeed displacements in time and place and into fiction virtually guaranteed complete freedom in the creation of a dramatic discourse whose implications were not lost on audiences alive to Spain's own problems. Censors, furthermore, concerned with representation rather than signification, by and large took no notice of such resorts as irony, play, contradiction and counter-currents: they could not hear them, or they did not have time to notice them, or they thought them above the heads of those they might unsettle. In any case these are of their very nature elusive techniques, more readily perceived than pinned down, and impossible to 'prove'. As long as the surface of a play complied with their requirements – and this normally meant what was actually articulated in any single set of words, or in a single action or string of actions – then they were satisfied enough. The theatre's discourse on kings, in any case, does not invariably address problems directly relevant to the historical moment. But it is always rooted in an acute sensitivity to the painful disjunction between the contemporary ideal of kingship and the disturbing reality with which Spain from the beginning of the seventeenth century on was trying to come to terms. It was a fictional replication of the theoretical and popular concerns of the real world. The plays are enactments of possibilities envisaged by political philosophers, emblems, in a sense, of the issues which informed contemporary politics.

Interestingly enough, one of the problems inherent in the depiction of princes on stage which was not really addressed and which few seem to have been even aware of was that it ran counter both to received notions about majesty and its current practice. Saavedra Fajardo observed 'Dentro de los palacios son los príncipes como los demás hombres; el respeto los imagina

[23] Stradling, *Philip IV and the Government of Spain*, 15. Mariana, however, by then already in his seventies, was imprisoned for two years in 1609–11 for his earlier attack on the copper coinage issue in his treatise *De Mutatione Monetae* (1602).

mayores, y lo retirado y oculto encubre las flaquezas' (*Empresa* XXI, 836). It is a theme he returns to again and again: 'si no se conserva lo augusto de la majestad no habrá diferencia entre el príncipe y el vasallo' (*Empresa* XXXIX, 99b), 'Lo que no se ve, se venera más', 'Más se respeta lo que está más lejos. . .No apruebo el dejarse ver el príncipe muy a menudo en las calles y paseos' (*Empresa* XXXIX, 101b). In other words, majesty requires distance if the royal aura is to be fully maintained. Kings must not be seen to be the men they are. Sir Thomas More captured the conundrum exactly in his tale of the peasant who came to town and happened to see a royal procession. When he hears the crowd shouting 'Long live the king,' he inquires eagerly 'Where is the king? Where is the king?' When one of the crowd points out the king riding by on his horse, the peasant, disappointed, replies, 'Is that the king? I think you are fooling me. He seems to be a man in an embroidered garment.'[24] Little wonder that Renaissance monarchs in their royal progresses strove so hard to appear more divine than human. The popular idea that princes are, or should be, somehow out of the course of ordinary human nature is present in the Spanish drama as well. When Casilda in Lope's *Peribáñez y el Comendador de Ocaña* sees the king for the first time she cannot believe her eyes, '¿Que son/ los reyes de carne y hueso?' And when Costanza asks 'Pues ¿de qué pensabas tú?' Casilda charmingly replies 'De damasco o terciopelo', an entirely appropriate conviction in a play where differences in social status are textually imaged in clothes and trappings throughout (Act I, lines 986–9).[25] Casilda's tone here is perhaps slightly elusive – she is after all an intelligent woman and the words could well be delivered in fun – but Lope does not leave the matter there. When Inés announces that the king is leaving, and Costanza regretfully remarks,

> Tan presto
> que aún no he podido saber
> si es barbirrubio o taheño,

the worldly Inés has this to say about the mystery of majesty:

> Los reyes son a la vista,
> Costanza, por el respeto,
> imágenes de milagros,
> porque siempre que los vemos,
> de otro color nos parecen. (Act I, 997–1004)

[24] *The Latin Epigrams of Thomas More*, ed. and trans. by Leicester Bradman and Charles Arthur Lynch (Chicago: University of Chicago Press, 1953), 205–6; referred to by Stephen Greenblatt, *Renaissance Self-Fashioning: From More to Shakespeare* (Chicago/London: University of Chicago Press, 1980), 27.

[25] Ed. J.M. Ruano and J.E. Varey (London: Tamesis Texts, 1980).

The reality of majesty does not live up to the idea of it, but even so the awareness of majesty dazzles. More's peasant sees the man and not the king because he is not expecting to see the king, and does not know how to recognize him. Lope's rustic Salvano in *El villano en su rincón* regards a king as being scarcely subject to natural processes at all:

> Salvano. ¿Éste es el Rey?
> Fileto. Aquel mancebo rojo.
> Salvano. ¡Válgame Dios! Los reyes, ¿tienen barbas?
> Fileto. Pues ¿cómo piensas tú que son los reyes?
> (Act I, 1180b)[26]

Drama, of course, removes kings from their palaces and shows them to be not merely men but much of the time to be men as others are. Their very appearance on stage at the mercy of an audience's pleasure diminishes them, perilously narrowing the distance between the enactment of kingship and its substance, between theatre and ritual. It offered a peculiarly exact representation of the idea of monarch as *persona*, of kingship as role, of royal behaviour as performance, and of royal sufficiency as image – analogies explicitly recognized by Machiavelli and endorsed (albeit without Machiavelli's strategic recommendations) by Spanish monarchs and theorists alike. This process of demystification has been nicely summarized by Stephen Greenblat, 'to conceive of kingship as a dramatic part. . .is potentially at least to demystify it, to reduce its sacred symbolism to tinsel'.[27] That Philip II realized as much is obvious from his ban on stage portrayals of himself during his lifetime as being inconsistent with his dignity. How, after all, should a common actor impersonate the king? How should a king be depicted as a man with the stature of other men and retain his mystery? Yet if a stage king is to be more than a cipher his dramatic effectiveness lies precisely in his humanity. The *comedia*'s constant vision of the twin nature of a king does not, of course, rely on the promptings of contemporary political theory, on the views of jurists and theologians. Observation and shared human experience constituted prompting enough. But that twin nature was a very live contemporary political concern in seventeenth-century Spain and the theatre's constant stream of fallible kings could have done little to reinforce the aura of mystery and impenetrability cultivated by the Spanish Crown. Segismundo's formulation of the humanity of a king at the end of Act II of *La vida es sueño*, 'Sueña el rey que es rey', is an extreme one. To equate kingship with dream and with role play may be theologically impeccable but it is politically quite daring, seeming to be saying as it does that a king is a social convenience, a political

26 *Lope Félix de Vega Carpio. Obras escogidas*, I, *Teatro* I, ed. Federico Carlos Sainz de Robles (Madrid: Aguilar, 1990; first edn. 1969).

27 *Renaissance Self-Fashioning*, 27.

necessity, nothing more. It would have met with Mariana's stern approval, but it must have caused a momentary frisson in the *corral* when the play was first performed. Lope de Vega had already, in the early years of the century, exploited the idea with dazzling virtuosity in his remarkable Roman play *Lo fingido verdadero* (1608), where actors and emperors step in and out of each others' realities with disturbing ease.

It is intriguing that, in a society in which interest in politics ran high and the problems of kingship loomed large, the licence the theatre took to itself in the depiction of princes should not have been regarded as unsuitable and undesirable, if not harmful. It may be seen as another indication of the special position the theatre enjoyed, constituting as it did an institution subject to rules and regulations but by no means entirely controlled by them. Indeed the king clearly found his two identities very useful where the *corrales* were concerned, with one of them ratifying measures of control, reform, even on occasion closure, with the other attending public playhouses and palace theatres to see the plays for himself. But the theatre's immunity with respect to its depiction of princes is largely explained by the fact that, far from regarding the dramatization of kingship as performing a disservice to real-life princes, contemporary commentators chose to see flawed and fallible kings in a quite different way. Within the accepted tradition that it was incumbant upon the subject to offer his prince *consilium* – a duty taken seriously by seventeenth-century Spanish *arbitristas* – one of the standard arguments throughout the seventeenth century of those who defended the theatre against its opponents was that drama, by providing examples of both suitable and unsuitable behaviour, acted as a mirror for princes. According to López Bravo princes needed to be educated into their weighty task, 'Alcánçase la facultad del govierno (como todas las demás) con naturaleza, arte y exercicio' (99) – this is indeed the opening statement of *Del rey*. The reasoned arguments of purpose-written treatises were one instrument of instruction – Mariana's *De rege* was written in response to a request from a friend, García de Loaisa, preceptor of the heir to the throne, who felt that a work combining moral philosophy and historical example would be a valuable aid in preparing the young prince for rule.[28] Another, more palatable and therefore possibly more effective one was the theatre itself, for the reasons given by Melchor de Cabrera y Guzmán:

> pues el Príncipe, viendo representar acciones heroycas de otro, templa las que más le apassionan y halla quien sin nota le acusa de error ú descuido, y toma modelo para adelante. El señor mira como en vn espejo lo imperfecto de su proceder y como buen pintor borra el defecto y fealdad para quedar sin la mancha que le desdora.[29]

[28] See Alan Soons, *Juan de Mariana* (Boston: Twayne, 1982), 47.

[29] In his defence of the *comedia*, *Defensa por el uso de las comedias y suplica al Rey nuestro señor para que se continuen* (1646), Cotarelo, *Controversias*, 93–103.

The theatre's adversaries, concerned with its general immorality and without ever using its unflattering portrayal of kings as ammunition (to suggest that contemporary princes were corruptible would hardly have been tactful), consistently identified the effectiveness of stage mimesis as one of the most dangerous things about it. Seeing impropriety and wrong-doing acted out before their very eyes was bound to be corrupting for audiences, for rhetoric and representation affected the emotions and persuaded spectators to sympathy and imitation. Gonzalo Navarro Castellano is adamant on this point:

> La historia es necesaria en este mundo, la comedia no: aquélla refiere los vicios: ésta los irrita; aquélla los representa a la memoria con la relación, ésta a la voluntad con la imitación, que despierta y mueve el apetito. Mayor batería hacen los ojos a la voluntad que las orejas, como dice Horacio.[30]

The debate had to be conducted in moral terms by the theatre's defenders in order to counter those who attacked it on moral grounds, and both sides were in agreement over the effectiveness of visual enactment. For one of the theatre's few Jesuit defenders, P. José Alcázar, spectatorship involved another form of perception: 'son las comedias espejo de la vida humana, en que hallarán muchos avisos morales y políticos los que lo quisieren considerar con los ojos del entendimiento'.[31] This statement with its final, happy conceit tacitly concedes that the theatre's first purpose is to entertain but at the same time firmly maintains that it has much to teach as well. Over half a century earlier Francisco de la Barreda in his 'Invectiva a las comedias que prohibió Trajano y apología por las nuestras' (c.1618), looking at the matter the other way round, admitted that the *comedia* had a moral function but argued that there was no reason why it should be converted into a tribunal or a pulpit, that it was enough for it to advise like a friend without threatening like a judge. He even suggested that the serene semblance of the friend might possibly achieve more than the terrifying one of the judge.[32] For the theatre's supporters the *comedia* was a friend to princes, indirectly and gently embodying the more daunting exhortations of openly judgemental treatises. Of course, if the theatre's defenders and detractors present pictures of the *comedia* that are diametrically opposed it was because it was in the interests of both to convey these differing impressions. Thus its defenders stressed its morality and exemplarity and presented characters as models of behaviour, to be followed or avoided as the case might be, because this is what was needed to counter

[30] *Discursos políticos y morales en cartas apologéticas contra los que defienden el uso de las comedias modernas que se representan en España* (1682), Cotarelo, *Controversias*, 148.

[31] *Ortografía castellana* (c.1690), Cotarelo, *Controversias*, 53–4.

[32] *El panegírico de Plinio en castellano, Discurso IX* (Madrid 1622), 249ff.

the denunciations of the theatre's critics. It was all part of the rhetoric of controversy and debate; each side saw what it wanted to see. The possibility that art was not a moral issue at all was not contemplated, not just because the *comedia* was not accorded the status of art by its critics but because all art was still seen as having to have a justifying moral dimension.

As it happened, those who saw in the theatre an invaluable source of instruction for princes could invoke an unexceptionable authority in their support – that of history. History itself was regarded as a text-book in the art of government, a form of rhetoric which provided examples of ethical and practical conduct in public life, a source of information which encouraged the induction of general rules. Kings not only read *Kings* in the Old Testament, taking note of the lessons it had to offer, but sought models of royal behaviour in medieval chronicles and the writings of classical antiquity.[33] In his 'Autosemblanza' Philip IV itemized for Sor María de Ágreda all the histories he had read, 'pues ellas [historias] son la verdadera escuela en que el Príncipe y Rey hallarán ejemplares que seguir, casos que notar, y medios por donde encaminar a buenos fines los negocios de su Monarquía'.[34] Political commentators agreed with him. The words of Luis Cabrera de Córdoba, for whom history was a 'preparación importante para los actos políticos', in 1611, were echoed in the middle years of the century by Jerónimo de San José, 'en su escuela se aprende la política del gobierno' and by Saavedra Fajardo: 'La historia es maestra de la verdadera política y quien mejor enseñará a reinar al príncipe, porque en ella está presente la experiencia de todos los gobiernos pasados y la prudencia y juicio de los que fueron.'[35] It is a point Saavedra reiterated in his dedication of his treatise to Prince Baltasar Carlos, then eleven years old, '. . .porque ninguna libertad más importante a los reyes y a los reinos que la que sin malicia y pasión refiere cómo fueron las acciones de los gobiernos pasados, para enmienda de los presentes'. The theatre took full advantage of this liberty. Contemporary treatises on kingship draw heavily on historical example to illustrate and legitimate their argument throughout the sixteenth and seventeenth centuries, but from the end of the sixteenth century on the increasing intellectual enthusiasm for Tacitus enshrined history, along with nature, as a flexible and malleable model for the political life of a nation, in opposition to the rigidity of Machiavellian political theories and principles. The theatre's historical or quasi-historical plays therefore guaranteed it a certain amount of respectability and intellec-

33 See Margaret Aston, *The King's Bedpost: Reformation and Iconography in a Tudor Group Portrait* (Cambridge: Cambridge University Press, 1993), 26.

34 Seco Serrano, ed. *Cartas de Sor María de Jesús de Ágreda y Felipe IV*, 232.

35 Luis Cabrera de Córdoba, *De Historia, para entenderla y escribirla* (Madrid, 1611), folio 9; Jerónimo de San José, *Genio de la historia* (Zaragoza, 1651), 4; Saavedra Fajardo, *Empresa III*, 19 a–b. See Santiago Montero Díaz, 'La doctrina de la Historia en los tratadistas del Siglo de Oro', in his edition of Cabrera de Córdoba (Madrid: Instituto de Estudios Políticos, 1948).

tual weight. At the same time, the philosophy behind these plays, by and large, was the intellectual conviction that history was deeply relevant to contemporary politics. It little mattered that history in the theatre wandered off into legend and literature, or underwent the transformations of the imagination – although the more extravagant examples were denounced by the theatre's opponents – for the boundaries between these domains were in any case blurred and uncertain. For contemporary spectators equipped with only a hazy notion of history and geography, a king on stage was to all intents and purposes a king in time, in history; those they had heard about gave substance to those they had not. And for the purposes of the playwright with kingship in his sights the fictional king would usually do as well as the fictionalized – Francisco de Cascales's enthusiastic exhortation of 1634 does not distinguish between the two:

> Vamos, vamos al teatro escénico, que allí hallará el rey un rey que representa el oficio real; adónde se extiende su potestad; cómo se ha de haber con los vasallos; cómo ha de negar la puerta a los lisonjeros; cómo ha de usar la libertad, para que no sea avaro ni pródigo; cómo ha de guardar equidad, para no ser blando ni cruel.[36]

Any story of a king, after all, contains lessons in kingship of some sort. If princes become what they are expected to become, or are encouraged to become, as Saavedra Fajardo (apparently a firm believer in nurture rather than nature) held, then to enshrine the expectations in their entertainment, as well as in their lessons, made excellent sense:

> Apenas tiene el príncipe discurso, cuando, o le lisonjean con las desenvolturas de sus padres y antepasados, o le representan aquellas acciones generosas que están como vinculadas en las familias. De donde nace el continuarse en ellas de padres a hijos ciertas costumbres particulares, no tanto por la fuerza de la sangre, pues ni el tiempo ni la mezcla de los matrimonios las muda, cuanto por el corriente estilo de los palacios donde la infancia las bebe y convierte en naturaleza (*Empresa* II, 12).

Plays, like palaces, communicate messages.

The process of royal education envisaged here by Saavedra Fajardo was one of largely unconscious assimilation, and such a process would certainly have been at work in the prince's exposure to the chronicles and fictions of the theatre, 'este recreo/ de príncipes empleo' in the words of the Conde de Urgel in Tirso's naturally partisan *La firmeza en la hermosura* (c.1621, Act I, 170a).[37] However, Bances Candamo's comment about plays written for kings

36 Francisco de Cascales, *Cartas filológicas* (1634) (Madrid: Espasa Calpe, 1961), II, 54.

37 *Obras* VII, Biblioteca de Autores Españoles, 243 (Madrid: Atlas, 1971). The French

(and there is no reason to suppose that by this he did not mean plays written with kings in mind, as well as just court drama) being a means of saying without saying, 'decir sin decir', suggests something rather more directed and purposeful. It reveals the conviction that it was entirely possible to convey in a digestible and diplomatic way messages that needed to be heard, and envisages the playwright actually setting out to convey them. As for the person at whom such plays were directed, deliberately sensitized as he had been from birth to the problematical nature of the responsibilities he had inherited, he can hardly have failed to reflect upon their implications for himself. Just as it is impossible for anyone to read or to watch unfold and remain unaffected a narrative that bears closely on that person's own experience, so every such play the king saw must, as he sat watching, have stirred up in his mind some sort of dialectic between his own situation and the events he was witnessing on stage. It was not even as if he could complacently take refuge in the comforting anonymity of shared human experience – a king is unique in his own country. He sat there knowing that the role that he and only he occupied was under debate, and that the other spectators knew that he knew. Self-consciousness and identification were unavoidable.

There can be little doubt, I think, that Calderón saw the court theatre's role vis-à-vis the Crown as being that of educator as well as celebrant, pointing out in suitably discreet fashion the dangers that beset the prince, the strain between private inclination and public duty, the need for self-knowledge and self-control. But in the public playhouses, too, the figure of the king and the nature of kingship, dramatized in different ways and for different purposes, played a significant part in the theatrical diet of Spain from the end of the sixteenth century on. This was partly a function of the sheer usefulness of such a protean character to a contriver of plots – a king was at once a man and a universal figure, capable of occupying a place anywhere on the scale from paragon to tyrant. But it also undoubtedly reflected the importance of the monarch to the Spanish imagination, an importance fuelled by the rapid growth of court life after the death of the austere Philip II, as well as by an acute concern with the nation's ills and a consequential interest in its heroic past.

Tirso de Molina's criticism of the government of Spain in his plays in the 1620s is well known – it effectively cost him his theatrical career – and, as work on his plays proceeds, Ruth Lee Kennedy's description of his theatre as a theatre of opposition becomes ever more convincing.[38] Calderón's gloomy

dramatist Lazare de Baif declared that tragedies were invented to teach 'roys et grands seigneurs' ('Dedicace au Roy', *La Tragédie d'Euripide nommée Hécuba*). In England Philip Sidney was more explicit: 'Tragedy maketh kings fear to be tyrants and tyrants to manifest their tyrannical humours', 'The Defense of Poesie', *Literary Criticism from Plato to Dryden*, ed. Allan H. Gilbert (Detroit: Wayne State University Press, 1962), 432.

38 *Studies in Tirso*, I, 211–14.

preoccupation with inadequate and misguided rulers is similarly well recognized and equally, if more obliquely, eloquent. But what of that apparent opportunist of popular prejudices and beliefs, Lope de Vega, proclaimed by Amado Alonso to be 'El más grande poeta de la conformidad', a genius of conformity?[39] If we take T.S. Eliot's view that the business of the poet is to express the greatest emotional intensity of his time, based on what that time happens to think, then perhaps we should be satisfied to look no further, though that apparently easy and innocent phrase 'what the time happens to think' is in fact a Pandora's box of begged questions and should give pause for thought. What seventeenth-century Spain thought about monarchy and what it thought about its own government were not one and the same thing. It might be as well to remember, too, that both Shakespeare and Molière were at one time also seen as natural, uncritical geniuses unselfconsciously expressing the will of the people. We now take a different view, and a similar reassessment of Lope de Vega's art is underway. With it must inevitably come a reassessment of his long-standing reputation as the seventeenth-century Spanish theatre's conformist *par excellence*, a judgement traditionally used in a spirit of affectionate admiration which in recent years has acquired a more critical, even sinister, edge through association with the propaganda–conspiracy theory.

For Hermenegildo, as we saw,[40] Lope was a compliant pedlar of official views and values, though whether for commercial, strategic reasons or through ideological conviction, he does not specify: the grammar of the Spanish – 'Lope de Vega, poniendo su arte al servicio de la ideología dominante, consiguió un público' – allows the creation of an audience to be either the purpose or the consequence of Lope's conformism. Such a view, however, sits ill with the fact that when in 1644, eleven years after Lope's death, the Council of Castile launched a concerted attack on the theatre, using the war with Portugal as an excuse for recommending that the playhouses be closed down, Lope's plays were identified as being amongst the worst offenders of those 'que tanto daño había hecho a las costumbres'. He was certainly not seen in his own day as friend of the system. It also takes no account of the fact that he was an extraordinarily complex and contradictory individual. Desperately eager as he was for social and literary respectability, stronger compulsions repeatedly pulled him away, and his life *and* his work show the urge to rebellion and self-expression time and again triumphing over the weight of orthodoxy and convention. He doffed his hat respectfully in the direction of the classical precepts, yet went entirely his own artistic way, producing a drama based on views that were, in their implications, brilliantly original and daring. He mingled with the rich and great without ever being one of them, and his scandalous personal life ensured that, in spite of

39 'Lope de Vega y sus fuentes', *Thesaurus* (Bogotá) 8 (1952), 1–24, p.3.

40 See chap.1, 7.

being a national hero, he never attracted patronage from within the court's narrowest confines. As a patriot and as a poet fulfilling commissions for the authorities and the court as well as the public playhouses, he naturally paid his dues by writing poems and plays to mark national events and celebrations, plays such as *La nueva victoria de Don Gonzalo de Córdoba*, 1622, which celebrates the victory over Mansfeld's Protestant forces at Fleurus, and three years later, in 1625, *El Brasil restituido*, which dramatizes the recovery of Brazil from the Dutch at Bahía. He took part in the social life of the court and sometimes accompanied it on royal visits and progresses. But in 1621 he had publicly solicited in one of his court plays, *El premio de la hermosura*, the post of royal chronicler, without success, and although for a while in the early 1620s he assiduously dedicated works to the Count-Duke and Countess of Olivares in an attempt to attract their patronage,[41] he reaped scant reward other than a small royal pension in Galicia. In some of his verse in the twenties (in his *Epistle to don Antonio Hurtado de Mendoza*, and in his poetic celebration of the foundation of the Colegio Imperial in Madrid in 1629, *Isagoge a los reales estudios de la Compañía de Jesús*) his praise of Olivares is somewhat muted, partly perhaps through disappointment, but also because his patron of long standing, the Duke of Sessa, upon whom he seems to have been financially dependent in 1627–28 when in ill health, was a committed opponent of Olivares and the patronage game therefore had to be played with considerable diplomacy and discretion. In a letter to the Duke of Sessa in January 1630, Lope denounced a recent tract (*El chitón de las tablillas*) written anonymously by Quevedo, defending the Olivares régime from the attacks launched upon it in another clandestine work, as 'lo más satírico y venenoso que se ha visto desde el prinçipio del mundo'. These words, which may well have reflected Lope's own opinions, were certainly what his patron wished to hear, although Lope is careful not to impugn Olivares himself and he goes on to counsel Sessa to make strategic peace with the Count-Duke, 'que la mayor discreçion es hazer de los enemigos amigos y humillarse como el caldero al pozo para sacar el agua'.[42] It is not at all wise, however, to depend on his correspondence for a reliable reflection of his views. He gives little away in his letters, not least because Sessa, the principal recipient of those that survive, was by temperament, intelligence and interests not a person to inspire or warrant political confidences or intellectual discussion. In his comments on contemporary figures and events Lope says what Sessa wanted to hear – patronage was all and could not be placed at risk – although where his views echo what are clearly Sessa's own he is prepared to be more

41 For example, *El premio de la hermosura* (performed 1614, published 1621) and *Circe* (1624) to the Count-Duke and his collection of verse *Triunfos divinos con otras rimas* (1625) to the Countess.

42 *Epistolario de Lope de Vega Carpio*, ed. A. González de Amezúa, 4 vols (Madrid: Real Academia Española, 1935–43), vol.4, no. 523, 142–43.

critical. From the latter end of the reign of Philip III the standard obsequies are tinged with a prominent note of being hard done by and neglected by the king and Lerma, and in one he explicitly accuses Lerma of promising much and giving very little.[43] Another reveals that his bitterness was not entirely due to paranoia: Sessa had obviously reported back to him unflattering things being said about him at court, 'de que vine triste, pensando qual es mi dicha, que en Palacio no se acuerdan de lo que he seruido en tantas ocasiones para remediar mis necesidades, y para caluniar mis costumbres esté tan en la memoria, siendo átomo de la Corte y del sol de aquella grandeza', a clear reference to the lifestyle that almost certainly hindered his advancement at the highest level.[44] Veiled, or not so veiled, remarks such as that in *Lo fingido verdadero* (c.1608) referring to the time of Alexander the Great: 'que los príncipes entonces/ honraban los que lo eran [gran poeta]' inhabit the play-texts like a nagging tooth. In 1620, when he published Parte XIII of his plays, the prologue openly reveals his bitterness at the lack of official recognition and reward accorded him and these complaints were to continue throughout the rest of his life, intensifying in later years when he often found himself in desperately straitened circumstances. In his will he states that a promise made to him by the king of a post for his daughter Feliciana's husband was never fulfilled, and the abduction and subsequent abandonment in 1634 of his beloved seventeen-year-old daughter, Antonia Clara, by a noble member of the royal household who was not punished for the crime, grievously soured his attitude to his king in the last year of his life.[45] The exceedingly handsome reward he received simply for dedicating his epic poem about Mary Stuart, *Corona trágica* (1627), to Pope Urban VIII – a warm letter of thanks, the title of doctor of theology and the Cross of the Order of Saint John – merely emphasized the Spanish Crown's continuing neglect of him. He was not granted the accolade of membership of one of the military orders, the seal of approval without which no gentleman felt socially secure, and apart from a few honorific appointments of little standing he collected only two minor benefices. As a result, the circumstances of his life, as well as his temperament, nurtured in him extremely ambivalent responses indeed to authority and convention, an ambivalence which is very apparent in his inhibited and contradictory manifesto, *Arte nuevo de hacer comedias en este tiempo*, and which often becomes a palpable presence in his plays. And the ambivalence detectable in his depiction of kingship closely resembles, interestingly enough, the grave, if diplomatically expressed, unease of political theorists such as Rivadeneyra and Mariana.

The problem about Lope's drama, of course, is that the sheer size of his

43 González de Amezúa *Epistolario*, vol.3, no.184, 179.

44 González de Amezúa *Epistolario*, vol.4, no.434, 57.

45 See also chap.4.

output makes safe generalization impossible. Yet generalizations inevitably are made, often on the evidence of a few of the better-known plays. Where views regarding Lope's attitude to kingship are concerned, it is no coincidence that three of Lope's most celebrated plays – *Peribáñez y el Comendador de Ocaña*, *Fuenteovejuna*, and *El mejor alcalde el rey* – effectively enshrine declarations of faith in an idealized monarchy. Although very individual works of art written over a span of roughly eighteen years between 1605 and 1623, and set in different periods of Spanish history, they have a common preoccupation – power – and a common theme – the democratization of honour perceived in terms of class conflict and dramatized in terms of sexual aggression. In each one, a sexually obsessed nobleman comes into conflict with his peasant vassals and in each one the king, as God's vice gerent, plays a crucial strategic role as dispenser of justice, in *Peribáñez* and *Fuenteovejuna* ratifying without condoning the violent measures taken by the desperate peasants to protect their women, in *El mejor alcalde el rey* even taking an active role in the provision of a resolution. Critics never tire of pointing out that in spite of their superficially democratic, even revolutionary, spirit, the plays are, if anything, anti-feudalism but pro-monarchy. And, of course, this is indeed the case. But this does not mean that they are a defence of absolutism, as many commentators take for granted.[46] Neither, as I shall argue in due course, does it mean that they are not politically alert and searching. Lope's perspective on the feudal rights and privileges of the medieval nobility is the necessarily anachronistic one of his own age – they take second place to the centralized authority that is the surest guarantee of justice. For a king to subject a noble to the rule of law, as happens in *El mejor alcalde el rey*, is certainly not absolutism in the sense in which it was understood in the seventeenth century – that the king's will was paramount whatever the needs of the state or the opinion of his subjects. Spanish political theorists explicitly rejected such an interpretation of monarchy. These dramas, like Shakespeare's historical plays, celebrate the stable centralization of authority in the crown. This was not because monarchical authority or succession were in question in Spain – they were not, and sedition, as a result, was not the urgent concern it was elsewhere in Europe. Mariana's treatise on kingship, which holds that the authority of the republic is greater than that of the prince and condones in extreme cases the removal of the monarch, by force if necessary, was declared seditious in France in 1610 after the assassination of Henry IV and consigned to the flames. In Spain, on the other hand, although it caused a considerable stir and its vivid references to Jacob Clément, assassin of Henry III of France, had to be removed, the censor who

46 For example, José Mª Díez Borque, 'Estructura social de la comedia de Lope: a propósito de *El mejor alcalde el rey*', *Arbor* 85 (1973), 453–66.

licensed its publication in 1599 declared it an exemplary guide to proper and successful government.

If Lope's three plays celebrate monarchy it is because its indispensable role as guarantor of a healthy state was a tenet of political faith that Lope, along with his troubled age at large, needed to believe in. And given such a belief, of course, the dramatic usefulness of kings is self-evident – like gods in classical drama, they made excellent *dei ex machina*, dispensing justice and facilitating resolutions, if not always solutions. If the projection of kingship was a feature of seventeenth-century monarchies in Europe, the reason was that the monarch's ideal role as provider of national health and harmony was a difficult one to achieve given the vicissitudes of government and the questionable suitability of a hereditary ruler. And the drama, along with the widespread disillusionment, even cynicism, that characterizes seventeenth-century Spanish thinking generally, indicates that the people were not fooled. As Elliott has said, 'The example of the Spain of Olivares suggests that the new propaganda resources of the seventeenth-century state [and amongst these Elliott rightly includes the court theatre] were perfectly capable of being counter-productive and of damaging the very cause they intended to promote.'[47] The theatre was only partially in thrall to the power of court patronage and even then readily discovered strategies of evasion when it wished to do so. The plays of the leading dramatists represent a body of writing that enshrines what amounts to a betrayed vision of kingship. Explicit criticism of the monarch, even had it been possible in a theatre where each play had to be licensed for performance as was the case in Spain from 1615 on, was unnecessary when plays depicting fictional or historical kings could comment with impunity, by negative or positive example, on the split between an accepted ideal of kingship and the compromising reality. In the presence of an aware audience, even model kings could serve as a technique of subversion. And model kings are very thin on the ground indeed in the Golden-Age theatre, for princes one would have to categorize as 'good' are, for the most part, portrayed in a nuanced and rarely uncritical way. Even kings with a stable historical profile are made to bend to the dramatic imperatives of the moment. It may be that in Lope de Vega, at least, the depiction of princely imperfection started out as the dramatist's instinctive recognition that, since kings are men, the ideal of kingship must carry within it the seeds of its own defeat, that the vision itself is flawed. But after the accession of Philip III it would have been impossible for plays to maintain an air of political innocence in their depiction of kings, not least because they would not have been received innocently. It is always a mistake in any case to underestimate Lope – even *Peribáñez*, *Fuenteovejuna* and *El mejor alcalde el rey* betray a powerful nostalgia for a more personal form of rule, for a time when

[47] In 'Power and Propaganda in the Spain of Philip IV', *Spain and its World 1500–1700*, p.163.

kings were more actively involved in the processes of justice, and they smack therefore of a comment on the increasing distance between monarch and people that characterized Habsburg rule. That this was a reflection of contemporary concern is clear from Rivadeneyra and Mariana, both of whom warned against the dangers of over-delegation, and stressed that a prime requisite of successful monarchy was continuing accessibility; Rivadeneyra, in his extended treatment of justice and judges, went as far as to maintain that the only way the prince could ensure that the judicial processes were in good order was to take part in them himself from time to time (541). Lope's expression of belief in personal kingship is stated more strongly in each successive play of the three, with the last, *El mejor alcalde el rey*, depicting a monarch who in fairy-tale fashion actually goes in disguise to the peasants' village to make sure that justice is done: a potent indicator, not of a progressive flight into fantasy on Lope's part, but of the Spanish monarchy's growing remoteness. Romance merely serves the purposes of reality.

Having pointed out the dangers of generalizing about Lope's theatre, I am now going to generalize and say that the three peasant honour plays which tend to dominate traditional thinking about Lope's portrayal of kingship are not at all representative. Contrary to the generally held perception, his monarchs in fact tend to be a bad, or at least a severely compromised lot, particularly those who play a substantial, rather than minor strategic, role in the plot.[48] Lope's kings do not at all fit the following statement made by J.H. Elliott about the writers who held positions in the personal service of Philip IV and the royal family: 'In their books and plays these men would sing the praises of the Planet King and project to the world the brilliant image of Spanish kingship which the régime of Olivares was seeking to promote.'[49] Here in all likelihood lies a large part of the explanation for Lope's frustrated ambitions. His treatment of kingship in general is irreverential and he often goes out of his way to create his own dramatic reassessments of historical processes specifically in order to make observations pertinent to contemporary Spain. Thus in one of his many medieval plays, *Las almenas de Toro* written 1610–19, probably 1610–13,[50] half way through the reign of Philip III, he produces a beautifully equivocal portrait of Sancho IV, an eleventh-century king whose historical concern for the integrity of his realm may be seen as either legitimate or predatory, but whose murder, reputedly at his brother's command, has given him a generally sympathetic profile. By por-

48 Margaret Wilson, in *Spanish Drama of the Golden Age* (Oxford/London: Pergamon Press, 1969), 159–60, takes the typical line when she remarks that unlike Lope's kings, who are seen as the ministers of divine justice, Calderón's 'are only too fallible'.

49 'The Court of the Spanish Habsburgs', *Spain and its World 1500–1700,* 159.

50 Unless otherwise stated, dates given for Lope's plays are those found in S. Griswold Morley and Courtney Bruerton, *The Chronology of Lope de Vega's 'Comedias'* (New York: The Modern Language Association of America, 1940).

traying a Sancho who is insecure, duplicitous and lacking in judgement – the very reverse of Rivadneyra and Mariana's ideal prince – while at the same time suggesting that loyalty to the authority of monarchy is a necessary prerequisite of ordered government, Lope focuses on one of the central dilemmas of monarchy. It is a brilliant piece of tight-rope walking that draws attention to the dilemma posed by kingship without ever allowing the mask of ingenuousness to slip. In *El Duque de Viseo* (1604–10, probably 1608–09), which will be looked at more closely in due course, that forceful and much admired Renaissance monarch, John II of Portugal, is similarly transformed into a weak, insecure and ungrateful king, who stabs to death an admirable and innocent man he believes to be plotting against him. Here too history has been turned on its head – Viseu in fact did conspire against John II – and Lope's purpose is clearly to reveal the dangers both of lack of princely fortitude and of favouritism, correctly foreseen by Rivadeneyra and Mariana as being inevitable features of the reign of Philip III. It is a bold treatment of the kingship question, for in it loyalty to God's representative on earth breaks down, the disobedience is seen to be justified, and the person responsible is plainly the king himself. The message is implicit but clear; the relationship between monarch and vassal is essentially a contractual one; the loyalty the vassal owes his king must be earned. As Mariana warned, 'El poder de los príncipes se destruye y se debilita desde el momento en que les falta el apoyo del respeto y del amor en los súbditos' (chap. VI, 112), and again, 'También es necesario sujetarse a la opinión pública de los cuidadanos' (chap. IX, 169). Since *El Duque de Viseo* belongs to the same period as *Las almenas de Toro* the lessons they contain have an obvious relevance to the reign of an ineffectual king who had eagerly handed over power to a favoured and extremely exploitative minister.

Such concern on Lope's part does not, I think, reflect just some passing irritation with the régime nor does it surface merely in a few of his better-known plays. As with most Spanish plays of the period, the location of his play-texts within a specific historic moment is too often approximate at best, but his kingship plays in general reveal, throughout the last four decades of his career, a continuing and thoughtful engagement with the issue as well as considerable familiarity with the views of contemporary theorists and commentators. It is even possible that in the depiction of some of his villainous nobles he had in his sights specific government and court figures of the day, although unless there is some reliable indicator such as an equivalence of office – as in the case of favourites for example – such readings can only be interesting conjecture. It was not in Lope's interests to be openly provocative about identifiable individuals, and more reliably eloquent of the way in which his plays become part of contemporary political debate are the considerable number of them which either openly address the problems of kingship or contain a covert dialectic on the theme whose premises could be supplied at varying levels of complexity, sophistication and specificity by the audience itself. These plays constitute a body of writing which contains clear evidence of the influence of contemporary political thinkers upon him, and which at the same time shows Lope unerringly in command of the means whereby popular entertainment could be made a conduit of comment and discussion, even personal resentments. Such a discourse became fully legible only in the presence of the audience for whom it was intended, but even now these texts, many of them relatively little known, may be seen to offer in some way or other a critique of the contemporary situation in seventeenth-century Spain and to present a challenge to the view that Lope was a political poodle intent on propagating an official ideology, or at best an unthinking imbiber and dispenser of political orthodoxies.

There are a number of plays by Lope about kings or with kings in them, it has to be said, which scarcely seem to engage with political issues at all. They tend to be relatively early plays; the following are examples. In *La campana de Aragón* (1596–1603; 1598?–1600?) Lope dramatizes the legendary story of King Ramiro the Monk of Aragón who dealt with the ridicule of his nobles by cutting off their heads and piling them in the shape of a bell. *Los Ramírez de Arellano* (1599–1608) is an early version of the rivalry between King Pedro and Enrique de Trastámara. *El rey sin reino* (1597–1612) – a badly constructed play in which three people die for the convenience of the plot, and for no obvious medical reason, and no fewer than three characters have the same name – is about a king who dies for breaking a sacred oath and a boy-king who finally regains his throne. *Carlos V en Francia* (1604) depicts the relationship between Carlos V and François I, showing the latter in a very flattering light, presumably for diplomatic reasons during a period of relative harmony with France. In the quasi-historical *La reina doña María* (1604–08 if indeed by Lope), the King, don Pedro, is a womanizer who will not go near his queen and has to be tricked into impregnating her (a plot which might carry resonances of Philip IV if it was written later.) In *La batalla del honor* (1608), the king lays military siege to the Almirante de Francia and then sexual siege to the Almirante's wife. *El mejor mozo de España* (1610–11) romanticizes the courtship of the young Ferdinand and Isabella. In *La sortija del olvido* (1610–15), a silly story salvaged by some effective comedy and writing of very high quality, the King of Hungary is incapacitated by a poisoned ring and loses his wits. In *El galán de la Membrilla* (1615) Fernando creates problems for a pair of socially unequal lovers but eventually acknowledges his mistake. These plays exploit the appeal of the courtly and the historical to create stirring plots of love and adventure, taking what liberties they will with any source material and otherwise showing strong leanings towards the novelesque. By and large, as we might expect, they proceed in accordance with implicit assumptions about such things as legitimacy and suitability – fortitude, fairness, responsibility, magnanimity, keeping faith, and so on – but they do not actively concern themselves in any serious or arresting way with the issue of kingship. They do serve to show, however, the glamour royal characters held for contemporary audiences and their usefulness, therefore, to Lope when he settled down to write in a more reflective way. In a voracious commercial theatre ruled by the law of supply and demand, Lope naturally no more turned out kings of unvarying interest than he did plays of unvarying quality.

It is not my intention here to provide a catalogic study of all those plays by Lope which feature kings in a search for evidence for the contention that a considerable number of them constitute a telling political critique, because the level of interest with regard to kingship and government varies considerably depending on the play and in any case that way indigestion lies. Nor is it my intention to study his treatment of particular kings or to sieve through plots and dialogue in order to rehearse his broad views on monarchy in general – which were inevitably those of his time – for such studies already exist.[51] I wish instead to concentrate on those which engage with the then current debates in what seem to me to be significant ways, in the process revealing not only Lope's adroitness at contriving quasi-historical or romantic plots which could be seen to be making political points, but also the stratagems he used to negotiate a path of prudence between the acceptable and the unacceptable in political discourse. Since the normal function of language, in both its literary and non-literary forms, is to communicate – information, views, intentions, hopes, visions, anxieties and fears, understanding, insights – then I think we can assume that Lope meant to communicate something through the medium of his king-plays. Clearly access to any contemporary horizon of expectations and preoccupations is bound to be compromised by our own; but reconciling the two is the duty of the literary interpreter who takes history seriously. And essential to that reconciliation is an acknowledgement that things might not always be what at first sight they seem; that there are multiple ways of communicating meaning which evade the sort of explicitness which in certain circumstances can prove undesirable or even unwise. Interpretive archeology does not necessarily involve, therefore, either critical special pleading or anachronism – pitfalls neither more nor less to be deplored than the assumptions that the past has nothing in common with the present and that its literary texts mean only what they seem now to say. Chapters 3 and 4 examine a variety of procedures employed in the general corpus of Lope's king-plays for the oblique exploitation of history and pseudo-history to make political points. Chapter 5 suggests a way of under-

[51] See for example, Frances Exum, *The Metamorphosis of Lope de Vega's King Pedro* (Madrid: Colección Plaza Mayor Scholar, 1974); Miguel Herrero García, 'La monarquía teorética de Lope de Vega', *Fén* I (1935), 179–224, 303–62; Antonio Gómez-Moriana, *Derecho de resistencia y tiranicidio: Estudio de una temática en las 'comedias' de Lope de Vega* (Santiago de Compostela: Porto y Cía, 1968); Richard A. Young, *La figura del rey y la institución real en la comedia lopesca* (Madrid: Ediciones José Porrúa Turanzas, 1979); also, more generally, Otis H. Green, 'La dignidad real en la literatura del siglo de oro: noticias de un estudioso', *Revista de Filología Española* 48 (1965), 231–50.

standing these stratagems for successful communication in an age of political vigilance as part of an overall strategy of prudence in a carefully judged engagement with power, and chapters 6 and 7 then in the light of this shaping strategy discuss some of Lope's best-known and most potent political plays.

3

HISTORICAL TRANSFORMATIONS: FRACTURED ICONS I

At first sight, *La corona merecida*, a sombre, tragic play traditionally ascribed to 1603, does not seem to have much relevance to the matter in hand despite its title. It is a tale of royal lust, dramatizing the story of a legendary Sevillian heroine, María Coronel, who saved her husband's life by consenting to sleep with her importunate sovereign, then saved her honour by ulcerating her flesh with boiling oil. The heroic crown of the title is hers. The few critics who have looked at the play, usually in the context of tyranny, have been at a loss to explain the fact that these events, traditionally ascribed to the reign of the fourteenth-century king Pedro I of Castile, are reassigned by Lope to the twelfth century and the much admired Alfonso VIII, and that the famous María Coronel, in consequence, has to become a fictitious Sol. Lope was fascinated enough with the Janus image of Pedro – sometimes *el cruel*, at others *el justiciero* – to write no fewer than eight plays about him dramatizing his strengths and flaws, and was quite prepared in *Los Ramírez de Arellano* (1597–1608, prob.1604–08) to present him as a king unfit to rule. There can be no question, therefore, that he was merely trying for some reason to whitewash Pedro's reputation.

The only plausible explanation for this otherwise bizarre and unnecessary meddling with tradition is that a king remembered for his youth – Alfonso VIII succeeded to the throne as an infant – better suited Lope's purpose, for the play's subtext deals not so much with tyranny as with the relationship between the monarch and his favourites, with the way in which the young Alfonso – and his youth is much stressed – is aided and abetted in the pursuit of his unlawful appetites by pandering favourites. In 1603 Philip III was twenty-four, not at all a vicious young man but certainly a weak and idle one, who had been under the influence of the Duke of Lerma since well before his father's death. Rivadeneyra, while insistent that all princes, being human, need the prudent counsel of wise men (553–6), warns that since their position and responsibilities render them unusually susceptible to human passions, bad counsel is disastrous for the republic. He specifically denounces courtiers, who flatter and fawn upon their king and persuade him that he is inviolate (559–60). Flattery is a constant theme in Mariana, too, who warns that it makes kings arrogant (168) and that no single individual surrounded by compliant courtiers can guarantee the prosperity and well-being of the state (163).

Their dilemma is obvious – the very weaknesses in Philip III which made guidance essential rendered him doubly susceptible to the wrong *sort* of guidance. Lope's play is a dramatization of just these concerns, deftly weaving into a plot apparently far removed in time and action from seventeenth-century Spain strands of unmistakable significance for the day. The re-ascription of events to a youthful monarch brings closer to home the messages they carry and the king's sexual misbehaviour operates not literally but allusively, signalling the presence of the dysfunctional. A year earlier Lope had not minced his words when in *El príncipe despeñado* (1602) he put in one of his character's mouths this swingeing denunciation of court politics:

> Están las cosas en tan triste estado,
> que no hay hidalgo ya que corresponde
> a sus obligaciones ni a sus leyes:
> ¡Tanta codicia es ya privar con reyes! (Act II, 323b)[1]

Its blatant relevance to the new Lerma régime then clearly struck him as imprudent, for in the autograph manuscript 'privar' is amended to 'tratar'.[2] One of the ways in which displacement, temporal and geographical, works in these plays is to take kingship out of its familiar, pragmatic context and allow the audience to view it in a different, more objective light. In the background, however, the pragmatic will always hover, stimulating the drawing of inferences and the perception of connections between fictional and real worlds.

Interestingly, Lope widens the focus of debate in *La corona merecida*, showing the dangers of courtly counsel to be inherent in the unequal relationship between courtier and monarch. Thus while one of the young King's favourites, Manrique, is from the start a cynical schemer intent on currying favour, the other, Pedro, disapproves of the King's behaviour and says so. When the King insists that a lord's will must be obeyed in everything, good or ill, Pedro's reply might have come straight from Rivadeneyra:

> El consejo en el privado
> es ley de buen caballero;
> un privado lisonjero
> es un veneno dorado. (Act I, 233a)[3]

Lope's king-plays are threaded with similar *sententiae* with their roots in contemporary political philosophy. Pedro's affirmation later on that only lawful acts are appropriate in a king (Act III, 596b) directly echoes the chapter of Mariana's entitled 'El príncipe está sujeto a las leyes', where Mariana

1 *Obras*, Biblioteca de Autores Españoles, 197 (Madrid: Atlas, 1966).
2 See Menéndez y Pelayo's footnote to this line.
3 *Obras*, Biblioteca de Autores Españoles, 24 (Madrid: M. Rivadeneyra, 1853).

insists that the King is accountable not only to God and to morality but to public opinion. Pedro takes easy refuge in obedience nonetheless, and both favourites not only suggest means whereby the King can have his way but actively enable the deceit afoot. By Act III Pedro, too, has effectively become a complete accomplice in the King's immorality – the plan to arrest and frame don Alonso for the King's misdeeds is his. His actions have ceased to match his words of recrimination and concern, and even when supposedly trying to reason with the King after don Alonso has been arrested his words change, slide and slip:

Don Pedro.	Luego ¿la razón no puede nada?
Rey.	¿Qué puede la razón si está sujeta?
Don Pedro.	No puede estar sujeto el albedrío.
Rey.	¿Nunca has sabido tú lo que amor puede?
Don Pedro.	Ya sé que puede amor lo que la ira y otras pasiones naturales nuestras, que se pueden sufrir y resistirse; pero ¡ay de quien se deja llevar dellas!
Rey.	Pesado estás, habiéndome tú puesto en aquesta invención.
Don Pedro.	Harto bien dices, y esto es lo mismo que te dije.
Rey.	¿Cómo?
Don Pedro.	Que ya dices que yo la culpa tengo.
Rey.	Pues ¿ para qué me matas y me animas?
Don Pedro.	Porque negar no puedes que te engaña la luz de la razón, que no conoces, en viéndote perdido de remedio. (Act III, 244b–c)

As an explanation of his own shabby behaviour this specious answer is hardly adequate to meet the circumstances. In placing the blame squarely on the shoulders of the King, don Pedro slides out from beneath his own share of the responsibility. In doing so, however, he speaks in fact nothing but the truth. If favourites corrupt then it is incumbent upon a king to resist that corruption. Everything in the text conspires to condemn the King – his own attitudes and actions, the comments of others, the sequence of events, the extremes to which Sol is driven in order to protect her own honour and that of her husband. In denouncing him as 'ciego' (Act III, 245b), a habitual metaphor in the *comedia* for the moral disengagement caused by passion, rage or disordered ideas, she denounces his imperviousness to the requirements of his royal role. For this, it is made clear in the play, there are no excuses. If the corrupting influence of royal favour upon the courtier as well as the monarch is explored, so too, albeit more sketchily, is the exonerating circumstance of royal youthfulness. Alfonso's courtiers generally excuse the King's behaviour and justify their own complicity by invoking his youth. But Pedro clearly feels that the King's age does not exempt him from the claims of reason and self-control, and the Queen's lady-in-waiting, sympathizing with her mistress's distress at arriving from England to find her new husband only a reluctant and hasty visitor to the royal bed, scornfully dismisses the excuse of youth as inappropriate in a bridegroom with royal responsibilities. The King himself, in a rare moment of self-knowledge, accepts responsibility for his own actions, reassuring Pedro, when he gloomily observes that once the King's desires are satisfied he will regard him as an infamous pimp, that Pedro in doing his will is just the virtuous means to vicious ends which are all his. Is this, one wonders, Lope's way of laying responsibility for government firmly in the royal lap? Certainly this neglected play is saying, implicitly and explicitly, some extremely interesting things about the role of the favourite in government five years after the era of the royal favourite had begun. At one point in Act I there is even open criticism of the expense and extravagance of royal wedding festivities – a reference perhaps to the marriage of Philip III to Margaret of Austria in 1599.

The behaviour of the Alfonso VIII of the play is reprehensible in the extreme. He sins against a sacrament, against his responsibilities to his queen, his nobles and his country, against the code of honourable behaviour. He abuses his power and his contractual relationship, based in morality, with his subjects, as Sol points out; he is hypocritical, he dissimulates, lies and frames an innocent man. Clearly no simplistic equivalence with Spain's pious and innocuous reigning prince would either have been intended or detected. The behaviour is villainous because Lope wished, albeit with consummate tact, to drive home the point that youthful princes are extremely vulnerable to the influence of favoured advisers. The excuse of youth is dismissed as invalid because kings cannot afford to be young, they cannot behave as other men. As doña Costanza comments in Lope's *Las paces de los reyes y judía de Toledo* on the *savoirefaire* of another dramatic manifestation of Alfonso VIII, 'Los reyes nacen con canas'. This play (1604–12, prob.1610?–12) dramatizes the famous story of Alfonso's love for his mistress Raquel, the Jewess of Toledo, who was killed for reasons of state. In Lope's version Alfonso's passion leads him to neglect his kingdom for seven years, while he lives apart with Raquel, until the Queen has her killed, whereupon Alfonso comes to his senses and the royal pair are reunited. The play operates satisfactorily and coherently at the level of stirring historical romance. But of course here again we have a conflict of personal inclination and royal responsibility, and an extravagant neglect of government. In the following reign Luis de Ulloa's epic poem about Raquel and Alfonso VIII, *Alfonso Octavo Rey de Castilla* (published in 1650), known as *La Raquel*, would be directly relevant to the philanderings of Philip IV. Ulloa, a moralist and political pessimist who was entrusted with the education of Juan de Austria, Philip IV's son by the actress María de Calderón, and who gave refuge to his protector Olivares when the latter fell from power, comments acidly on negligent kingship in the poem: 'y en la vida culpable de los reyes/ no son vicios los vicios sino leyes'.[4] It would be going too far, perhaps, to see the beautiful, tragic Jewess Raquel as a deliberate, if incongruous, cipher for the greedy self-serving Duke of Lerma, but the relevance of a king allowing himself to be distracted from his duties by an attachment to a subject so great that the Queen can claim that it is Raquel who rules Castile, could not have been lost on the audience. The king-plays are fictions but they opened a door onto reality, revealing to their audience things about real-life kings and kingship. Act I of the play – quite unnecessarily in terms of the plot which then has to take a chronological lunge forward – presents Alfonso as a youth displaying all the initial royal promise which as a man he will, for an extended period of his reign, betray, so here again contemporary issues do not seem to be far removed from Lope's mind. Indeed the inclusion of Alfonso's youth suggests perhaps that the play was written nearer 1604 than 1612, for Lope wrote a number of other plays figuring youthful kings in the late sixteenth and early seventeenth centuries – *La varona castellana*, *La fortuna merecida*, *El rey sin reino*, *El príncipe despeñado* and *La inocente sangre* amongst them. Philip III, at twenty, was not particularly young by the standards of the day when he ascended the throne – his grandfather Charles V had been sixteen and his own son would be the same age – but he was in terms of maturity, experience and dedication the equivalent of a youth, and Lope was not slow to exploit public interest in the new king in the early years of his reign.

Of the titles listed above, *La inocente sangre* (prob.1604–08, but almost certainly retouched in 1622) is the most obviously, not to say crudely, didactic in that it depicts the king, Fernando IV of Castile, being struck down by God in his sleep for his misdemeanours after one of his victims appeals to divine justice. Fernando is so incensed by the murder of his favourite that he condemns two innocent brothers to death for the crime. His desire to find the culprit clouds his judgement: he ignores the advice of a senior counsellor, he permits himself to be deceived by two malicious and unprincipled men without establishing the truth, he allows his personal feelings, in short, to gain the upper hand. He believes he can arrive at the truth by gut feeling, 'Que no quiero información/ mayor que mi corazón' (Act III, 367a),[5] which of course will not do at all. One of the brothers reassures the woman he loves that a king is a godlike being (Act II, 359a) – committed, is the implication, to justice and truth. He will soon discover to his cost, however, that Fernando is only a man (this ironic technique of asserting in the dialogue what is denied by the action, of having it both ways in other words, was a favourite strata-

[4] Biblioteca de Autores Españoles, 29 (Madrid: M. Rivadeneyra, 1854), 479b. See Josefina García Aráez, *Don Luis de Ulloa y Pereira* (Madrid: Consejo Superior de Investigaciones Científicas, 1952).

[5] *Obras*, Biblioteca de Autores Españoles, 51 (Madrid: M. Rivadeneyra, 1860).

gem of Lope's to which we shall return later on). Justice and prudence were the twin cornerstones of contemporary monarchical theory: in López Bravo's words, 'incapaz es del reyno el príncipe sin prudencia y indigno dél sin justicia' (116). The messages for the monarch who is a dispenser of justice here come loud and clear: 'Conde: Si agravia el Rey la justicia/ ¿Quién habrá que la defienda?' (Act III, 367b), and again,

> [Voice off] Los que en la tierra juzgáis, . . .
> No os ciegue pasión ni amor.
> Juzgad jurídicamente;
> que quien castiga sin culpa
> a Dios la piedad ofende. (Act III, 371c)

So does one about a specific form of justice, one very close to Lope's heart – the need to reward services rendered to the country in the fields of arms and letters:

> Siempre los reyes los premian,
> porque están a cargo suyo
> ya las armas, ya las letras. (Act II, 363b)

The brothers put to death are Pedro and Juan Caravajal, and Lope dedicated the play to a descendent of theirs, Sebastián de Caravajal, who was a member of the Council of State. In the dedication, published in *Parte* XIX of Lope's plays in 1623, he deplores the hasty judgement of a king in a way that suggests that some particular contemporary reference might have been intended, as well as a more general comment on kingly behaviour: 'el juez temerario más daña al que juzga que al que es juzgado'.[6] There is of course no way of knowing this without an exact dating, both for the play itself and the dedication. On the other hand there can be no doubt about the nature of the play's advice nor its target: irresponsibility, impetuousness, personal feelings and wishes, above all the excessive attachment to one particular counsellor that leads to a clouding of judgement, had no place in the conduct of a king, a warning applicable to the reigns of both Philip III and Philip IV. The dedication explicitly emhasizes that bad counsel does not exonerate a king: 'No le hallan los historiadores al Rey disculpa con haber sido engañado.'

The action in *La corona merecida* and *Las paces de los reyes* turns, as we have seen, on sexual unruliness. The depiction of princes offered the seventeenth-century theatre plenty of scope with regard to the sexual or love interest that was so crucial an element in the *comedia*'s recipe for success, so

6 *Obras*, Biblioteca de Autores Españoles, 51, 349. In the dedication Lope elaborates the point and reinforces it with Latin quotations from Aristotle, St Augustine, Tertulian and St Gregory.

crucial indeed that it was included at times even at the risk of incongruity. Pertaining as it did, however, in the case of the king, to the individual rather than the role – royal marriages were affairs of state not the heart – the love motif possessed a double appeal for playwrights, allowing them as it did entry to an aspect of kingship that preoccupied political thinkers in the Early Modern period, particularly during the reign of a monarch not cut out for rule: the uneasy relationship between the man and the role, between the private and the public persona. The image of kingship established by Lope is an essentially human image with a man at its very centre, albeit a man with a special relationship to all that constituted humankind's existence – God, country, law, society, family and nature. The kings who stride through Lope's plays are lovers, husbands, fathers, dispensers of rewards and punishments, rulers misled and manipulated by scheming enemies and favourites, leaders winning and losing wars. Only very occasionally do we see them iconographically as remote, divinely appointed arbiters and distributors of justice and even then they are usually robed in some way or other with their own humanity. In such a role they cannot occupy the centre of the action, for centrality necessarily brings exposure – the man who is an image of God cannot withstand the close scrutiny of other men.

Since even a king is subject to the law, stage kings are not excused their misdemeanours by dint of being kings. The public role does not remove or even diminish the imperfections of the individual – in the drama there is a productive tension between the two. The king is greater than his flaws, but not as great as he would be without them or as great as he ought to be. For the English Puritans' 'We fight the king to defend the King' Lope would undoubtedly have substituted, in answer to any charge that his depiction of kings was less than flattering, 'I criticize kings to defend the King.' Lope depicts kings engaged in sexual and romantic dalliance as a way of revealing the man beneath the crown, and of commenting upon the way in which the man who is a king comports himself. Time and again in the plays the stress point is passion, which thus becomes a systematized indicator of the monarch's fragile human nature. The individual's behaviour in this area of human activity serves as a paradigm of his behaviour as a public person, for of course a king is a public person first and only second a private individual; accordingly behaviour unsuitable in any honourable man is reprehensible in a prince. Rivadeneyra painstakingly pointed out to his young prince that not only were princes, by reason of their position and responsibilities, more susceptible to human passions than other men, but weakness in them was correspondingly more dangerous for the republic (559–60). The depiction of sexual misdemeanours therefore becomes in Lope a codified critique of princely conduct. Lope is saying, 'Kings are men; but they must be kings first, and their behaviour and their actions must always acknowledge that special role.' Of course the process of humanization that drama requires of the depiction of a king necessarily diminishes the public persona. To place a king on the stage is to reveal his smallness, to portray him as a desperate, importunate or jealous lover is to strip him, temporarily at least, of majesty, for it encourages a withdrawal not just of awe but of respect: self-control is essential in one who controls. And a just prince depends on the respect as well as the love of his subjects, dignity is essential in one who reigns. All the Spanish theorists of the time made this point, including Vives in his *Concordia y Discordia* in the early sixteenth century: 'La grandeza de un príncipe consiste en ver las cosas mejor que el vulgo y en regirse a sí mismo serenamente, puesto que tiene bajo sí a tantos que gobernar. De esta grandeza no debe descender el príncipe por las iras o los odios de los demás, porque entonces abdica de su rango y se convierte en un cualquiera' (417). But Saavedra Fajardo, with his greater knowledge of the world, would make the point most strongly: the *benignidad* in a prince that inspires the love of his vassals must be accompanied by *gravedad* and *autoridad* if he is to inspire respect, 'porque si éste falta [respect], es muy amigo el amor de domesticarse y hacerse igual. Si no le conserva lo augusto de la majestad, no habrá diferencia entre el príncipe y el vasallo' (*Empresa* XXXIX, 99b). He goes on to make a plea for moderation in all things but, 'En lo que más ha menester el príncipe este cuidado es en la moderacián de los afectos, gobernándolos con la prudencia, que nada desee, espere, ame o aborrezca con demasiado ardor y violencia llevado de la voluntad y no de la razón' (*Empresa* XLI, 104a). Depicting a king as unwisely in love, as an individual shorn of his sense of royal responsibility, clearly invokes this levelling process. Politically the dangers of such a process were seen to be extreme. Kings in their comportment and demeanour must stand out as beings apart if they are not to appear not merely human but mortal. As Saavedra Fajardo goes on, 'Muchas vezes en Francia se atrevió el hierro a la majestad real.' The assassination of two successive Henrys, the Third and the Fourth, in France in 1589 and 1610, served as a sharp reminder that even hereditary monarchy guaranteed no absolute protection against mutability and that kings were indeed men.

The tenet that the prince who sacrifices prudence to preference places his realm at risk is enshrined in Spain in that archetypal legend of royal lust, the Visigothic King Rodrigo's seduction of the daughter of Count Julian, governor of Ceuta, who subsequently wreaked his revenge by inviting the Moors into Spain. Lope's dramatization of the tale, *El postrer godo de España* (1599–1603, possibly 1599–1600), or *El último godo* as it is otherwise known, is revealing for the way in which it focuses blame on the king and exonerates La Cava, as the Count's daughter came unflatteringly to be called. With the passage of time she had become a more acceptable scapegoat for a nation's humiliation and defeat than a king seen eventually to represent the idea of Hispano-Christian legitimacy. In the Moslem chronicles and the earliest Christian accounts the Count's daughter is unequivocally raped by Rodrigo. Later Christian accounts proceeded to embroider the narrative in predictable ways, maintaining that she put up little resistance, even led the king on, and felt ashamed of her behaviour afterwards. The embroideries better suited the way in which late-medieval Spain chose to view its past, as well as medieval ideas about the way in which kings should and women did behave. It was at this stage in the blackening of her character that La Cava acquired her name, Arabic in origin curiously (an attempt perhaps at greater vilification), meaning whore – the name, illogically, is given her by the chronicles, and by Lope along with them, even before the king has set eyes on her. In the play the perspectives of history and plot converge when Florinda laments the fact that she will in future be given this damning nickname (Act III, 375b).[7]

In Lope's version a king's blatant abuse of his power to gratify his sexual whims hands his country over to the enemy. Himself newly married to the king of Algiers' daughter, Rodrigo promises the beautiful Florinda, who has been entrusted to his care by her father, that he will never, as she puts it, 'ask for her hand' – a young girl's euphemism for sexual favours. As the King later cynically points out, to promise is not to swear; in any case in the event he asks for nothing, he simply rapes her. When she denounces him as a tyrant and a traitor, he expresses regret that he did not kill her into the bargain. He is portrayed, therefore, as an out and out villain, entirely incapable of self-governance who breaks his word and commits treachery, and unheedingly sells his kingdom and his religion for a moment's self-gratification. His decadent court is characterized by the 'sedas y damascos' which offend Spain's saviour, the noble Pelayo, whose vigour and wholesome values are embodied in the 'peñascos' amongst which he prefers to live (Act II, 374b). None of this censure is explicitly articulated in the dialogue – direct attack was not Lope's way. Although Florinda is an innocent victim, already within the play's narrative it is she whom, according to the testimony of her father, both Christians and Moors revile; and although the Count's treachery is denounced and punished, the King escapes verbal censure. However, an apparently triumphalist dramatization of the events that were supposed to have led to the invasion of 711 is lent critical depth and edge by this very clash of official and subversive perspectives. The audience knows Florinda to be innocent, yet even Pelayo the hero refers to her as 'la vil Florinda'. Count Julián betrays his country, but his understandable anger, his love for his daughter and his wife, his horror when the consequences of his actions sink in, the suicide of his daughter and the death from cancer, raving, of his wife, escape the confines of a laboured poetic justice to provoke our sympathies and endow his character with an element of the tragic. The characters' perception of events is therefore not necessarily the play's and the audience's. The real culprit escapes explicit blame, but nemesis does its work and the lack of comment from any character in the play other than the injured daugh-

[7] *Obras*, Biblioteca de Autores Españoles, 195 (Madrid: Atlas, 1965).

ter and father constitutes an eloquent silence through which Florinda's accusations echo after the play's close. A concealed dialectic is set up by the play-text and the audience is left to draw its own conclusions from the way words spoken connect, or fail to connect, with what it sees unfold before it. The inscribing of ironic contradictions, sometimes subtle, sometimes stark, to create a space in which inference might operate was a key feature of Lope's political agenda.

Lope's source for the play seems to have been Miguel de Luna's *Historia verdadera del rey don Rodrigo y de la pérdida de España*, effectively a work of fiction built on chronicle and legend that purported to be a Castilian translation of an Arabic history.[8] Here Florinda (it was Luna who invented this name) blames herself for the destruction of Spain and calls herself 'la más mala mujer que hubo en el mundo', a consequence of the guilt she had acquired in the later versions of the story. Lope, however, pointedly omits this self-immolation. Florinda's last speech indicates that she takes her own life because she cannot bear the revulsion and opprobrium she realizes she will inspire in others through being regarded as 'el cuerpo enemigo,/ que fue de España castigo' (Act II, 375b). To be the instrument of Spain's downfall, however unwilling and unwitting, is, she realises, guilt enough.

So why did Lope rewrite legend by opting for an innocent La Cava and a ruthless, cynical, irresponsible king? Presumably to direct the spotlight of guilt upon the king himself. The title of the play is our clue: Rodrigo is the last gothic king, that is, the end of a line of kings represented here as unruly and decadent, as unfit to govern. The invasion is at once an ending and a new beginning as Pelayo emerges to lead Spain on the road to reconquest and greatness, 'puesto que Rodrigo se resuelve, de sus cenizas nacerá Pelayo' (Act II, 392b). Rodrigo does not have the kingly qualities for monarchical success, and in this telling of his story sexual misdemeanour is once again employed as a paradigm for the lack of those qualities of self-regulation, judgement and responsibility essential in a prince. The sexual misdemeanour here is of the most blatant and reprehensible sort – a misuse of the power invested in a prince for the protection, not the betrayal, of his subjects. The play dramatizes, early in a new king's reign, the dangers seen by political commentators in Spain to be inherent in absolutism. Rivadeneyra explains it in terms of regal tenancy, 'Ningún rey es absoluto ni independiente ni propietario, sino teniente y ministro de Dios, por el cual reinan los reyes, y tiene ser y firmeza cualquiera potestad' (475). Lope might have paraphrased the message of *El postrer godo de España* in López Bravo's words, written a few years later: 'Podríase, pues, decir varón justo el príncipe que se juzgare sujeto a las leyes y que, aunque de poder absoluto lo pueda todo, sólo entienda que

8 See Menéndez y Pelayo's prologue to the play in *Obras*, Biblioteca de Autores Españoles, 195, 19–56.

pueda lo que es loable y justo porque, en el sumo poder, ha de ser menos la licencia. Ésta es voz de rey, y de tirano aquella (*Del rey*, 112). While Philip III certainly showed no signs of a propensity for tyranny – he did not have the energy for it – he was prepared to licence a situation whereby the man in effective control of Spain, Lerma, used the royal prerogative to further his own personal interests in a quite blatant and disgraceful way. Mariana, after all, held that rule by favourite was 'el mal más terrible que se puede imaginar' and associated it unequivocally with tyranny (61–2). However, more significant than this for the theatre, in all probability, was the generally heightened interest in politics and the problems of kingship that the accession of Philip III and the rise of Lerma provoked. It is significant how many of Lope's kingship plays do belong to the first decade or so of this reign, and one of their central preoccupations is precisely the question of what qualities in a prince make for successful rule.

The theme of sexual unruliness reappears in two other early seventeenth-century plays, *La fe rompida*, where the king himself in typical *comedia* fashion seduces then abandons the heroine, and *El príncipe despeñado*, where the king tries first to seduce, then rape the wife of his major-domo and foremost supporter. And again the message is that the ruler who will use his power for sexual ends will stop at nothing, for he spurns morality, responsibility, honour and respect for his subjects. In such plays, sexual politics act as a mirror of national politics. The conflicts and strains inherent in kingship are mapped onto the timeless narrative of sexuality and passion rather than onto the existing political system itself, and misplaced desire in kings functions as a technique of demonization. While the body of the king relates to his private self, with all the needs and desires of the man, that body is also the incarnation of the state. It is entirely appropriate, therefore, that the body itself becomes the locus where the tension between man and role is played out.

La fe rompida (1599–1603) is a pseudo-historical romance with a sharp little moral. The King, Felisardo, discovers to his cost that his personal philosophy of kingship 'Lo que es mi gusto solamente es justo' (Act II, 567a)[9] provokes, as Mariana warned it would (120), the fury of the people. After he has enjoyed and abandoned Lucinda, she and her outraged father stir the people to revolt and force the King to sign a document denouncing his behaviour – misbehaviour leads to political mutability in its most dreaded form, civil war. The chastened King learns his lesson,

> No puede, Celio, un rey tener más miedo
> que parecer tirano. (Act II, 558a),

and does his duty by Lucinda. He marries her, although she is of lowly status,

[9] *Obras*, Real Academia Española (nueva ed.), V.

and she then helps him regain his throne when he is given up for dead. As kings go, Felisardo is not a bad one; his behaviour is reprehensible only in relation to Lucinda. But that is enough in a king to make him unfit for rule. The burden is that a king may be a man subject to a man's temptations, but he is also subject to man's laws and conventions of behaviour. Their observance in him is indeed all the more crucial because the consequences of non-observance are commensurably much greater, affecting as they do not merely a handful of people but a whole nation. As we have already seen, Rivadeneyra denounced weakness in a king as highly dangerous for the state. The prince has a duty not only to morality, to decency, to honour, but also to princely obligation.

El príncipe despeñado (1602) goes further than this in its depiction of royal sexual transgression. This is a play of considerable quality, the plot taut and well-paced, the dialogue strong and sinewy, the characters interesting and with some complexity. It figures a king neither black nor white who agonizes over his own sexual misbehaviour and its implications; two very strong female roles in Queen Elvira and the raped Blanca; a rational husband whose love for his wife survives her rape and who chooses to avenge himself on the King instead; some impressive scenes exploring the nature of love, sexual attraction and the relative merits of love-matches and arranged marriages; an on-stage birth; and an unusual opening scene that begins with an off-stage conversation. The play's thematic focus is the question of royal legitimacy. The King of Navarre dies unaware that his wife is pregnant. The nobles proclaim his brother Sancho, his chosen heir, king, but the Queen gives birth to a boy in hiding and eventually regains the throne after Sancho is assassinated by his premier supporter, don Martín, for raping Martín's wife, Blanca. The plot is loosely based on a supposedly historical event of 1076 involving Sancho II of Navarre, but the succession question was a fictional addition of Lope's. Menéndez y Pelayo considered that this aspect of the play, although very well done, destroyed the work's unity and therefore radically flawed the play.[10] But the business of the play is in fact entirely coherent. It is misleading to see it primarily as an honour–vengeance play, a play about a royal rape, as Menéndez y Pelayo clearly did. It is a play about monarchical legitimacy in which a royal rape plays a crucial part, in which the wilful abuse and dishonour of two subjects, a woman and her husband, are a signal of unfitness to rule. This in turn signals illegitimacy. It is not just that a king who behaves like Sancho has forfeited the right to rule; Lope seems to be suggesting that Sancho behaves as he does because he is not the legitimate king. If he is, then he goes further along this line of reasoning than did contemporary political thought. The abiding concern of Mariana's deliberations on kingship is political stability, and while acknowledging that hereditary rule has its dis-

10 *Obras*, Biblioteca de Autores Españoles, 197, 22.

advantages he recommends primogeniture as the greatest guarantee of law and order (79). He explicitly concedes, however, as do all the treatises on the education of princes implicitly, that the heir to the throne might well have to be educated into suitability to rule. Saavedra Fajardo stated specifically, 'El arte de reinar no es don de la naturaleza, sino de la especulación y la experiencia' (*Empresa* V, 20). Philip IV, as a young man deeply unsure of himself, speaks in his 'Autosemblanza' of having had systematically to 'aprender mi oficio de rey' on his succession because his father had died before he could educate him in kingship (231–2). Lope's play, on the other hand, would seem to assume that legitimacy confers suitability, an idea that is only a logical extension of the widespread belief of the day that social superiority and moral superiority went hand in hand, a belief linguistically embodied, of course, in the very concept of the noble and the gentleman. Nobles were noble because nobility was a duty not just learned but bred into them as being the proper price of privilege, 'que si hay alguna cosa en la nobleza, es solo el poner cierta necesidad a los nobles que imiten a sus pasados, y no desdigan de aquella virtud y grandeza que ellos les dejaron' (Rivadeneyra, 526). By the same process of genetic determination, kingliness was inherited along with the bluest blood, the blood of direct descent, a romantic notion which, it has to be said, Lope rarely seems to favour elsewhere in his theatre. The blood that flows in his kings' veins is usually the rich red blood of common humanity. Lope's purpose here, therefore, may well have been a subtler one – to promote the idea that legitimacy should signify suitability, that suitability is the duty that comes with the role. Time and again in Lope's king-plays, with their struggles and squabbles over royal succession, instability yields to legitimacy, and legitimacy and suitability are seen to be bedfellows. Legitimacy was certainly not a problem in contemporary Spain, which was virtually alone in Europe in this regard, but suitability certainly was. But while the advantages of a stable monarchy might far outweigh any reservations as to suitability and merit celebration, the lesson was there to be learnt that legitimacy imposed its own burdens. Gross sexual misdemeanour was a major failure of prudence, the exercise of judgement and foresight, as well as a failure of virtue, and prudence was in Saavedra Fajardo's words 'aguja de marear del Príncipe' (*Empresa* XXVIII). Medieval princes, warring dynastic leaders, are judged against Renaissance ideas of the king as the embodiment of the state and found wanting. But the comparison, paradoxically, produced in the process a critique of contemporary monarchy as well; the superimposition of contemporary ideals upon the past was an enabling stratagem which allowed misgivings about contemporary realities to be aired.

In *El príncipe perfecto* (Part I of which was written in 1614, Part II in 1616), Lope moved nearer his own time and in the process of doing so showed his hand more plainly. Here he exposes the yawning gap between the ideal of kingship and its contemporary reality by painting an idealized picture of an ancestor of Philip III's which skilfully forces Philip to identify with the princely paragon and yet at the same time implicitly emphasizes the yawning gap between them. The plays effectively constitute a *De regimine principum* very thinly disguised as historical romance, the nearest Lope came to writing a treatise on kingship. The ancestor and perfect prince is the very John II of Portugal whose character we see radically rewritten in *El Duque de Viseo.*[11] Here, a few years later, he reassumes his familiar identity as the forceful Renaissance ruler who in the late fifteenth century subjected the powerful feudal dynasties of Portugal to the centralizing authority of the Crown, then carved up the non-Christian world into two hemispheres with Spain. His cousin, Isabella of Castille, herself no weakling, admiringly dubbed him 'el hombre', for all the world like some early spaghetti-western hero. The plays were thought by Menéndez y Pelayo to have been directed at the young heir to the throne, the future Philip IV. However, I think a distinction must probably be made between the two parts. Since the young prince was only eight in 1614 and his father thirty-seven, it is much more likely that, at a time when Crown expenditure was unacceptably high and worries about the economic state of Spain were growing, the target of Part I, at least, was the malleable, pleasure-loving King himself. Part II, on the other hand, which portrays John II's son as well, opens with the young man receiving lessons in kingship from his father (lessons which we know from the testimony of his own pen Philip IV bitterly regretted not having received), and is studded with short episodes traditional in origin which are, to all intents and purposes, morality tales. It is very likely, therefore, that Part II was indeed written with the young Spanish prince in mind. Certainly Lope's prologue to the published text in 1623 refers to him, although by then of course he was seventeen and a king of two years' standing.

Lope's characterization of John II in Part I is unashamedly didactic. The ruthlessness and arrogance associated with the historical figure are omitted from his picture of the ideal prince who overcomes the foibles of youth (an illegitimate child, night-time escapades) to become the perfect man and leader: temperamentally and physically strong, just, prudent but resolute, interventionist, a dutiful son, and so on – the very incarnation of Rivadeneyra and Mariana's model king. By the time he came to write the sequel play two years later, Lope seems either to have lost faith somewhat in the perfectibility of princes, or to have balked at the idea of rerunning such dramatically unrewarding material, for the characterization now becomes more nuanced and more believable. Much is made of John's piety (which establishes a direct link with Philip III) and of the God-like nature of a king, and he remains all knowing, all seeing, all wise. Nonetheless, his firmness here descends at times into a historically authentic harshness, as when two dissident nobles are put to death – we remember Mariana's shrewd judgement (122) that Pedro el

[11] See chap. 6.

Cruel was deemed cruel by those intemperate nobles who forced him into being so. At the same time his generosity takes on – and the shadow of Philip III, who showered extravagant gifts on his favourite Lerma, is again very strong here – an air of imprudent extravagance as he impulsively doles out posts and favours. A pompous, self-congratulatory side to him emerges, but so too does a nice line in heavy irony; he is even on one occasion unnecessarily rude to the Queen. The composite portrait remains, nonetheless, an idealized and glamorous one, for that is what serves Lope's purposes. It is also, however, an extremely artful one, for while Lope emphasizes all the qualities desirable in a king which even Philip's greatest admirer would not have claimed for him – energy, resolution and effectiveness amongst them – it also carefully selects from the chronicles Lope used as his sources qualities which Philip did share with his ancestor – religious devotion, generosity, prodigality (according to the chronicle of Ruy de Pina, John was a 'liberal e mui manifico gastador'),[12] dancing and riding skills, a love of hunting. At the same time it plays down the pleasure-loving side to John's nature: 'en las cosas de placer/ es afable aunque modesto' (I, Act II, 100b)[13] his ambassador assures King Ferdinand of Spain, not a qualification applicable to Philip III, who spent his whole life in pursuit of his own pleasure. In other words Lope produced a portrait which, with the careful diplomacy which was the guiding principle of his dramatic engagement with power, said to his king 'Look this is you, but you as you ought to be, and not as you are.' A portrait of what the king ought to be like masquerades as a portrait of what he is like. And in case Philip or the audience were slow to make the connection, Lope provides them in Act II of Part I with a piece of contemporary royal iconography to encourage them to do just that. When John prepares to meet the Ethiopian king, Benoí, he adopts the dignified position – standing, with one hand on the back of a chair (or corner of a table) – with which the Habsburg monarchy chose to present its face to the world in a succession of now famous portraits, Titian's Philip II and Velázquez's Philip IV, Olivares and Queen Isabella amongst them. As he looked at the stage Philip III could not help but see staring back at him an image of himself. Once he had done so, it was clearly Lope's hope that the relevance of a great monarch shown in control of himself and his country, in spite of being surrounded by men who are self-serving, blinkered, even corrupt, would not be lost upon him.

John II, like most European monarchs credited with bringing their countries out of the Middle Ages, lends himself to ambiguous dramatization. While Lope could not in Part II entirely resist the challenge presented by his character, he uses the Portuguese king in *El príncipe perfecto* essentially as a medium for giving advice to his own sovereign. Philip must have been used

[12] See *Obras*, Real Academia Española (nueva ed.), X (Madrid: 1930), cxlii–cxliv.
[13] *Obras*, Biblioteca de Autores Españoles, 51.

to the idea that he was descended from those heroes of Spain's recent past, the Catholic Monarchs Ferdinand and Isabella; now Lope was reminding him, at some length, that the blood of another outstanding ruler ran in his veins. To us now such theatrical lessons might seem ingenuous as well as futile, but the persistence with which Lope and his contemporaries by means of different stratagems urged self-reform and improvement upon monarchs temperamentally incapable of taking any notice of their advice and flanked by favourites who did not wish them to do so, was a measure of their desperation rather than their naïveté.

If *El príncipe perfecto* lays its wares out plainly on the king's table, an earlier example of Lope's interest in the behaviour of princes is more convoluted in its methods, although it too makes use of the device of the portrait to get its message across.[14] *El servir con mala estrella* (1604–12)[15] tells a strange tale about a French noble who gives years of service in peace and war to Alfonso VIII and who thereby becomes his confidant and premier general, without receiving any reward whatsoever. Eventually Rugero, in despair, decides to return to France. The King, who has a great reputation for generosity and for recognizing indebtedness, a reputation which is borne out by his behaviour to many others in the course of the play, realizes that he has not given Rugero his due, wonders why, decides that it must be the fault of Rugero's 'mala estrella', and then determines to put this conclusion to the test. He engineers his return to Toledo and offers him two identical caskets to choose from. When Rugero chooses the empty casket without his beloved Hipólita's name on, this proves to the King's satisfaction that the culprit is not he, that Rugero's misfortune is indeed the result of Rugero's 'mala estrella'. He then proceeds to overturn the logic of this decision, and indeed of his behaviour throughout the play – he wanted to reward Rugero many times, he claims but something always prevented him – by giving Rugero the casket full of jewels and Hipólita's hand:

> porque entiendas y veas
> que puede más mi valor
> que el rigor de tus estrellas. (Act III, 390b)[16]

[14] For a study of the importance of portraits in the *comedia* in seventeenth-century Spain at large, see Melveena McKendrick, *The Revealing Image: Stage Portraits in the Theatre of the Golden Age* (London: Queen Mary and Westfield College, 1996).

[15] Morley and Bruerton's preferred date within this time span is 1604–06. I feel that in view of the strong sense of injustice the play exudes it is more likely to be late than early. Its French associations, too, suggest proximity to the marriage alliance contracted in 1612 between the royal houses of Spain and France. Olive Wilson in her University of London doctoral thesis, 'An edition of *El pleito por la honra*' (115–16), also postulates a date of composition of 1612–14 for *El servir con mala estrella*.

[16] *Obras*, Biblioteca de Autores Españoles, 247 (Madrid: Atlas, 1971).

What are we supposed to make of all this? The lack of logic in the King's argument is totally transparent, so what conclusion are we meant to draw? The one that we inevitably do draw is that it was in the King's power all along to reward Rugero properly. So why does he not do so? His magnanimity is never in doubt. What we have here, almost certainly, is another example of Lope doublespeak – of his desire to make a point directed at the King's ear while maintaining the face of loyal innocence and avoiding direct criticism. Philip III had the reputation of being liberal to a fault, so it is very obvious from this play that Lope felt that someone was being grossly and unfairly overlooked.

His strategy is a duplicitous and elaborate one. Rugero's behaviour is immaculate. Although he grumbles behind the King's back and becomes increasingly disillusioned, he never reproaches the King and never allows disgruntlement to affect his total loyalty and obedience to his monarch, even when the King's gross neglect of him is obvious to all. The loyalty and obedience owed a prince, the unquestionable authority of the monarch, are verbally stressed time and again, a favoured technique of Lope's when he wished to get some counter-point across – he protects his back as he covertly moves onto the offensive. At the same time, the supreme authority of monarchy is ingeniously conveyed in pictorial terms at two different points in the action. When the King secretly visiting doña Sancha is surprised by her brother Tello, he reacts, not by hiding, because 'Nunca los reyes se esconden' (Act I, 345a), but by 'freezing', by standing absolutely still, 'Escondido estoy así' (Act I, 345b). By abandoning his humanity by neither hiding nor protecting himself, by turning himself into an icon of majesty, he can command complete respect and, with respect, immunity. Don Tello takes his cue, realizes that in behaving thus the King is assuming that he, Tello, is a man of honour and a loyal subject who will react honourably and loyally to the image of majesty before him, and he behaves accordingly. He pretends that the immobile King is indeed a portrait of the King and takes no action. The King, out in pursuit of sexual adventure like one of his subjects, to protect himself assumes his universal persona as if it were a theatrical role. It was not quite what Saavedra Fajardo later on had in mind when, using a similar metaphor, he recalled, 'En su retrete solía enojarse Carlos V, pero no cuando representaba la persona de emperador. Entonces más es el príncipe una idea de gobernar que hombre; más de todos que suyo' (*Empresa* VII, 24). This perception of the prince's dual identity as private person and public icon involves a necessary repression of the man's passions and inclinations in order adequately to play the part of monarch, not a flight into royal authority as cover for unworthy personal actions. Accordingly, the scene in the play that so loyally proclaims royal authority also simultaneously subverts it by condemning the manner and purpose of its use. Alfonso is patently misusing his position as king to extricate himself from a situation created by his own unkingly behaviour. Tello is put on the spot, his honour and loyalty invoked by a sovereign who does not himself feel bound by the same values. And he certainly does not fail, for all his obedience, to make that point. He observes, as if to the air, how much more appropriate it would have been had the King been painted as a warrior and leader rather than as a gallant visiting a lady's house – an exquisitely tactful but barbed rebuke that exploits the King's own little charade in order to repudiate his renunciation of responsibility. In this very striking scene sexual impropriety once again operates as a signal of negligent kingship.

Later, when Rugero returns to France he takes with him a portrait of the King, which he unrolls when he is feeling aggrieved and bitter so that it will inspire respect and quell resentment, 'que son retratos los reyes/ de Dios y a Dios alabamos' (Act III, 381b). Once more the image of the king is disassociated from the individual man and his shortcomings, and assumes the iconic presence and power of *la majestad real*. But of course once more Lope has things both ways because the contrary point is simultaneously being made: Rugero should not have to go to such absurd, almost fetishist, lengths to remind himself that the man who has shown himself so incognizant of the great services he has done him is a king and therefore beyond resentment. For all the caveats regarding royal generosity in *El príncipe perfecto*, liberality was for theorists of kingship one of the essential, great princely qualities. Implicated as it was in the proper rewarding of virtuous actions, so essential to the welfare of the state, it was seen to be closely linked to the key concept of justice, considered the basis of all successful government, 'la madre y ama de los imperios', in López Bravo's words (*Del rey*, 114). Duke Sinibaldo in Lope's *La sortija del olvido*, invoking the idea of distributive justice, puts it plainly: 'Que es la justicia un ser distributivo,/ que a cada cual le da lo que merece' (Act II, 612a).[17] The prince who did not recognize the public services of a man who had served him as well as Rugero was not merely unjust but himself did disservice to the kingdom, seen here in Rugero's renunciation of his offices. Public illiberality was of greater consequence to effective rule than private immoralities. Alfonso's philandering is in human terms understandable, if disruptive, but for his lack of generosity to Rugero there is no conceivable excuse. Since it falls outside reason and natural justice, attributing it to Rugero's *mala estrella* is entirely logical but, at the same time, entirely spurious. The play-text subverts the play-title, which ends up encapsulating not what the play has shown but the opposite of what it has shown. It is a technique of *quod non est demostrandum* which nonetheless provokes firm conclusions. Lope would use it again later on in his wife-murder play *El castigo sin venganza*.

[17] *Obras*, Real Academia Española (nueva ed.), X.

There are other subverted obeisances, too, to the authority of a king; doña Sancha persuades herself,

> Amar al Rey es del mundo
> precepto en primer lugar;
> servirle tras el amar,
> es mandamiento segundo.
> Pues darle lo que ha de ser
> para su gusto y su intento,
> es tercer mandimiento;
> y el cuarto es no le ofender. (Act I, 343b–4a)

But a judgement on the validity of these partisan words is provided by their consequences – a seduction, an illegitimate child,[18] and Sancha's murder of the brother who is the obstacle to her affair. Alfonso condemns his irresponsibility out of his own mouth when he fraudulently makes light of the effect it has on the family's honour:

> Los que a los reyes provocan
> mejor es que los igualen
> al sol, pues entran y salen
> sin manchar en lo que tocan. (Act I, 349b)

A king can do no harm, commit no sin – the claim is preposterous. And his behaviour provokes adverse comment from his nobles: '¡Oh, cuánto a un príncipe afea/ una liviandad!' (Act III, 373a). There are sharp remarks, too, in the play on adulation, falsehood in furthering ambition, and the effectiveness of flattery. The lackey Turía's following barb would not have missed its target with a seventeenth-century Spanish audience:

> No es mal principio, señor,
> la lisonja para entrar
> al alma de un rey. (Act I, 336b)

In *El rey sin reino*, written probably during the same period (1597–1612), the consequences of the negative manifestation of flattery – silence – are uncompromisingly spelt out:

[18] The child fathered on doña Sancha by Alfonso is the 'desdichada Estefanía' of Lope's play of that name (*El pleito de la honra* completes the Estefanía *la desdichada* trilogy). Much is made of this in the text, initially by a Moorish maid with prophetic insight. As Morley and Bruerton point out (241), the story's chronology does not mean that *El servir con mala estrella* necessarily preceded *La desdichada Estefanía* (written in 1604). The strength of the play's criticism of the court and particularly of the lack of recognition given the truly deserving would suggest a date of composition later rather than earlier in the reign of Philip III and the time-span (1604–12) suggested by Morley and Bruerton.

Huniades. Todos los más que sirven a los reyes
hacen traición, Matías, en dos cosas:
la una en que jamás al Rey le acuerdan
que ha de morir; la otra, que le encubren
por su gusto las cosas en que yerra. (Act II)[19]

The rhetorical heart of *El servir con mala estrella* is provided by an extended soliloquy of Rugero's, outside the court on the point of his return to France. It is a denunciation of the disappointments, pitfalls and corruption of court life and the power of envy to impede the progress of the deserving:

En tanto que me aperciben
este famoso caballo,
que es en la casta español,
y en artificio troyano
(pues si de tantos servicios
viene a ser carta de pago,
no pone en menos incendio
la Troya de mis agravios),
quiero quejarme a tus puertas,
¡oh casa, ataúd dorado
de muchos que entierran vivos
y que muertos viven sanos!
Dióme la esperanza un hilo
con que, en el viento fiado,
entré en este laberinto
por la puerta del engaño.
Fui dando a sus salas vueltas,
de la experiencia guiado,
que es el mozo de los ciegos
que rezan en los palacios.
Topé el favor cauteloso,
que me enseñó dos retratos
de la guerra y del consejo:
hice reverencia a entrambos.
Vi la soberbia ambición
y la lisonja, contando
sobre una mesa de viento
muchos contadores falsos.
La puntualidad miré,
que se estaba levantando
antes que el sol; que el sol guarda
las leyes que Dios le ha dado.

19 *Obras*, Biblioteca de Autores Espaõles, 191 (Madrid: Atlas, 1966), 317a.

La ceremonia pasé,
que estaba con el cansancio,
repitiendo reverencias
a unos ídolos de mármol.
La solicitud tras ella,
que con notable cuidado
se desvelaba en juntar
honra y provecho en un saco.
Llena de dos mil papeles
vi la pretensión, llorando,
mesándose los cabellos,
más que los papeles canos.
A la desdicha en un río,
con mucha flema y espacio,
vi pescar con una caña
peces, pero sin sacarlos.
Vi al olvido que borraba
los números desdichados
de los servicios, y sólo
iba los ceros dejando.
Vi al poder que estaba haciendo
figuras y hombres de barro;
mas los que una mano hacía,
deshacía la otra mano.
Vi sobre todas las puertas
siete letras en sus arcos:
envidia. ¡Envidia decían!
¡Ay de los que van entrando! (Act III, 380a–b)

The length, intensity and impassioned misery of this speech are, I think, the key to the play's curious plot. The work, as we have seen, has aspects of considerable interest and the writing and some of the scenes are very strong. It is, however, a strange mixture of the carefully directed and crafted and the inconsequential and incomplete, of political seriousness and novelesque extravagance. The main action is superficially limp and contradictory, yet it has in its cruel neglect of a good man an invisible inner thrust that makes itself palpable; the true feeling in the play is not the feeling of the love affairs, but the feeling generated by an understandable sense of injustice. The only persuasive way of reading the bizarre unfolding of its central strand, therefore, is as the expression of some contemporary grievance. If we look for comparable seventeenth-century equivalents to Rugero whom Lope might have cared enough about to pen Rugero's monologue, it is difficult to detect whose that grievance might have been. The person concerned is hardly likely to have been the Count of Lemos, a patron of Lope's for a while, for he was a son-in-law of Lerma's and one of the numerous relatives and supporters with whom the favourite surrounded the young king to consolidate his own power;

he was appointed *gentilhombre de cámara* in 1600. Nor is it likely to have been the young Duke of Sessa, who was to be Lope's long-term patron, to whom he acted as personal secretary from around 1605 on. He too was a rich and powerful man with titles and estates, and could hardly have been the model for the role of the neglected, unappreciated Rugero. It is always possible, of course, that Lope was championing someone else's cause, but the most likely contender, in view of Rugero's attitude to the King as well as his heartfelt speech of despairing rejection, has to be Lope himself. He, Spain's leading poet and dramatist, was the one who danced attendance at court, whose plays and *autos* were performed on public occasions, and who yet received no official recognition from a king who showered rewards on lesser talents. Unable to take issue with the king directly, wary even of openly voicing a complaint at all for fear of forfeiting any future reward, he devises a convoluted strategy ostensibly to absolve the play-king of responsibility while making it clear that it is within a king's power at any time to choose to honour a subject. The reluctance to lay blame at Alfonso's feet, the very resort to the fiction of fate, to the idea of manifest destiny, and to that eternal scapegoat, envy, themselves suggest that to Lope's mind the issue presented problems of diplomacy too delicate for him to deal with in a more open, immediately legible way. Very plausibly, feelings of hurt and bewilderment really did struggle with loyalty to his king, in the way Rugero's do; no doubt the envy of others did seem a plausible explanation, it was certainly a face-saving one. Pride must anyway have inhibited the overt expression of a sense of injustice. As the years went by that sense of injustice would become more bitter and more open, but at this point Lope chose to transfer his feelings to a medieval Frenchman, resorting to a subterfuge which would cover his tracks while discovering his message. Few who knew him could have overlooked the parallels or misjudged his purpose, but outwardly at least his face was saved and the royal prerogative remained intact.

El servir con mala estrella offers an interesting comparison with *La fortuna merecida*, a play with a similar proposed date-spread (1604–15, ?1604–10). If the former portrays a favourite who goes unrewarded, *La fortuna merecida* portrays one who is rewarded too much. Both present extreme cases and it is difficult to believe, since both are in their different ways 'odd' plays – *El servir con mala estrella* for its apparently illogical plot, *La fortuna merecida* for its apparently unnecessary historical distortions – that this concern with merit and reward bore no relationship to contemporary court circumstances. *La fortuna merecida* directly addresses the problematical question of *privanza*. It is one of a pair of plays planned by Lope to depict the rise and fall of Alfonso XI's steward and favourite, Alvar Núñez de Osorio, here called Álvaro Núñez de Sarria. Alfonso was only fourteen when he took up the reins of government in 1322 and appointed three principal advisors; one of them, Alvar Núñez, a leading figure in the entourage of the young king's uncle and former regent, the Infante don Felipe, became his favourite. Considerable animosity and rivalry existed between the three advisers, and between them and the king's uncles and their factions, all of whom seem to have been an unsavoury lot who constantly plotted against the king. In 1325, at the height of Alvar Núñez's influence and having already acquired vast wealth in money and land, by fraud according to his enemies, he was created Count of Trastámara, of Lemos and of Sarriá.[20] He himself had requested a reward for his services which would put him on an equal footing with the *ricoshombres* of the realm, and for strategic reasons, in order to strengthen Alvar Núñez's hand against his enemies, the king complied, although so long was it since any man had been created count in Castille or Leon that a special ceremony of investiture had to be devised for the occasion. This advancement so incensed the Infante don Juan Manuel that he set out to bring Alvar Núñez down. The story was put around that Núñez was to marry the king's sister, and this caused so much political unrest that in order to avoid open rebellion on a large scale the king consented to dismiss Núñez and reclaim his lands. Alfonso eventually had him killed on the grounds that Núñez would not hand over the castles the king had put in his charge. The *Crónica de Don Alfonso el Onceno*'s accumulated account, in other words, exonerates the king and presents Alvar Núñez as indeed a favourite on the make who amassed a great fortune at the Crown's expense, although early in the narrative he is presented as a worthy and powerful adviser helping the king cope with a dangerous opposition. The burden of the chronicle is that by insisting on becoming a count Núñez made a crucial miscalculation and went too far for his enemies to stomach.[21]

Since Alvar Núñez was an ancestor of the Count of Lemos, for some time Lope's employer and patron, Menéndez y Pelayo sees the play as an exercise in whitewash: 'A esta corriente de rehabilitación genealógica pertenece la ingeniosa comedia de Lope de Vega, dócil siempre a tal género de impulsos' (96).[22] He goes on, 'no es posible perdonarle los desafueros que esta vez cometió contra la historia (tan respetada por él en otras ocasiones)', and he upbraids Lope for making don Juan Manuel, one of medieval Spain's most distinguished men of letters, a villain of the piece – an unfair criticism, since the prince behaved as badly as did most noblemen in those centuries of internecine strife and Lope was merely being liberal with the truth. On the other hand, since the play does not hide Núñez's relatively obscure origins, but on the contrary exaggerates them, Menéndez y Pelayo somewhat irrelevantly sees the play as being 'en el fondo muy democrático'. It is illuminating to see

20 Historically the name was Sarriá. That Lope, however, thought of it as Sarria is clear from the assonance scheme used at one point where the name appears in the text (see the quotation later in this chapter, 69).

21 Menéndez y Pelayo gives the historical account in *Obras de Lope de Vega*, Biblioteca de Autores Españoles, 211 (Madrid: Atlas, 1967), 86–98.

22 *Obras*, Biblioteca de Autores Españoles, 211, 96.

him providing the bricks and mortar for what would become, largely thanks to him, the standard view of Lope as a natural genius of haphazard and sometimes irresponsible methods, a closet democrat without the courage of any of his convictions, eager only to please. Since Menéndez y Pelayo expected historical plays to follow their sources, he neglected to ask why, if Lope could perfectly well be historically accurate when he chose, he chose not to be so here. Lope, of course, was skating in this play on thin ice. He certainly could not afford to risk the displeasure of his patron Lemos and the Lerma régime – Lemos was, it will be remembered, Lerma's son-in-law and a *gentilhombre de cámara*. Yet the play is inescapably an exploration of a subject of intense contemporary comment and concern, however disguised, and simply could not have been seen without stirring thoughts relevant to that situation in the minds of its spectators.

Given that Núñez was an ancestor and the play certainly flatters his character, motives and rise to power, in one sense *La fortuna merecida* was indeed an elaborate compliment to the Lemos family, as Menéndez y Pelayo maintained. The play's circumspect credentials in this regard are established immediately in the first scene by the appearance of an earlier, fictional Count of Lemos (the title did not at that stage exist) and by heavy references to Sarriá, the Lemos family's ancient seat. But if flattery was Lope's sole aim, it could have been easily achieved without recourse to the distortions which aroused Ménendez y Pelayo to such indignation. What, therefore, is behind Lope's reworking of his source material? In the play, Álvaro Núñez, an obscure member of a cadet branch of the Lemos family and formerly page to the Conde de Lemos, comes to court as a young man in the hope of serving the count. He saves the King's life without knowing his identity, and ends up in his service. The King, in the play a grown man with a queen, a mistress and children by both, develops an inordinate affection for Núñez, and in spite of his youth and complete inexperience proceeds to make him his *valido* and to shower him with rewards which include some of the highest positions in the land. Álvaro Núñez's behaviour throughout is impeccable. He is virtuous, selfless, reasonable, unassuming and submissive to the point of servility, and when his appointment to the *maestrazgo* of Santiago proves contentious, he graciously forfeits it in order to avoid civil strife. His enemies are confounded, and on this high note the play ends, though a sequel depicting his fall is promised. This sequel, as far as is known, never materialized; perhaps Lope tactfully decided for the sake of his patron Lemos that discretion was the better part of invention here.

Lope paints a rather different picture, therefore, from the powerful adviser of the chronicle who, overtaken by greed, amassed a great fortune at the Crown's expense and himself provoked the nobles to revolt by insisting on a title. And it is in the play's altered characterization that its other, covert, identity lies. The mature, established adviser to the Infante don Felipe, regent during Alfonso's minority, is here an obscure young man straight from the country. In reverse, the fourteen-year-old Alfonso is in the play a mature, experienced adult. And whereas the young historical Alfonso from the start was ruthless, unscrupulous, astute and politically adroit, ready when the time came to have Alvar Núñez killed, Lope's mature Alfonso is irresolute and full of doubts, politically blind and foolishly self-indulgent in heaping favours on an amiable man who has done nothing other than accidentally save his life. The King's extreme affection for the young man is, significantly, an embroidery of Lope's – the chronicle mentions no such attachment.

The reversal of ages and the changes in characterization have two effects. They deflect any implied reference in the play to new or youthful kings, they deflect what would otherwise have been obvious connections between a historical greedy favourite (Núñez) and a contemporary one (Lerma), and, more crucially in terms of the play's exploration of the relationship between king and favourite, they focus responsibility for what happens firmly on the King himself. Núñez is young, inexperienced and selfless, and if he seems ready to shrug off the young woman he loves in order to marry the lady of higher birth chosen for him by the King, then we are probably meant to put that down to Núñez's recognition that he is the King's creation and therefore owes him complete obedience. There are nice touches of humour and irony at Núñez's expense in the romantic sub-plot and there is something slightly dissonant, perhaps, about his extreme servility – a mild dig possibly at the fawning flattery denounced by Rugero in *El servir con mala estrella* and regarded by all political theorists as the corrupter of kings. But there can be no doubt that Lope wishes to present Núñez by and large as an admirable youth. He is a favourite who morally deserves his good fortune – a useful deflective tactic on Lope's part to avoid incurring powerful displeasure in a favourite's régime. At the same time he undoubtedly has too much of it for the good of the realm. The play unequivocally showed that however deserving a *privado*, the monarch must realise that there had to be a proper balance in such matters, that the *privanza* system, breeding as it did jealousy and divisiveness, created problems even if the *privado* himself did not. Lope's Álvaro Núñez is the perfect *privado*, but the realities of politics, state affairs and human nature have nonetheless to be allowed to act as brake. Thus Lope's *privado* willingly renounces a great honour for the sake of law and order, and the King has enough sense to accept. He learns to subordinate his own will and wishes to political necessity. It is self-evident that there was an unmistakable message here for Lope's own time, a message decently arrayed in difference – the mature king this time, the young, self-denying favourite – but immediately apparent to anyone within the circle of the court and to many outside it. Philip III was irresponsibly generous and to none more irresponsibly generous than to the Duke of Lerma, whom he held in the greatest affection and esteem. Excessive generosity in giving has traditionally been considered reprehensible for whereas generosity recognizes obligation and is therefore morally desirable as a reward for services rendered, an excess of generosity is an attempt to purchase loyalty and therefore a form of self-interest.[23] Saavedra Fajardo, however, very possibly with the recent past in mind, would later distinguish liberality in a prince from prodigality in a more pragmatic way than this. Identifying liberality as a characteristic of kings because, 'Con ella, más que con las demás [virtudes], es el príncipe parecido a Dios, que siempre está dando a todos abundantement' (101b), he pronounces prodigality to be not only undesirable but dangerous because, 'Un vasallo pródigo se destruye a sí mismo; un príncipe a sí y a sus estados' (102b). Alfonso's prodigality generates civil strife, Philip's was seen by many to be depleting the financial and human resources of the Crown at a time when Spain could ill afford either. Within a short time of Philip's accession Lerma was not only a much richer man even than he had been before, but he had been allowed to replace all the experienced stalwarts of the previous reign with his own family and supporters. Royal favourites in their turn have favourites who become rich and powerful on the back of their patrons – in Lerma's case don Pedro Franqueza and above all don Rodrigo Calderón, both of whom rose swiftly to great influence and fortune under Lerma's protection. Calderón gained complete ascendency over the royal favourite – living proof of the danger inherent in *privanza* with political influence being exerted, as it was, at two removes from the throne. The dispersal even more widely of the Crown's resources down the pyramid of grasping collaborators was another urgent concern. Quevedo, admittedly a partisan commentator, in his *Grandes anales de quince días* subsequently put it very bluntly, 'quedó Su Majestad desnudo en pocos años de la mejor herencia de su gran padre'.[24] And some satirical verses usually ascribed to the court satirist and wit the Count of Villamediana make it abundantly clear where people thought it had all gone:

> De que en Italia barbados
> anden obispos y papas,
> y en Castilla anden sin capas
> y los más dellos rapados;
> y que en Lerma con candados
> esté de España el dinero. . . [25]

By 1612 Lerma's ascendency would be such that a royal decree was promulgated declaring that orders from the Duke carried the same authority as those

[23] See Marcel Mauss, *The Gift: Forms and Functions of Exchange in Archaic Societies*, trans. Jan Cunnison (London: W.W. Norton, 1967).

[24] *Obras de Francisco de Quevedo y Villegas*, Biblioteca de Autores Españoles, 23 (Madrid: M. Rivadeneyra, 1852), 212.

[25] See Teófanes Egido, *Sátras políticas*, 82.

of the king himself.[26] Lerma was shameless in pursuit of wealth and in his abuse of royal patronage and favour. On the death of the Count of Fuensalida, not long after Philip II's own death in 1598, the new king bestowed upon Lerma the largest *encomienda* in Castile, belonging to the Order of Santiago. The largest in the Order of Calatrava went to Lerma's second son, Diego. Not for nothing in *La fortuna merecida* is the distribution of such honours a major issue, the Grand Priorship of the Order of Saint John going at Álvaro Núñez's request to his cousin. Not lost either on Lope's audience would have been the significance accorded in the play to the fact that Álvaro Núñez has an old castle restored at his own expense with the aim of presenting it to the King. In historical terms, fortified castles were a symbol and facilitator of armed rebellion, which is why the real Alvar Núñez's refusal to relinquish his led to his death; the wholesale destruction of castles was one of the strategies used by Ferdinand and Isabella in the fifteenth century in their move to curb the power of the nobles and stabilize the realm. In the play, Álvaro Núñez's gesture symbolizes his total commitment to his king, his lack of personal ambition and greed; he himself uses the restored fortress as a metaphor for the restoration of his family fortunes by the King. This was a far cry from the entrepreneurial activities of Lerma who in 1601, when the court moved to Valladolid, quickly acquired a large amount of property in that city, restored it and then sold it to the king, who had no palace of his own there and was staying in borrowed lodgings. The Duke, indeed, was an enthusiastic property developer on a large scale, spending huge sums of money which after his fall he would be accused of obtaining from the Crown by fraud, and like Álvaro Núñez in the play he accumulated numerous towns, palaces and forts, including the castle of Simancas. The old fortress of Lerma itself was converted into a complex of ducal palace, church, convents, gardens and park by the architect Francisco de Mora; work began in 1613, but discussion and planning started considerably earlier, and given the play's proposed *terminus ad quem* a sly echo of the grand refurbishments and reconstructions at Lerma might well be contained in the incident of Álvaro Núñez's efforts in that direction.[27]

Lope's facade of respect and dutifulness in the play never cracks, but is always smoothly maintained by the diplomatic techniques of deflection, distortion, reorganization and recreation he had at his command. Anything else was unnecessary in a capital as highly sensitized as was Madrid to the activities of a man who in his rise to power had made, and continued to make, many enemies. The analogy did not need to be anything like exact to strike home; and if analogies were there for the detecting, we can be sure that Lope

[26] See Francisco Tomás Valiente, *Los validos en la monarquía española* (Madrid: Instituto de Estudios Políticos, 1963), 71–2.

[27] For further details of Lerma's building and restoration activities, see R. Menéndez Pidal (ed.), *Historia de España*, vol.XXIV (Madrid: Espasa Calpe, 1979), 461–8.

intended them to be there. He was fully aware that the merest possibility of contemporary relevance was enough to reflect and incite feelings, not necessarily even of hostility but of misgiving and concern. The artificial exoneration of a distant ancestor of the Count of Lemos (and in the play not even a direct one) could not, after all, have been a pressing concern, although there was clearly nothing ever to be lost from pleasing a powerful friend. What much more plausibly focused Lope's attention on Alvar Núñez's story was the idea of a favourite indulged to the point of imprudence. He does not argue, as he might have done, that such preference was unjust, so much as (mis)use history to show that it was politically unwise – a safer tactic and a more effective one. Even so, Álvaro Núñez on more than one occasion does openly acknowledge the justice of other nobles' complaints, even if the King chooses to ignore such arguments until forced by circumstances to take action:

> Tello, tan gran caballero
> como sabe toda España,
> los Algarves de Algeciras
> y las galeras de Malta,
> pretende ser Gran Prior.
> Pienso, señor, que ya estaba
> en buena opinión contigo:
> yo entonces, con ignorancia,
> por mi primo te pedí,
> don Sancho Núñez de Sarria,
> la gran cruz, de que nació
> justa queja y justa causa. (Act II, 43b–4a)[28]

By neglecting the human face of politics, Alfonso, and by implication Philip with him, was ignoring the promptings of that 'guía y maestra de todas las virtudes naturales',[29] prudence, without which good government was impossible. A knowledge of the hearts and ways of men and the ability to put that knowledge to use was a necessary part of the exercise of prudence. *La fortuna merecida* enjoins upon a king prudence in the management of a favourite, and it was just not possible to write an 'innocent' play about a favourite, historical or otherwise, in the reign of Philip III. We do not find in Lope's theatre the intrepid forthrightness of Mariana, who baldly argued in his *De Rege* that state affairs in Spain were conducted 'al arbitrio del rey y al capricho y voluntad de unos pocos' (chap.VIII, 161) and that a single ruler surrounded by compliant, flattering courtiers could not guarantee public well-being. But in the theatre such forthrightness was rendered superfluous

[28] The text of the play is in *Obras*, Biblioteca de Autores Espaõles, 212 (Madrid: Atlas, 1968).

[29] Rivadeneyra, *Obras escogidas*, 552–3.

by methods more artful than those available to the writers of learned treatises. Drama could say quite as much as discursive prose yet run scant risk of censure. After all, to denounce a theatrical plot for its contemporary 'point' is an admission of resemblance and therefore relevance. On the other hand any fiction officially maintained can be an efficient and useful instrument of truth. Drama, by marginalizing authorial responsibility – the mouth that speaks the words is never the playwright's own – establishes a complicity which it is difficult to challenge.

Even so, when Sir John Hayward's *The First Part of the Life and Raigne of Henrie IIII* was suppressed in 1599, not long after it had been licensed, Attorney General Coke, who prosecuted Hayward, assumed the intent of relevance: 'the Doctor selected a story 200 years old, and published it last year, intending the application of it to this'.[30] Since the capacity of historical or quasi-historical plays to engage with the political present was explicitly and repeatedly conceded in England,[31] it is hardly likely that it went unrecognized in Spain. Since monarchs drew their legitimacy from the nation's past, the association of past and present kings was a natural one for dramatists and spectators alike – occupying the same throne was an invitation to comparison. Accounts of the censorship of plays in England during this period are a telling indication of how much Spanish plays were allowed to get away with. A lower degree of sensitization to political dissent in the more stable monarchy must have played its part here (though even in England most plays passed muster), but a greater degree of self-censorship involving the use of complex and diffused stratagems of criticism, such as that at work in *La fortuna merecida*, undoubtedly also permitted the greater latitude allowed the Spanish playwrights, thereby facilitating the safe and successful communication of political messages.

30 Janet Clare, *Art Made Tongue-Tied by Authority: Elizabethan and Jacobean Dramatic Censorship* (Manchester/ New York: Manchester University Press, 1990), 26.

31 See Clare, *Art Made Tongue-Tied*, 27.

4

HISTORICAL TRANSFORMATIONS: FRACTURED ICONS II

Reclaiming Spain's past for the purposes of the present provided Lope with an almost inexhaustable supply of dramatic material. In the context of a commercial theatre his selection and manipulation of that material obeyed not only his own interests but the interest of the audience as well. Had he not considered that the discourse of kingship was of continuing concern to his public he would certainly not have devoted so many lines of verse to the repeated and explicit airing of the same set of political issues. *Privanza* and all its political ramifications was not just a live but an extremely contentious issue throughout the two reigns that coincided with Lope's mature writing career. His interest in royal favouritism may be traced again some years later in an oblique way in a play of courtly romantic intrigue, *Querer la propia desdicha* (1619–20). Lerma had fallen in late 1618, when the intrigues of his son, the Duke of Uceda, and Fray Luis de Aliaga, the royal confessor and Inquisitor General, culminated in a message to Lerma from the king giving him permission to put aside the cares of office and to enjoy the peace and tranquility of retirement. Uceda and Aliaga succeeded to the royal favour, though without enjoying the ascendency of Lerma, and held it through two and a half years of intense political manoeuvring at court until the death of Philip III in 1621 at the age of forty-two, and the succession of his sixteen-year old son, opened the door to power for the young prince's gentleman and mentor, the Count of Olivares. The political energy, the reforming zeal and the visionary ruthlessness with which Olivares was to rule Spain for over twenty years would stir up animosities far bitterer than Lerma's lazy, self-indulgent greed had done, and ensure that royal favour and delegated power remained a topic during Lope de Vega's lifetime. It was in the balance between the two that contemporary anxieties continued to lie. The Spanish commentators of the age might differ somewhat in their interpretation of royal sovereignty, but they all acknowledged that in practice no man could or should govern alone. Single rule as such was a tenet of faith in that it was seen to reflect the natural order and the divine, but the burden of power was by general consent too Herculean a task to be borne without the advice and support of others. Favouritism and flattery, however, were the Scylla and Charybdis of this necessary process of consultation; the one ran the risk of abdicating power into another's hands, the other encouraged arrogance and that identification of the individual will with the interests of the state which constituted tyranny. For Rivadeneyra the way for a prince to acquire prudence was not to trust in himself but to take wide counsel (566), a view partly prompted of course, like the similar views of other theorists, by the perceived inadequacies, for reasons of youth or temperament, of Spain's own monarchs. In *Querer la propia desdicha*, written, if Morley and Bruerton are right, not long after the fall of a great favourite, Lope muses on some aspects of *privanza*.[1]

The plot is a curious one. At the court of Alfonso of Castile and León a lady rejects her lover because he receives too many favours from the king and only accepts him when he finally negotiates his own disgrace. Ángela's reason is that she fears success will change don Juan and therefore their relationship, for a man with influence and power, she thinks, will undoubtedly wish to influence and control everything, including his wife,

> porque ha de querer
> tener el imperio en todo;
> y no quiere de ese modo
> querer ninguna mujer. (Act I, 444a)[2]

Ángela, furthermore, is a rich heiress whereas Juan initially is poor, and she realises that the power to give gifts changes the nature of the gift of love. For Ángela, born wealthy, being willing to marry a poor man is a measure of her love and an acknowledgement of his instrinsic worth. His willingness to marry her is an abdication of male pride for the sake of love, a sacrifice she appreciates since she has no little pride herself. The love intrigue is complicated, with little or no action and virtually no historical underpinning. It relies scarcely at all on the familiar devices of comic misunderstanding – dropped letters, forced lies, mistaken identities – and a great deal on the complexity and unreliability of human motivation. It probes the nature of love and jealousy in an unusual and thoughtful way. Ángela has no wish to dominate her husband through her wealth and position but neither does she wish to be possessed, dominated, outranked (a motive revealingly denounced by an indignant Cotarelo y Mori as patently absurd).[3] She wants a person, not a *persona*, a construct of titles and riches. Don Juan early on identifies two forms of jealousy – one rooted in suspicion which discredits the loved one, the other in a sense of one's own inadequacy. It is this second form of jealousy that Ángela

1 In his dedication of the play to Claudio Conde, Lope pens a warm and elegant tribute to a friend with whom he shared some of the dangers and reversals of youth, saying that its title, if not the play's content, is appropriate to this time in his past because he values the adversities they experienced together and because these were the chosen adversities of youth.

2 *Obras*, Real Academia Española (nueva ed.), XIII (Madrid, 1930).

3 In his introduction to the play, *Obras*, xxvi.

is afraid of feeling – she has no wish to experience the jealousy of inequality and inadequacy. Paradoxically she is happy to accept don Juan when he is poor, before and after his intervening period of success, although this places him in the very position which she refuses to occupy. The difference in her eyes is that she is already rich and has enough for both. She is the person she was born, the person don Juan fell in love with, whereas success has given him a different identity; it has even in her eyes begun subtly to change his character, making him more assertive and dominant than before. The couple's explicit privileging of love over social and material considerations (Act III, 464b–6b) is impassioned and impressive and the thread running through their thinking is that titles and possessions, particularly when acquired, lead to pride and thence envy, 'la nobleza rica/ desatinos sueña' (Act III, 466a). Ángela's attitude is clearly contrasted with that of the self-interested doña Inés, for whom love is a form of social currency. Inés sets her cap at her cousin don Juan when he is rich and powerful then abandons him when he loses everything again at the end; in the process, ironically, she loses the respect of the King who, unbeknown to her, is in love with her.

The underlying emphasis in the play is on the arbitrariness of worldly rewards and the swiftness with which they can come and go. The King's lavishing of favours, titles and money on don Juan after the completion of a simple diplomatic mission to Aragón is impetuous and ill considered. He conceives an instant affection for the young man and makes him a knight of the Order of Santiago without knowing the least thing about him. On learning that he is poor he immediately makes him a count without giving him a specific title or the lands to go with it – he has no idea what is available – and when he finally fills in the blank on the memorandum that requires him to do so, he capriciously uses up the extra space on the parchment by making don Juan a duke into the bargain. Don Juan's servant, Tello, makes malicious fun of all this whimsical prodigality, and when rebuked by his master for reacting to the news of his dukedom with an obscene expletive he counters unequivocally, 'Aquestas cosas no son,/ señor, para hablar en seso' (Act II, 453a). The work is a striking example of the way in which, even in a play apparently centred elsewhere – here in the sexual politics of love and jealousy – Lope's obsession with favouritism and favours could be a major shaping influence. The word obsession is not too strong, I think, for there can be little doubt that Lope's attitude to political favouritism was inextricably bound up with a strong, personal sense of royal neglect. Here the play of the ideas of over-reward and under-reward that we see at work in different ways in *El servir con mala estrella* (under-reward) and *La fortuna merecida* (over-reward at the expense of the more deserving), is constantly present in the dialogue. The embarrassment of favours that threatens don Juan's happiness is the subject of his conversations with Ángela throughout the action, whereas Tello continually complains that he receives nothing for his services and attempts to wrest something out of the King for himself. The frequent unfairness as well as the selective excess of royal favour was, it is clear from these plays, an on going gripe of Lope's, and in *Querer la propia desdicha*, as in other plays, he offers an explanation in which criticism masquerades as excuse – royal isolation. The following interchange between Tello and the King develops this idea and is a typical example of Lope's technique having it both ways, of weighting censure with flattery in order to cover himself:

Tello. Aquí estaba el rey; no sé
si me atrevo a entrar. ¿Qué importa?
Si su grandeza reporta,
su benignidad se ve.
Rayos, como el sol, ofrecen
los reyes, cuando los miran;
mas ¿por qué causa me admiran,
si tanto a Dios se parecen?
¡Qué gran ser la monarquía!
Si fuera rey, no durmiera,
por no pensar que no era
rey el tiempo que dormía.
Con justos, con altos modos,
hizo Dios un rey, un hombre
que fuese igual en el nombre
y en la grandeza entre todos.[4]
Ya me ha visto.
Rey. Tello amigo,
¿Cómo no nos vemos ya?
Tello. Por que un rey, señor, está,
como es rey, sólo consigo.
Y he notado, o son antojos
de mi ignorancia fingidos,
que oye con otros oídos
y que ve con otros ojos.
Rey. No te entiendo.
Tello. Si ha de oír
un rey, es lo que otro oyó,
porque al rey se lo contó,
no porque lo oyó decir.
Si ha de ver, fuerza ha de ser
que es por lo que el otro vio.
Rey. No te explicas.
Tello. ¿Cómo no,

[4] The meaning here is unclear, and the text possibly corrupt. Lope could scarcely have intended to say that a king is equal in name and greatness to either God or other men, or even that he is equal to God amongst other men, although this is more plausible. It is unlikely, I think, to be a disingenuous joke of Tello's.

si es tan fácil de entender?
  ¿Anda el rey por la ciudad,
para ver, ni para oír?
Rey. Ya te entiendo.
Tello. Esto es decir
que está en duda la verdad.
  Cierto emperador había
que tal vez se disfrazaba
y por la ciudad andaba,
donde él mismo oía y vía.
  Murmuraban a un rey griego
una noche unos soldados,
por mil pantanos cargados
de una máquina de fuego,
  y él, que iba entre ellos desnudo,
'Del cetro y la monarquía
murmuralde – les decía-;
mas no de mí, que os ayudo'.
Rey. Tello, ejemplos de tu mano
no pueden tener valor.
Tello. Gran razón tienes, señor.
Hable del campo un villano.
Rey. ¿Qué hay por allá, que también
informa algún desigual?
Tello. Señor, decir mucho mal
y hacer siempre poco bien.
  En estos dos polos solos
se mueve, aunque injusta ley,
una corte.
Rey. Pues el rey
tiene diferentes polos.
Tello. ¿Quién, señor?
Rey. Premio y castigo. (Act II, 449)

The King is naturally allowed to have the last word, but what Tello, with the *gracioso*'s traditional licence, has said remains said. The remoteness of the monarch was a cause of concern to political theorists at the beginning of the reign of Philip III; by 1640, when Saavedra Fajardo's *Idea de un príncipe político-cristiano* was published, the aura of impenetrable royal dignity cultivated by Philip IV made it seem not only inevitable but desirable. Vives (247) and Rivadeneyra (541) had enjoined vigilance and participation upon the monarch, Mariana accessibility (chap.V, 97), and here in these remarks of Tello's the nostalgia for these royal values that is detectable in such plays as *Fuenteovejuna* and *El mejor alcalde el rey* is unequivocally articulated. If the king neither sees nor hears, he is out of touch with reality and then the wishes of others prevail; this, as Rugero in *El servir con mala estrella* indicates, is where favour, flattery, neglect and envy – all synonymous with court politics in seventeenth-century Spanish writers – take over. The distribution of reward and punishment was indeed the business of a king, but Alfonso has missed the full implication of Tello's observations – in a court royal isolationism makes it impossible to identify the good and the bad that need to be rewarded and punished. Here, as in the *comedia* generally, the *gracioso* is the ideal scapegoat, the voice of unpalatable truth out of a mouth that is able to disclaim responsibility for what it says precisely because it is denied validity: 'ejemplos de tu mano/ no pueden tener valor'. Tello's pious mouthings about kingship move effortlessly into a warning about the consequences of ignoring that essential requirement of good government, knowledge of what was happening and of what people were thinking – the lack of which was seen at the time to be connected with both tyranny and ineffective monarchy. He builds a safeguard into his homily – the fault lies with the system and not the monarch, the good will of the King himself is not in question – but Alfonso's opaque response itself reveals how pressingly the point needs to be made. The *gracioso* device, of course, is an unsubtle and transparent one which would have fooled no one, indeed its effectiveness lay in its very predictability. Plain speaking and home truths are the *gracioso*'s stock-in-trade, his unfettered opinions at once licensed and safeguarded by his comic role; convention guaranteed immunity. He is the common man expressing the common man's view of things, possessed of an autonomy which the other characters, more circumscribed by their roles in the play, do not enjoy. What he says could be conveniently dismissed, but it could not be erased because his observations are crystallizations of preoccupations embodied in the play as a whole and in its parts.

The problem presented by the necessary or inevitable isolation of the monarch, the idea that kings see only through the eyes of others, crops up again in another play about a royal favourite, *Porfiando vence amor*, written in the 1620s (1624–30, 1624–?1626). The King of Hungary banishes his favourite Carlos on the basis of a false accusation of treason. Carlos is a good and able man, the King is just, an astute judge of men and their ability, and full of good will. In the very nature of things, however, kings are susceptible to the malice and envy of others and truth often eludes them:

> El vivir de engaños llenos
> los reyes, causa también
> que todo lo que no ven
> lo ven con ojos ajenos. (Act I, 278b)[5]

Lope's great political tragedy *El Duque de Viseo*, written a decade and a half

5 *Obras*, Real Academia Española (nueva ed.) (Madrid, 1930), XIII.

or so before, turns on this very premise. The conceit in the later play is Alejandro's, Carlos's rival, coined to do Carlos down, but events prove him right – with the difference that the real creator of deception, of what the King cannot see because it is not there, is not Carlos but himself. Strictly speaking, *Porfiando vence amor* is a play about love and fidelity, envy, and the politics of favouritism, in that order. But to characterize it thus is to misrepresent its identity. The politics of *privanza* and Lope's own reservations and convictions about kingship, court life and favouritism seep into many of his plots, shaping or partly shaping the narrative and providing a sub-text to the work's apparent concerns sometimes so clamorous that it threatens to appropriate the play. The interconnected structures of merit, reward, envy, loyalty and favouritism, in the general as well as the political sense, gnawed at his imagination and they push their way through his plots almost inspite of him. *Porfiando vence amor* is such a play.

This work, authentic albeit undated, has been assigned to the mid to late twenties, a time when the aging Lope had not yet given up the hope of advancement, and his flattering portrait of the life of a royal favourite was clearly meant to curry favour with that only effective channel of royal preferment, Olivares:

Carlos. Quien sirve, señora mía,
no es libre; y aquí en palacio,
aunque es verdad que cautivan
grillos y cadenas de oro,
tan dulcemente nos quitan
el tiempo y la libertad
que antes se acaba la vida
que gocemos sin descanso
un día de tantos días. (Act I, 276b)

It is only fair to say that Lope spoke here nothing but the truth – not even Olivares's worst enemies ever accused him of neglecting his post. Carlos's subsequent exchange with the King is, in terms of flattery of Olivares, more ingratiating:

Rey. No tengo
otro mayor descanso en mis cuidados,
cuando contigo a conferirlos vengo,
que verlos, si no en todo remediados,
en parte de su pena remitidos
y a mejor esperanza levantados.
Carlos. Siempre están mis deseos prevenidos
a tu servicio, como dueño solo
del alma, que gobierna mis sentidos.
Único rey, como en el cielo Apolo,

das luz a todo el orbe de mi vida.
Su movimiento es tu dorado polo. (Act I, 277b)

Privanza, furthermore, a quarter of a century or so after the accession of Philip III and the rise of Lerma, is taken absolutely for granted: one favourite without question succeeds another. Alejandro's confidant at court, Armindo, even produces an extravagant religious analogy for *privanza* when Alejandro complains enviously about the way in which so many court ladies defer to Carlos:

¿Qué quieres, si Carlos priva?
La república del mundo
la de los cielos imita.
¿A los santos no rogamos
para que ellos a Dios pidan
lo que habemos menester?
¿Pues de qué, señor, te admiras
que imite la tierra al cielo
y que ruege a los que privan? (Act I, 277b)

But Armindo is a something of a cynic and his words here are undercut by a barbed tone of irony which is then echoed in Alejandro's disgruntled rejection of the rationalization offered: 'Si; pero estoy envidioso,/ y en el cielo no hay envidia.' The joke proves irresistible, and deference slides into artful humour. This subtle shift, in fact, initiates a move away from diplomacy, and from this point on *privanza* and *privado* are treated less generously. Lope had made his self-protective gesture of obeisance and now felt able, it seems, to introduce into the work, implicitly by means of charaterization and plot and explicitly in the dialogue, what he felt to be a few home truths. In Carlos deference verges on the unctuous: having strongly recommended Alejandro as the best general to lead the troops to battle, his response when the King tentatively raises Otavio's name is, 'Será mejor si a ti, señor, te agrada./ Otavio es valeroso, cuerdo y sabio' (Act I, 278a). The King is prepared to defer to Carlos's judgment and choose Alejandro, but Carlos insists, 'Recibiera, señor, tu gusto agravio,/ pues a mi humilde voto le prefieres.' Carlos's responses are revealing. In the first, with that conditional 'si', worth is made contingent upon preference, a preference which in Carlos's opinion, clearly, is not grounded in this instance in worth. In the second, royal pleasure becomes a whimsical thing centred not in judgement but in pride. Whatever the circumstances a king's wishes must not be denied. It is an odd little episode, on the surface of it unnecessary – the good working relationship between King and favourite has already been amply demonstrated in their exchange of mutual praise – but with the effect of making Carlos, the King's valued adviser, appear willing almost to abandon reason and good sense and to abase himself to please his master. He is prepared to sacrifice the country's good to the monarch's fancy. The point of the episode emerges only as the action unfolds. The King's wishes prevail, as they should have done, because, for all Carlos's virtues, it is the King who turns out to be the better judge of character: Otavio goes to war and brings it to a successful conclusion for Hungary, Alejandro is not the honourable man Carlos describes him as being. Carlos arrived at the right conclusion for the wrong reason. What he saw as a simple matter of royal *gusto* was in fact a crucial question both of judgement and of authority. A king must rule, taking counsel but making his own judgements and taking his own decisions. The favourite is and must remain a subsidiary figure. The message is directed not only at Olivares but at the young Philip.

In his preference for the sharp, self-serving Leonarda, Carlos proves as innocent a judge of women as he is of men, and shortly after his conversation with the King his servant Fabio reprimands him for neglecting Lucinda, who dearly loves him. Fabio then proceeds to making a general point of the particular case, by taking up the idea of the favourite's satellite role and warning him in no uncertain terms,

A tu persona gallarda
se inclinan cuantas te ven
discreto y valiente también;
pero el ser favorecido
del Rey la más parte ha sido
para que te quieran bien.
Las gracias de Efestión
Alejandro las hacía.
La aurora en que viene el día
bostezos de Febo son.
De un príncipe la afición
es pragmática inviolable;
que como él de un hombre hable
y le acredite su gusto,
a todos, señor, es justo
que les parezca admirable.

Carlos. ¿De manera que el favor
me ha dado merecimiento?

Fabio. Es de tus partes aumento
el tenerte el Rey amor.
¿Qué ingenio no hará mayor
su afición, qué gentileza,
qué virtud, gracia y destreza?

Carlos. Sí; pero en toda ocasión
ha de dar más opinión
la verdad que la grandeza,
si bien le debo al favor
cuanto presumen de mí.

Fabio. Esto considero en ti,
sin ofender tu valor. (Act I, 280a–b)

Now this is very plain speaking indeed, particularly from a playwright actively seeking preferment. If the play was indeed written in the middle to late years of the 1620s – a time when he was honoured by the Pope[6] and when old scandals were receding – its frankness makes one suspect that Lope's forked-tongue technique of interleaving criticism with praise might well have been a contributory factor in his continuing failure to achieve the recognition he felt he deserved. Olivares was not a man to cross, as Tirso de Molina's banishment from Madrid testifies, and he might understandably have taken offence at being preached at publicly by a playwright. The very forthrightness of this speech, however, suggests a date of composition towards the end of the decade – 1630 is the latest possible year in Morley and Bruerton's view – by which time Lope's efforts to win the favour of Olivares and his wife had patently failed, and he was beset by financial troubles. There is no question here of coded messages; the cover normally provided by character and plot is virtually non-existent. Fabio's words are an uncompromising (and in the event prophetic) reminder to Philip IV's favourite that he is the king's creature, that he is what he is solely by royal permission – as Lerma, like Antonio Pérez before him, had learned to his cost. Carlos's fall itself then begins to read like a warning about the fragility of delegated power. The favourite's dependence is brought into further relief by the articulation of royal authority invested in the image of the sun king. Carlos, indeed, in the first shock of dismissal seems mesmerized by this apparently arbitrary display of royal power: 'Oh Rey, al sol semejante' (Act I, 281a) and, soon afterwards,

Sol el Rey, palacio esfera,
sube terrestres vapores
a sus claros resplandores,
y aunque él padece desmayos,
tal vez que se engendran rayos
dan en las torres mayores. (Act I, 282a)

In the dialectic inspired by the co-existence of an ideal of kingship and the realities of rule, the institution is absolved of responsibility, yet at the same time seen as inherently flawed because certain consequences and effects flow from it. For the time kingship, as the plays show over and again, presented two problems: the humanity of the individual who inhabits the king, and the dangers inherent in the system itself – there can be no kings without a power structure, there is no power structure unaffected by human envy and desire.

6 See chap.2, 34.

Both at bottom involve the complex interconnections between ideologies, mental constructions, and self-interest and self-expression. The fall from royal favour of even a noble and well-loved minister is at once a directed warning and a general statement about a notoriously vulnerable political system, as Leonarda points out:

> ¿qué valimiento
> de la envidia se escapó?
> ¿Qué virtud no derribó,
> qué verdad, qué entendimiento? (Act I, 281b)

Carlos is deserted by his friends when he falls from grace – and his servant Fabio is shunned by his fellow servants. Even Leonarda deserts him in favour of the new favourite, Alejandro – Lope's phrase for such women is 'de las de "¡viva quien vence!" ', used here of Leonarda (Act II, 294a) as well as of Inés in *Querer la propia desdicha* (Act III, 467a). Of course we learnt at the beginning of the play that she was initially attracted to him because of his position and then fell in love, but with Lope this admission in itself is a signal of the sort of restraint and self-interest which for him played no part in love. Lucinda, by contrast, is committed, unrestrained and generous in her devotion. Leonarda justifies her change of heart by resorting to the idea of mutability – all things, even kings, change,

> múdase un rey, que aunque es hombre,
> tiene, como las campanas,
> metal de divinidad
> con lo humano en partes varias. (Act II, 292b)

But her litany of traditional platitudes constitutes special pleading. The skies, seas and seasons she invokes change as part of the ineluctable patterns of nature and the cosmos, whereas Carlos loses the King's trust and falls through the wilful malice of an enemy. In obliterating the distinction she condemns herself. Real friends are not of the fair-weather kind she sees even the best friends to be. Lucinda remains true if Leonarda does not, and Carlos, once the King discovers the deceit, is reinstated. In the affairs of men, particularly those which involve the play of power, there is no need to turn to cosmic theories for answers when human nature itself provides them. Lope would not live to see the fall of Olivares himself, but had he done so it would have caused him no surprise. He had reminded him after all that favourites were made and unmade, that they were merely 'Figuras y hombres de barro' in Rujero's words in *El servir con mala estrella*,[7] the constructions of a more substantial and lasting power that embodied the state itself.

7 See chap.3, 62.

The political sub-text of *Porfiando vence amor*, although it contained as well a lesson for Spain's young king, focuses on favouritism. In *El poder en el discreto*, written possibly as little as a year earlier, the king himself takes the centre of the stage. J.H. Elliott has pointed out that Spain was 'never more truly a conciliar monarchy than in the last three years of the reign of Philip III',[8] after the fall of Lerma. However, with the accession of Philip IV and the rise of an active and energetic favourite who had ambitions for his country as well as for himself, and who was prepared if necessary to incur the displeasure of the establishment – and the rest of Spain for that matter – in order to implement them, the exercise of political power became an even keener issue than it had been during Lerma's heyday. Philip IV's reputation has undergone a revision in recent years – Stradling judges that 'all things considered he was the greatest of Los Austrias'[9] – but since he was only sixteen when he ascended the throne, the early years of his reign were anxious ones for those concerned with the state of Spain. Lope de Vega completed *El poder en el discreto* on 8 May 1623, when the new king was eighteen. Ostensibly another love plot, as a play about a young king it is a barely diguised *de regimine principum*, the title revealing unequivocally that the play's real business is kingship and the nature of power. Pedro Vargas Machuca, who wrote the *aprobación*, dated 18 January 1624, took the point, stating that 'está con mucho decoro y *buen ejemplo* el amor en este Rey que introduce' (my italics).

The play portrays the King of Sicily's prudence and discernment in deciding not to abuse his power in the conduct of his love for a young woman committed elsewhere. Inspite of being sorely tempted to pull rank, he eventually rejects the exercise of *force majeur* and opts instead for the sensible exercise of discretion, that habit of mind that enabled man to navigate a virtuous and circumspect course through life. In the process he learns to put public duty before private inclination, his subjects' well-being before his own desires. It takes him time to arrive at this wisdom, however, for all that he is presented throughout as a decent, reasonable youth. Only once does he show himself prepared actually to abuse his position: when Serafina marries in secret and her new husband is supposedly away, the King decides to press his suit and, when this is refused, to use force. His favourite, Celio – who is, unbeknown to the King, Serafina's husband – in desperation appeals to the King's sense of fair play by pointing out that he is indirectly responsible for the marriage, reminding him that he pretended to have lost interest in Serafina (his motive was in fact to find out whether Celio was in love with her). Persuaded by this reasoning, the King modifies his position and decides to press Serafina for sexual favours only if her husband is of the compliant type:

8 *The Count-Duke of Olivares*, 37.

9 *Philip IV and the Government of Spain*, xv.

> Sabe que hay dos maneras de maridos.
> Unos, a quien su honor, entendimiento,
> talle y autoridad, ser ofendidos
> defiende a todo injusto atrevimiento;
> otros, por su bajeza conocidos
> de tan poco valor y sentimiento,
> y en su casa y mujer tan descuidados,
> que aun lo merezca ser de sus criados.
> Esto se entiende con dejar aparte
> la ley de Dios, porque a ninguna ofensa
> da licencia jamás; pero es mostrarte
> lo que el discurso de los hombres piensa.
> Guardando, pues, de este respeto el arte,
> veré el marido de su honor defensa,
> y conforme le viere, te prometo,
> Celio, tener o no tener respeto. (Act III, 489a–b)[10]

He may doff his cap at the teaching of the Church but clearly he sees the practical issue for himself as a socio-political, not an ethical one, involving his responsibiliy to his subjects rather than his duty to sexual morality – if the husband is not offended then no offence is committed. Discovering that the husband is Celio, the King accepts the situation and gives the marriage his blessing:

> La discreción y el poder
> conmigo están compitiendo
> . . .
> . . .pero, en efeto,
> la esperanza que te ha dado
> mi valor y entendimiento
> me obliga a valerme ahora,
> más que del poder que tengo,
> de la discreción. . . (Act III, 492b–3a)

His conclusions contain an obvious lesson. Courage and understanding, qualities on which the King evidently prides himself, dictate in the circumstances the use of discretion, not power. By reverse reasoning the implication is that discretion demands both – the courage of self-denial and the understanding of what kingship requires – and is not to be taken as the resort of weakness. The key to the exercise of power is the knowledge when not to use it.

With the King's blessing comes a sharp reprimand for Celio who, instead

10 *Obras*, Real Academia Española (nueva ed.), II (Madrid, 1916).

of admitting to his love for Serafina when the King first mentions his attraction, creates with his subterfuges most of the problems that ensue. None of this need have happened, as the King points out. But Celio and the other characters proceed all the time on the assumption that the King will indeed use his power to achieve what he wants. Their manoeuvrings are merely attempts at circumventing it. At the same time they are surprised at how deeply he is affected by his love for Serafina, whereas the King himself is only too painfully aware throughout that he is human. His dilemma is fully apparent only to him and it is one he thinks through for himself, although Celio at one point, exasperated at having to act as the King's go-between, does burst out,

> ¿Piensas tú que tu poder
> se extiende más que a los cuerpos?
> Sólo Dios reina en las almas. (Act II, 470a)

With commendable restraint the King, who has merely asked him for Serafina's response – she has thus far been courteously cool – crossly and sarcastically inquires whether Serafina is not 'señora de su albedrío'. When Celio bleakly points out that wills can weaken, the King is willing to concede that he does indeed have much to offer Serafina. By the end of the play, however, the King is not the only character to have learned the meaning of the proper exercise of royal power.

Poder is a word that occurs often in the text; another, in conjunction with it, is *gusto*. In the eyes of his subjects the King's pleasure is paramount, but the play makes clear that kingship itself necessarily places constraints upon that pleasure. There is a telling contrast between this emphasis on royal power and authority and the way in which the King behaves like a lovesick gallant, setting out in the dark for Serafina's house to catch a glimpse of her and courting a woman he is not able, for dynastic reasons, to marry. *Comedia* convention might be thought to be taking over here, but Lope was too experienced for this recourse to convention to be inadvertent in a play with such a clear agenda. He is using the camouflage provided by the love plot tactfully to address the problems posed by a young man who had recently ascended the throne and was being escorted round the streets of Madrid at night in search of adventure by his mentor Olivares. The royal favourite was actually rebuked by the Archbishop of Granada, the king's former tutor, for encouraging the king's extra-marital adventures.[11] The combined motifs of youth and power coincide explicitly and meaningfully in Serafina's expression of misgiving:

> Es mancebo tan soberbio

[11] See Gregorio Marañón, *El Conde-Duque de Olivares* (third edition. Madrid: Espasa Calpe, 1952), 38–9; also Elliott. *The Count Duke Of Olivares*, 112.

que en quitándole su gusto,
a su poder tengo miedo. (Act III, 492a)

She is unfair in her judgement of the King's character – he has shown little sign of arrogance – but she unwittingly puts her finger on the problem: it is hard for youth both to renounce its fancy and to 'domar y enfrenar el potro del poder', in Saavedra Fajardo's words (*Empresa* XX, 53b).

As a parable about kingship *El poder en el discreto* is neither a complex nor a subtle play. Indeed it is more direct than most of Lope's kingship plays, with plot and purpose coinciding more closely than in many and a title that immediately leads the audience below the surface business of the plot to the play's real agenda. Here, as in *Porfiando vence amor* and elsewhere, Lope's technique of camouflaged narrative, of using the plot for contemporary comment without overt contemporary reference, occasionally explodes into words as direct as the fictional dialogue allows, words that would have resounded from the boards to lodge within the consciousness of a knowing audience. Celio's charge about the limits of royal sovereignty, when he is provoked by jealousy and despair into a frankness he would normally never risk, is theologically impeccable and has to be conceded by the King, but in its impertinence, if nothing else, it is a trenchant statement about the delineation of power in an age when monarchs were increasingly encouraged to perceive themselves in cosmic terms. Pedro Crespo's words in Calderón's *El alcalde de Zalamea* are the famous articulation of this idea in the Golden-Age theatre,

Al rey la hacienda y la vida
se ha de dar; pero el honor
es patrimonio del alma
y el alma solo es de Dios. (Act I, 873–76)[12]

and as the considered judgement of an elderly and prudent man (in the play) they carry a weight and a rhetorical rotundity that this passionate outburst on the part of a young lover lacks. But Lope's Celio was there before him. Flora's comment to the King after learning that he has transferred his affections to another is scarcely less forceful:

Los grandes señores son
tan amigos de su gusto
que, sea justo o injusto,
disponen la voluntad
a cualquiera novedad,
cause o no cause disgusto. (Act I, 469a–b)

[12] *El alcalde de Zalamea*, ed. Peter N. Dunn (Oxford: Pergamon Press, 1966, reprint ed. 1977), 61.

Under cover of a scorned woman's bitterness Lope openly makes a damning observation about the great which few in his audience could have wanted to disagree with. And, of course, when it suits him the King does forget all about Serafina's free will when he later decides to use his power to possess her. He subsequently opts for a campaign of seduction on the strength of some very dubious reasoning and finally desists, not because to try to seduce a married woman is in itself unsuitable behaviour in a king, but because he discovers who Serafina's husband is. A question mark hangs, therefore, over the King – his is an interestingly ambiguous characterization – and another question mark hangs over that – did Lope perceive the King to be compromised by his privileging of discretion at virtue's expense? Of course adultery, in Spain as elsewhere in Europe, was at the time a crime that only a woman could commit in law, and male philandering, although theologically a sin, came very low indeed on the list of contemporary moral shortcomings. In the unravelling of the plot's complications and its celebration of the King's discretion, the finer issue of sexual morality is certainly lost from sight. This in all probability reflects Lope's cynical opinion that compliant husbands get what they deserve (given his own behaviour he could have thought little else), that men will be men, and that in this regard even kings have traditionally always been allowed, in practice if not in theory, their humanity. It certainly introduces a knowing irony into the play's perspective on the character formation of a king. There is nothing to suggest, however, that it was meant to be an issue. Lope is concerned here not with royal sexual peccadillos but with the need for youth to come to terms with political power, to learn the discreet exercise of authority, to see good government as lying in the balance between royal sovereignty and the will and welfare of the republic. *El poder en el discreto* is not a play to give much joy to those who seek to see in Lope an adherent of absolutism, for it presents royal power as being properly hedged about by restrictions that are indispensable for effective rule. The threat of *force majeure*, the mere assumption that it will be deployed, here leads only to confusion and deceit, to frustration of the king's desires, not fulfilment. It is, in other words, resoundingly counter-productive.

It will be very clear by now that Lope's concern with kingship was directed above all at the sorts of issues treated by the theorists of the day. They were ideological concerns about matters such as the nature and requirements of kingship, the king's two-fold identity, and *privanza*, for all that they were prompted by the contemporary situation and implicitly targeted individuals. The more particular and explicit political criticism and satire associated with Tirso de Molina was not Lope's way because it entailed greater risks and he had much more to lose than Tirso, firmly ensconced as the latter was in the security of his religious order. And since Lope was the one allowed to go on using the stage as a platform for political debate his was in the event the more effective policy. There is one notable play assigned to Lope, however, which departs from this general rule of foxy prudence in the choice and handling of political issues. The seventeenth-century manuscript of *El rey por semejanza* attributes the first act to one Grajales, though which one of several possible Grajales this might have been is not known.[13] At the beginning of Act II the play is attributed to Lope. Morley and Bruerton categorize the play as being of doubtful authenticity but ascribe it tentatively to the period 1599–1603. My own view is that Act I might well not be Lope's but that Acts II and III are more convincingly his. Act I has an uncharacteristic structural awkwardness and a lack of fluency in the writing, whereas thereafter the dialogue proceeds with silken fluidity and pace. Furthermore, the characters become more convincing and more interesting in the last two acts, and the love scenes between the Queen and the man masquerading as her husband the King are quite excellent and very reminiscent of *El perro del hortelano*, with the Queen feeling now strongly attracted, now drawing back in account of her honour. Lope of course did not often collaborate in the writing of plays, and it is by no means impossible that the play is entirely his; but it is not difficult to imagine circumstances which could have led, for example, to his continuing one already started.

The play is a novelesque romance about a queen who has her tyrannical husband murdered by an admirer and is then rescued from a very dangerous situation by the appearance of a royal look-alike, a *villano*, whom she persuades to take the King's place. The *villano*, Altemio, turns out, naturally, to have all the kingly qualities that King Antíoco lacked and he and the Queen eventually fall in love with each other and live happily ever after. The wickedness of regicide is dutifully pointed out, but the fairy-tale nonsense of the plot is in effect an unconcealed frontal attack on bad government. The ills which Altemio puts right are not only the moral tyrannies one would expect in such a tale – murder, deceit, rape – but, more prominently, a long list of specific socio-economic shortcomings as well as one or two familiar political abuses. The excessive wealth of the nobility comes under fire and the point is strongly made that their wealth and power increases only at the expense of the Crown. Excessive taxation is also hammered:

> Porque son tantos los pechos,
> tributos e imposiciones,
> agravios y vejaciones,
> con que los tienen estrechos,
>   echándoles cada día

13 The possible contenders for authorship of Act I, all contemporaries of Lope, are: the Graxales mentioned by Agustín de Rojas as being an actor who wrote plays; the *licenciado* Juan Grajales, author of a play called *El bastardo de Ceuta*, printed in 1615; and another *licenciado*, Juan de Grajal, author of the two-part play *La próspera y la adversa fortuna del Caballero del Espíritu Santo*. See Cotarelo y Mori's prologue to the play in *Obras*, Real Academia Española (nueva ed.), II, xii–xiii.

a fin de los consumir,
que no lo pueden sufrir. (Act II, 506b)

Indeed the dramatic core of the play concerns what is effectively a tax row, a confrontation between the nobles and the King, who states he is going to subject them to enforced taxation. Since, as aristocrats, they are tax-exempt, they regard this as an outrageous and illegal afront to their honour and rank. They only yield when he proceeds to erect a scaffold on which to execute them for not complying. He then reveals his intention of teaching them a lesson: they have no more right to ruin their vassals with ever-increasing taxation than he has the right to force them to pay taxes on pain of death – both actions are unjust and constitute an abuse of power, 'Yo os trato como vosotros/ tratáis a vuestros vasallos'(Act II, 513b). Social extravagance and ostentation, particularly at court, are targeted as well, as are excessive and unfounded favours, 'Las mercedes superfluas' (Act II, 509a), and the gross misdirection of money which should go to the poor, the deserving and the Church (another dig at the extravagance of Lerma and his protégés). The dangers of *privanza* and royal negligence are once more unequivocally pointed out:

Bien es, si en él [the *privado*] no hay lealtad,
que el Rey fíe de un vasallo
su reino, y por sólo honrallo
arriesgue su majestad. (Act I, 505b–6a)

and again,

¿No sabrá mejor juzgar
un Rey, vedlo, Conde, vos,
que es inspirado de Dios,
que un hombre particular? (Act I, 506a).

There is no question in this play of the audience being left to deduce from the contrast between the two kings how a king ought to behave and what he ought to stand for. The necessary reforms are spelt out. And in case the play's didactic intentions were somehow overlooked, a prince (the murdered king's son) witnessing lessons in kingship from an exemplary monarch is included in order to drive the point home. No spectator could possibly have seen such a play without drawing forceful contemporary parallels. In the early years of the reign of Philip III tax reform and cuts in government expenditure were amongst the measures recommended by *arbitristas*.[14] The target here is patently the Lerma government's ongoing failure to spread Castile's tax burden more equitably by introducing fiscal measures to reduce the huge imbalance

[14] See J.H. Elliott, *Imperial Spain 1469–1716* (London: Edward Arnold, 1963), 295.

between the nobility, who were exempt from most taxes, and the commoners who, in greatly reduced numbers since the plague of 1599, bore the brunt of the Crown's money-raising activities. Lerma and the king chose to deal with this pressing problem by ignoring it, opting instead for easier solutions such as the sale of offices and jurisdictions, the imposition of subsidies on Portuguese Jews and the manipulation of the Castilian currency.[15] Lope employs his usual diversionary tactics by deflecting criticism towards the nobles themselves, but nobody in his audience could have failed to realize to whom it was really addressed. Not only is the point about fiscal equity trenchantly made but here is an energetic king concerned enough about his subjects to take action. Philip III preferred to expend his energies on his own pastimes and leave the government of his kindom to Lerma. This was the reign that marked the rise of the *privado*, and Lerma and his family had very quickly become enormously rich on the back of the Crown, through royal favours, appointments and gifts. Court life, after the austerity of the previous reign, soon settled into a pattern of extravagance and ostentation, and this exacerbated the widespread bitterness caused by the government's unwillingness to address what Elliott calls the 'gross inequalities between the [tax] exempt rich and the penalized poor' (299). All the socio-economic and political concerns in the play point therefore, albeit not conclusively, to a date in the early years of Philip's reign – the second quotation above does not strike one as being the product of a period when the *privanza* system was well-established; and such a dating would of course fit in with Morley and Bruerton's own tentative dating for the play if it is Lope's and consequently make Lope's authorship more likely. It would be extremely unwise, I think, to infer from the play's engagement with socio-economic issues that Lope could not have written it. On the contrary, as we have seen, he wrote a number of plays which deal with contemporary political realities while masquerading as royal romances, and plain speaking, it should by now be clear, is not nearly as unusual in his theatre as has been conventionally thought. His plays denounce injustice, corrupt government, social and political irresponsibility, delegation of rule, excessive distribution of royal favour, and his characters attack the rich, the great, the court. At the same time it is certainly the case that the attacks here have a directness and above all a specificity which were not Lope's favoured *modus operandi*. The assault on the privileges of the rich and the advocacy of tax reform do not even issue from the mouth of a *gracioso*-servant, whose prattlings could be put down to foolishness or envy. They are an integral part of the play's dramatic structure, and they come authorized by the King himself. This might have served to neutralize anticipated censure (a standard ploy of Lope's) but it has also an exemplary function. Not only are these reforms necessary but the king is the person who

[15] See Elliott, *Imperial Spain*, 299.

should see that they come about. He is the fount of earthly justice, 'la principal virtud del príncipe' for López Bravo (*Del rey*, 114), and his is the responsibility to ensure that justice is distributed equally. Lope's Duke Sinibaldo would point out in *La sortija del olvido* 'Que es la justicia un ser distributivo', and there is, in fact, nothing of substance in *El rey por semejanza*'s critique of contemporary Spain which Lope at some time or another did not use his plays either to say or imply. It is in the manner of saying that the difference lies. Would Lope have dared to offend, at the very least irritate, his aristocratic patrons by declaring so forcefully that they should be exacting fewer taxes from their tenants and actually paying taxes themselves? Did he, perhaps, place too much confidence in the use of displacement, in the power of carefully worked fiction to provide camouflage and deflect criticism, and learn from reaction to the play that it was not an experiment he should attempt again? Did the play even get performed? Mariana in his treatise *De morte et immortalitate* had criticized the common people of Spain for imitating their betters in their wanton behaviour and extravagance, 'They recline at their banquets, besotted with food and wine, softened and corrupted by debauchery, after the example of their princes',[16] and been censored for his pains. The Lerma régime was not very energetic in pursuing such matters, however, and the theatre in any case enjoyed a licence denied the treatise inspite of its power to mimic reality, its power, as Mariana disapprovingly stated, to put incredible things together in such a way that they do not seem to be fictions but real happenings: 'cosas increíbles componerse y afeitarse de manera que no parecen fingidas, sino acaecidas y hechas'.[17] *El rey por semejanza* was almost certainly performed therefore. It could not, however, have made its author(s) many friends amongst Spain's élite, and if the play is indeed largely Lope's then it was not an experiment he would repeat quite so baldly again. If Act I was the work of a different pen, then perhaps the beginnings of a two-king plot, a perfect vehicle for political comment, and the example of political frankness (the critique gets underway in Act I) proved on this occasion just too tempting for Lope to resist.

There are no such ifs attached to a much later play, *El piadoso aragonés*, the autograph manuscript of which is dated 16 August 1626. The play, which depicts the rivalry between Fernando *el católico* and his step-brother Carlos, Prince of Viana, for the throne of Aragon, was denounced with virulent indignation by Menéndez y Pelayo for its wilful distortion of historical facts, its anachronisms and its fictional absurdities. He ascribed these crimes to 'la mezquina adulación palaciega' and dismissed the play as 'una obra baladí'. Proceeding as usual from his own assumptions both about Lope and about the

16 *Tractatus* VII (Cologne: Antonius Hieratus, 1609), 359b, translated in Soons, *Juan de Mariana*, 127.

17 *Contra los juegos públicos* (*De Spectaculis*), chap. V, *Obras del Padre Juan de Mariana*, II, Biblioteca de Autores Españoles, 31 (Madrid: M. Rivadeneyra, 1872), 410b.

proper relationship between history and fiction, he once again did not pause to wonder whether anything other than instinctive obsequiousness had led Lope to reconstruct history in the way he does. But this in fact is an extraordinarily interesting play, above all for what it reveals about Lope's capacity for dramatic duplicity, for engineering texts which fulfil multiple, often contrary, purposes.

Historical chronology and events are certainly refashioned in order to make Carlos, in the play a rebellious prince severely trying the patience of a long-suffering father, shoulder more responsibility for the shabby treatment he suffered in real life at the hands of his father and step-mother. Juan II of Aragon and his wife, Juana, were extremely ambitious, and Fernando, the younger, was always the favoured of the two sons, partly because of his superior political temperament and acumen. The historical Carlos did indeed take up arms against his father but only under severe provocation, not through ambition and petulence as at first sight seems to be the case in the play. He was duly defeated. Later on, he was deposed as Prince of Navarre and imprisoned. In 1460 Juan passed over Carlos in favour of Fernando when he named his lieutenant in Catalonia. War broke out in Catalonia as a result, and then continued after Carlos's death in 1461. A look at what had been going on in Spain in the year or so immediately before Lope wrote the play suggests what might have been in Lope's mind as he recast these events to bring about Carlos's transformation from somewhat elusive political figure to rebel.

The *annus mirabilis* of 1625 had brought victories over the Dutch in Flanders and Brazil, the English at Cadiz and the French in Italy. That same year also saw the finalization of Olivares' plans for the Union of Arms, a defence policy aimed at organizing military co-operation between the kingdoms of Spain in order to ease the burden upon Castile's financial and human resources. In late 1625 Philip IV and Olivares set out to visit the three states that constituted the kingdom of Aragon. The *cortes* of Aragon, Catalonia and Valencia proved difficult to convince, however. The Catalan *cortes*, fearing a concerted erosion of its traditional liberties – relations between Catalonia and the Crown had not in recent years been good – was particularly recalcitrant, but a guarantee of limited co-operation was in the event wrung out of the *cortes* of Aragon and Valencia. On 31 January 1627 the Crown went bankrupt and suspended payment to its bankers. This measure proved successful in the short term, however, and that year the king was able to remind the Council of State of the achievements of his reign thus far – military victories abroad, domestic reforms and financial improvement. In spite of setbacks and continuing problems, therefore, the government was riding high and the mood in Spain was buoyant. Was the play perhaps commissioned, therefore, as part of this triumphalist mood? That *El piadoso aragonés* was intended as a triumphalist play the ending leaves us in no doubt. After forgiving his dying son and being reconciled with him, Juan is about to arrange a marriage between Carlos and the mother of his child when the action is abruptly terminated by a fanfare of trumpets and doors open on high to reveal, in the words of the stage direction, 'El príncipe don Fernando y la reina doña Isabel, coronados, y a sus pies algunos moros y judíos, y España a un lado, y Castilla y Aragón al otro'. A quasi-apotheosis, in effect, of the Catholic Monarchs. *España* then addresses King Juan, gives a brief explanation of the tableau in case its significance has escaped anyone, makes an even briefer reference to the descendents of the Catholic Monarchs and then ends in a flattering obeisance to the reigning monarch Philip IV. This has all the flavour of a court play and strongly suggests that the play was indeed written with court performance in mind. The adjustments to history now become explicable: Lope set out to please the king by presenting events in the light most flattering to his ancestors.

This does not explain, however, why he chose an episode of Spanish history that needed rejigging to suit his purpose. If he were set on writing about Fernando he certainly did not need to remodel history in order to flatter him. Of course, those turbulent years of late medieval Spain when dynastic loyalties and interests cut across national considerations, and when princely scions had fingers in all the ancient kingdoms' pies, are not easy to make moral judgements about. It is difficult to reconcile Menéndez y Pelayo's moral outrage at Lope's version of events with the objective accounts of modern historians. The ambiguous and complex play of interests in a confused and ruthless political world in itself conceivably roused Lope's interest in the events he dramatizes. Or perhaps it was the human interest inherent in a story where a monarch is faced with a son's rebellion, a dilemma which Calderón would explore in a very different way in *La vida es sueño* a few years later. Clearly the younger son, Fernando, given the play's apparent purpose, has to be privileged by Lope and his father's actions whitewashed, but the really interesting aspect of this seemingly undistinguished play is how in the course of it, and without appearing to do so, its sympathies in fact slew towards Carlos, the Prince of Viana. And the conventional novelesque elements in the plot upon which Menéndez y Pelayo pours such scorn play some part in creating this effect. It is as if Lope, inspite of his brief, is pulled by his sense of historical fairplay towards an alternative, more balanced point of view. It is impossible to say what degree of conscious pleasure Lope took in this erosion of the play's *raison d'être* – the glorification of Philip IV's antecedents – but the resulting tension is what, *pace* Menéndez y Pelayo, makes this a work of considerable interest. Lope was certainly not writing 'obras baladíes' ten years before his death, and his complicated manipulations of history deserve some attention.

The tension centres on the figure of the Prince of Viana himself. He is presented from the start as rash, impetuous and ambitious, and his attempts to wrest the throne of Navarre from his father are predictably – how could it be otherwise? – unequivocally condemned, even by the mother of his child, who loves him. By the end of the play, though, the situation has radically altered: he has emerged as a man driven to treason by being deprived of his rights. He asks for nothing other than what is rightfully his, Navarre, to which he is heir through his deceased mother, Blanca, who brought the kingdom to her marriage with Juan II. Juan, for his part, in defiance of chronology and history, is here an indecisive old man who, against the wishes of Navarre, hands over the reigns of government in his absence, not to the rightful regent Carlos, but to his second wife, Juana, mother of Fernando. When Carlos charges him with proceeding improperly, the King neither justifies nor explains his action. In fact Lope signally fails to mention anywhere in the play the view that Carlos was considered by many to be less than ideal for rule because of his intellectual inclinations and lack of political ability. Since no justification is forthcoming for his exclusion, his accusations that the Queen has turned his father against him, which at first ring of pique and paranoia, begin to sound very convincing. As he himself very reasonably points out in a dignified speech in his own defence, explaining that his complaint is not against his father but against his step-mother:

> Los capitanes y vasallos sabios
> que en este grueso ejército he traido,[18]
> la causa justifican, pues que vienen.
> Valor, entendimiento y honra tienen. (Act III, 355a)[19]

In other words, his claim has legitimate and honourable support. The play ends with King Juan on the run from the combined forces of Aragon, Catalonia and Navarre, all of which see Carlos as heralding the dawn of a new era of peace. The situation is saved for Juan when his son is fatally injured in a fall from his horse (Carlos did in the event die an untimely death). Unable through his love for his son to deal harshly with him throughout the play – and his dilemma is movingly portrayed at times – he now forgives him in a scene of reconciliation. He is about to arrange his dying son's marriage to his mistress, doña Elvira, in order to legitimize their son when, as we saw, the action is brought to an end by the triumphant tableau, which materializes with almost cynical abruptness and speed. Lope, it seems, suddenly remembered what he was supposed to be doing and decided not to cloud the issue of the succession in the minds of his audience.

It is the slyness of Lope's procedure which is so striking. The text is peppered with all the correct expressions of admiration for Fernando and, in Act III, for his newly acquired kingdom of Castile, but Carlos is actually portrayed as being quite as courageous, forceful and determined a figure as his step-brother. What he lacks is Fernando's restraint and patience, that is, his

[18] I have not used modern accentuation here in order to preserve the rhyme scheme.
[19] *Obras* XII, Biblioteca de Autores Españoles, 213 (Madrid: Atlas, 1968).

political judgement. Fernando's role in the play, indeed, is somewhat restrained and marginal; he observes rather than participates in the struggle and concedes Carlos's rights while deeming it more sensible for him just to wait until his father dies to claim them. As the favourite son, he cannot, through a failure of imagination, understand Carlos's sense of outrage at seeing his stepmother rule his mother's kingdom. Lope, on the other hand, it is obvious, had considerable sympathy for this impetuous rebel denied his traditional rights for no good reason. His desire for a degree of independence from his appointed, or self-appointed, theatrical task is clear from the very novelesque elements that reduced Menéndez y Pelayo to scorn. They have, of course, a conventional dramatic purpose in that they provide the love interest required by Spanish audiences, but it would be quite extraordinary for a dramatist of Lope's stature, experience and maturity to introduce such scenes without giving them some voice in what goes on in the play. This applies particularly to the case of Fernando's bizarre bargain with doña Ana. We see him at the beginning disapproving of sexual affairs, but then, without seeming to feel any real affection for doña Ana, who adores him, he professes out of courtesy to love her, and promises at her request to marry her on the day he becomes king of Aragon – safe, as he thinks, in the knowledge that Carlos as his elder brother is heir. Now obviously Lope included this partly as a little piece of dramatic irony to be relished by his audience, but this does not entirely explain it away. Later on, Fernando accepts the hand of Isabel of Castile without a second thought for Ana, who bears his child. His behaviour is excused by his servant Nuño, but doña Ana is not mollified and much is made of the fact that Fernando has broken his word. Nuño, wriggling on behalf of his master, can claim he has become king of Castile not Aragon and therefore has not deceived her, but, like the visionary Ana, the audience knows that king of Aragon he will become. Now in the *comedia*'s ethos of honour a broken word is a significant flaw. Fernando at best shows a lack of judgement in the arena of sexual politics, and Lope frequently, as we have seen, uses sexual misdemeanour as a metaphor for princely unreliability in his depiction of kings. It is not that Lope is denigrating Fernando, but that in this particular portrayal of the very king associated above all others with the principle of political expediency he is trying to avoid a polarization of character and to remind the audience that even perfect princes are not in fact perfect men. Ana's conclusion could serve as epitaph for the play:

> No hay fe segura, amor ni confianza,
> en el hombre más noble de la tierra;
> y luego llaman la mujer mudanza. (Act III, 359a)

At this level of human activity political motives are paramount, and human and moral considerations often go by the board. By contrast and to help redress the balance, Carlos's behaviour to Elvira after the seduction is supportive and loving up to the point where she angers him with her rebukes for his behaviour to his father, and his intentions throughout are honourable. Her love for him survives their quarrel, and the play compells us to ask whether a man adored by a woman of spirit and principle and supported by the people of three kingdoms could be entirely bad. Even at a time when relations between the government of Spain and the eastern kingdoms were somewhat strained, this fact, together with Carlos's legitimate grievance within the narrative of the play, must have carried a lot of weight in shaping the audience's attitude to the events it portrays. Although superficially a hymn to Fernando and his father, this is Carlos's play. And although his rebellion – historically factual – is condemned, it is hedged round with mitigating circumstances which are of Lope's fashioning. The historical reality is that Carlos and his father ruled Navarre jointly after the death of Queen Blanca, that his stepmother was made governor of Navarre only after Carlos had taken up arms against his father, not before as happens in the play, and that the support he enjoyed in Navarre, Aragon and Catalonia, although considerable, was by no means unanimous. The distortions of history that Menéndez y Pelayo condemns are thus unfavourable to Carlos in some respects, but very favourable in others. Lope's Carlos is not the Carlos of history, an unfortunate if by no means guiltless pawn in the hideously complicated struggles between the ruling dynasties of northern Spain.[20] He is a man ambitious to possess what is his and prepared to commit *lèse-majesté* to achieve his aims. But moral right and legitimacy are on his side and his actions are therefore understood, even sympathized with, if not condoned.

The process afoot here, it has to be said, is complex and devious to say the least. Lope distorts one brother's character in the other brother's favour, then proceeds to counteract the distortion with other distortions and a partial return to historical truth. He ostensibly achieves his official purpose of demonizing Carlos, then in a sort of double bluff retrieves him for sympathy, even heroism. As a result, he has his cake and eats it, fashioning a story which seems to privilege Fernando and Juan but makes of Carlos the character we care about. The over-sentimentalized, late-medieval view of Carlos, while doing no harm to Fernando's reputation – for in fact Fernando was a boy when the historical facts involved here took place – did nothing for the aura of messianic legitimacy of the line which his seventeenth-century descendents sought to promote, and Lope prudently took another tack. King John, in reality an active politician with unpopular ambitions in Castile, similarly becomes an honorable old man, benign, loving and generous, with a worthy reluctance to punish an erring son – he is *el piadoso aragonés*. On the surface the royal line is exalted in a celebration of the united Spain instigated

20 For an account of the complicated historical events that form the background to Lope's play see Ramón Menéndez Pidal, *Historia de España*, XV (Madrid: Espasa Calpe, 1964).

by Fernando. Immediately below the surface, however, Lope pursues his own interests and sympathies, concentrating on the stepbrother who did not make it rather than on the one that did, and playing mischievously with the dynamics of human beings caught up in political situations. The play is fiction, inspired by history, with a political *raison d'être* but a distinct artistic purpose. It flatters and deceives simultaneously and shows just how practised Lope had become in pleasing others in ways that pleased himself more. He was always ready to use his art to please a king because he knew that the theatre possessed an unrivalled capacity to speak with more than one voice, that it was the puppet master and not the man who paid him who enjoyed the last laugh.

By now it will be evident that Lope entertained very definite ideas about kings, their role, their comportment, and their exercise of power, ideas which he worked into his plays in a variety of ways and with varying degrees of frankness. If the dates at our disposal, including Morley and Bruerton's datings, are reliable, then both the king-plays dealt with here and those not included indicate that Lope's interest in the theme was a continuing one, with, as we might expect, a marked concentration of plays in the reign of the ineffectual Philip III. The advent then of an extremely youthful king and a powerful reforming favourite maintained public interest in plays about kings and kingship, and Lope, as we have seen, continued to say what he wished to say in this regard even during the years when he was making his last all-out bid for preferment. It is a measure of his real – not convenient or commercial – interest in these matters that the play which I am convinced was his last specifically addresses the subject of kingship.[21] However, *La mayor virtud de un rey*, written almost certainly in late 1634 or 1635, the year of Lope's death (Morley and Bruerton's dating is 1625–35), approaches it this time from a very personal angle. In 1634, when Lope was seventy-two, his favourite daughter Antonia Clara, then a girl of just seventeen, ran off with – in Lope's eyes was abducted by – a nobleman in his thirties, don Cristóbal Tenorio, a protégé of Olivares who in 1623 had become an *ayuda de cámara* to the king and been made a knight of the Order of Santiago. Needless to say, although a widower he did not marry the girl; in fact he abandoned her several months later to marry doña María Suárez de Deza, and Antonia Clara died a spinster in 1664. The king took no action whatsoever, inspite of the fact that the abduction of a daughter from her father's home was a crime with severe penalities, and Tenorio continued to enjoy royal favour. Lope was devastated. The incident totally blighted the last year of his life, and perhaps indeed hastened his death as one account of his death maintains in the margin of the

21 J.H. Silverman's little-known 'Lope de Vega's Last Years and His Final Play', *Texas Quarterly* (Spring 1963), 174–87, came to my notice after I had come to this conclusion; *Las bizarrías de Belisa* is still normally held to be Lope's last dramatic work.

manuscript: 'Lope murió de pena de que Tenorio le sacó una hija.'[22] The last work he published, the eclogue *Filis* (1635), transposes the painful events into a pastoral setting, and his intensely moving short poem, *Huerto desecho*, published posthumously along with *La mayor virtud del rey* in *La Vega del Parnaso* in 1637, uses the metonym of the wasted garden to describe their impact on his own life. In *Huerto desecho* he makes it clear that he held the king directly responsible for the outcome of the disastrous affair. He was extremely bitter that Tenorio escaped scot-free and here, in this poem at the end of his life, the anguish caused by this recent terrible blow and the resentment bred in him over the years by royal neglect twine together into an inextricable knot of weary despair:

> Áspero torbellino,
> armado de rigores y venganzas,
> súbitamente vino
> a deshojar mis verdes esperanzas,
> haciendo el suelo alfombra de colores
> tantas hojas escritas como flores.
> No fuera el gran monarca,
> porque viviera yo, menor planeta,
> pues cuanta tierra abarca
> y ciñe el mar, se le rindió sujeta. . .
> Si bien hay tierra adonde
> ni aun con oblicuous rayos su grandeza
> a su nadir responde,
> tal es de mi fortuna la aspereza,
> que no me alcanza el sol, ni me ha servido
> haber junto a su eclíptica nacido.[23]

In *La mayor virtud de un rey*, however, the distancing process demanded by the dramatic form seems to have come to his rescue, for here at least Lope purged his bitterness in the story of a Portuguese royal favourite already officially betrothed by the King, who falls in love with a Castilian lady and, in his desperation to prevent her being taken back to Castile, abducts her. The details, it will be seen, are diplomatically recast. The action is set in the reign

22 See H.A. Rennert and A. Castro, *Vida de Lope de Vega (1562–1635). Notas adicionales de F. Lázaro Carreter,* (Salamanca: Ediciones Anaya, 1969), 316–26, and the note to p.317 on pp.548–9. See also Juan Manuel Rozas, *Lope de Vega y Felipe IV en el 'Ciclo de Senectute'* (Cáceres: Universidad de Extremadura, 1982). The first to solve the mystery of the identity of Antonia Clara's abductor was A. González de Amezúa, 'Un enigma descifrado: El raptor de la hija de Lope de Vega', *Boletín de la Real Academia Española* XXI (1934), 357–404 and 521–62.

23 *Lope Félix de Vega Carpio. Obras escogidas*, II, *Poesías líricas-Poemas-Prosa-Novelas*, ed. Federico Carlos Sainz de Robles (Madrid: Aguilar 1973; first edn. 1943), 298b–9a.

of King Emmanuel I of Portugal, the nobleman, don Juan, is a decent man genuinely torn between duty and a reciprocated love, and the need to save an unwilling Sol from being taken away from him for ever is pressing. Nonetheless, scarcely a member of Lope's audience could have failed to realise that the play was a coded address to Philip IV over the issue of Lope's own daughter. Not a few must have reflected on the irony of the fact that his declining years had been blighted by the action of a daughter doing exactly what hundreds of his theatrical heroines had done and got away with. But this was life not fiction, and for Antonia Clara there was no happy ending.

The play for all its simple plot is a very impressive one. The quality of the dialogue – dense and complex beneath a deceptive simplicity – is extremely high, the characterization, including that of the King, is sharp and unromanticized, the sexual politics are compelling. What concerns us here, however, is that it is saturated with the impact made on Lope by his daughter's misfortune – the coincidence of literature and life is just too great for an earlier date for the play to be convincing, particularly in view of the way in which Lope's anguish and preoccupation found an outlet in others of his writings as well at that time. Not merely the broad brush strokes of the plot but remarks in the dialogue as well repeatedly recall the episode and the lack of royal reaction to it, and the bitter musings on women and love reveal the disillusion of a disappointed father. The peasant-*gracioso* Mendo, when ordered by don Sancho to keep an eye on his daughters and the mysterious huntsman he has seen in their vicinity, retorts knowingly:

> ¿A mí me mandas que doncellas guarde,
> pobre, villano, rudo?
> ¿Quién en el mundo pudo,
> por más que fuese honrado, sabio y fuerte?
> La mujer más cobarde,
> en llegando a querer, y más doncella,
> su honor y el de sus padres atropella,
> ni repara en la fama ni en la muerte. . . .
> Verdad es que tus hijas
> son cuerdas como bellas;
> pero hay hombres demonios tan sotiles
> dando y enamorando,
> y más si topan las defensas viles
> que son, señor, criadas codiciosas,
> que no hay honra segura. (Act I, 622a–b)[24]

With Juana the maid soon afterwards he does not mince his words:

24 *Obras* XII, Real Academia Española (nueva ed.).

Tener hijas, o sean feas
o hermosas, es triste suerte.
Feas no las quiere nadie,
hermosas todos las quieren.
Guardarlas es imposible;
que son hombres y mujeres
ellas queso, ellos ratones;
unas callan y otros muerden.

Juana. También los suelen coger.

Mendo. Yo veo que muchas veces
queda el queso ratonado,
y ellos huyen y se meten
en sus agujeros libres. (Act I, 625a)

Sancho himself despairingly concludes later on, '¿Esto es hijas? Más valiera/ que nunca hubieran nacido' (Act II, 634a). There are strong echoes, too, of Lope's resentment at his own lack of royal recognition, which was clearly bound up in his mind, as we saw, with the king's indifference to Antonia Clara's fate. Mendo the *gracioso*, detained at the play-king's order for his apparent involvement in the abduction, begs plaintively,

Si el encierro va despacio,
no se olviden de enviarme
cuando coman algún prato:
será la primera vez
que me den algo en palacio. (Act III, 640b)

Don Sancho de Mendoza, the aggrieved father, overlooked by the King in spite of his distinction and achievements and now grossly wronged by the King's favourite, is transparently a projection of Lope himself.

The dramatic tension is created by the play between favouritism and justice, the balance of expectations being set up for the audience on the one hand by the assurances of the King's son, don Juan's close friend, who takes it for granted that favouritism will take its expected course, and on the other by Juan's clear perception of his moral dilemma and the danger it puts him in. How will the King react, how will the problem be solved? For the King here is by no means an idealized character – his is an over-hasty, impatient nature, and less than magnanimous. Significantly, however, for him the dilemma just does not exist. He proves to be an unequivocal subscriber to Rivadeneyra's tenet that justice is the very basis of government and that without it all else fails (526). He therefore behaves as he must, putting justice before personal preference. Indeed so concerned is he to pursue it that he has to be restrained from punishing both don Juan and his own son without knowing the full facts. But the crucial point is that he does want justice done and he is prepared to take action even against a favourite. He allows his legalistic instincts to be tempered by good counsel and then by clemency, all in accord with Rivadeneyra's prescriptions for the practice of justice (546–8), and a constructive solution is eventually found. The greatest virtue of a king is therefore shown to be justice tempered by mercy. True love and the eternal optimist in Lope triumph – there are no class barriers between don Juan and his Sol to strain the audience's credulity – and in literature if not in life bitterness finds at the last a benign resolution. But the abiding message is that the first instinct, the *sine qua non*, of a monarch, whatever his faults, must be to right wrong and to punish the wrong-doer. The play's many references to kings as images of God and to what a subject owes his monarch (629a,b; 630a; 642b; 643b; 645b; 646b) are not there solely to flatter to deceive, to allow Lope to reproach without giving offence, although they do patently fulfil that function. They also explicitly remind Philip IV that the responsibilites that came with the job were weighty ones indeed, that he was, after all, the representative within his dominions of God's justice. Sol's father, in pursuit of justice after her abduction, puts it plainly:

> que Rey que sabe el agravio
> no cumple su obligación
> si deja que pobre apele
> para el tribunal de Dios. (Act III, 643a)

The King agrees, condemning those nobles who commit offenses under cover of rank and favour:

> que son indignos resabios
> de hombres tan nobles y sabios
> el valerse del favor
> del poderoso señor
> para cometer agravios.

His assurance to Sancho,

> Conmigo no hay más amor
> que coronar el valor
> la espada de la justicia;
> no reinará la malicia
> donde yo reinare,

is the pledge of royal impartiality that Lope wished to see implemented in the affair of Antonia Clara. Sancho's reply is a grateful acknowledgement of the King's guarantee and, along with it, of the monarch's crucial role in the divinely ordered cosmos, 'Si vos sois Dios en la tierra,/ ¿quién no ha de fiar de Dios?' (Act III, 643b). However, one feels that by this stage in his life that 'if' carried for Lope a conditional rather than a concessive weight of meaning. If this is indeed Lope's last play then he ended a dramatic career marked by a sustained interest in the problems of kingship and the political issues of the day with a personal rebuke to his own king.

As a body the king-plays address head-on problems of authority and government – favouritism, royal inadequacy or distraction, royal immaturity, self-delusion, court intrigue, the dangers of rumour and opinion. In so far as it deals for the most part with ongoing, larger issues this is a drama of macropolitics. Micropolitical specificity was not necessary to sow in people's minds telling connections between the stage world and the world outside the *corrales*. This very lack of specificity indeed gave the theatre licence to explore issues of contemporary relevance without prejudicing the generally relaxed relationship between theatre and government. But there can be no doubt that the plays reflect the circumstances and concerns of Spain's own monarchy. The competition for the Crown reflected in Shakespeare's history plays is rarely an issue, neither is the question of legitimate succession – there were obviously very good reasons why the Elizabethan theatre engaged with such themes. In Spain's stable monarchy it is the qualities of the monarch and the conduct of state governance which reappear time and again, likewise for very good reasons. We can assume that in a culture in which the theatre was so important, what the theatre did and said was not irrelevant to the concerns and perceptions of the people of the day. After all, what contemporary hermeneutical identity do the plays have other than that inscribed within them by the shared knowledge and preoccupations of author and spectators? Many of Lope's king-plays have little real substance to them other than that constituted by the invisible connections between the world within the play and the world that contained the play. Dramatic representations of kings took on meaning from monarchy in the real world and gave meaning to it, but it is essential to look beyond the canonical texts to be in a position to produce a historical reading of any real credibility.

The king-plays are representations of the history of the very society at which the plays were directed. They contributed, therefore, to the Spaniard's consciousness of Spain's identity as a nation and of the historical continuum of the nation. Thus links were forged between past and present. That these representations were highly fictionalized was immaterial, for the audience's grasp of historical events – even the educated audience's – was necessarily partial and unreliable. The past is always in part a creation of the present, or a succession of presents, and Lope's recasting of Spain's history may be seen as an attempt to help audiences understand the present rather than the past – the issues they address are Renaissance issues dressed in medieval clothes. His creative manipulations of historical 'truth' are motivated by a desire to paradigmaticize the past, to make it an exemplar for present consideration. It is the past put to the service, not of absolutism, because that would have required a very different set of plays, presumptions and ideological iterations, but of good monarchical government. This is not to deny the plays' invocation of an exotic past, the entry they seemed to offer into a simpler yet more stirring world. Nor is it to deny that Lope had a historical understanding of the politics of the past – many of the plays dramatize precisely the struggle between the nobility and the crown, and plays like *Fuenteovejuna* (directly) and *El mejor alcalde el rey* (indirectly) celebrate the victory of benign centralized monarchy over feudalism. But the plays' central engagement is with the relevance of that struggle and that victory for contemporary government. The internal contradictions of monarchy were more effectively as well as more tactfully understood in the context of the more intimate medieval pattern of kingship than in terms of Renaissance political abstractions. Medieval kings are dehistoricized in order to create images of kingship convenient to the representation of general kingship issues. If, as Quentin Skinner states, 'political life sets the main problems for the political theorist, causing a certain range of issues to appear problematic, and a corresponding range of questions to become the leading subjects of debate',[25] then the same may confidently be said of the political theatre – its agenda was set by political life. But just as the relationship between these ideological structures and their social base is affected by the intellectual context within which political theorists write, so the relationship between our play-texts and their contemporary political base was complicated by both the traditions of drama and the requirements of the theatre. For these plays, as for very different ones, Lope used the comprehensible dramatic language he himself concocted from existing ingredients to create his *comedia nueva*. Hence the admixture of romance, pseudo-history and comedy to what is essentially political drama, drama which sets the problems of political life at the level of popular understanding, casting them not in terms of the scholarly and abstract but of the narrative and emblematic. To understand what they are communciating it is necessary to recognize the language they use – a language which might on the face of it seem inappropriate to the weightier issues that swirl beneath the surface of the plot – and to imagine how this language might have been negotiated by spectators reading it from within the political realities of their own day. In doing this, for all that the age was not characterized by a monolithic value system as used to be thought, it is essential not to lose sight of the ideals, assumptions and beliefs which Lope shared with his own society. It is against this framework that monarchs in the king-plays act out their parts and are judged. Lope explored the problems of kingship from a position within, but on the inside edge of, this socio-political frame. He presents monarchy as the providential form of government but problematizes it to an extent which raises questions for which he has no real answers.

25 Quentin Skinner, *The Foundations of Modern Political Thought*, 2 vols (Cambridge: Cambridge University Press, 1978), xi.

Lope's propensity to portray inadequate princes in fact relates to historical reality rather than to poetic justice, to the contingent rather than to the providential. Where not downright tragic (*El castigo sin venganza*, *El Duque de Viseo*), most of the plays end on a merely hopeful rather than a reassuring note. The uneasy alliance of historical player and providential role sets up a tension that is never resolved, because resolution is impossible. Whereas in the three famous peasant-honour plays the king is the agent, even when reluctant, of poetic justice (at the surface level of the plot at least), in the king-plays the symbolic role is not only notable for its absence but derives significance and prominence from its absence – it is precisely the inability or refusal to behave as a king should behave which is at issue. I am not suggesting that Lope wilfully set out to call into question the operation of providence in this regard, but for any who chose to ponder the implications of these plays his theatrical portrayal of monarchy undoubtedly raised uncomfortable questions about providential concern. Lope's history is a history shaped not by divine agency but by the ambitions and desires, the strengths and the weaknesses of men.[26]

Lope's acute preoccupation with the tension between the man and the role reflects the new perception of an antinomy between 'society' and the 'individual' that at the level of monarchy was given particularly sharp emphasis by what one might call the 'ideologization' of the leader in the new nation-states of the Early Modern period. His relentless demystification of monarchy almost begins to look in later years like a campaign to counteract the growing move, if only within the court, towards absolutism and quasi-divinization. For all their Machiavellian emphasis on human rather than divine agency – and of course Lope's engagement with kingship would hardly have been possible but for the debate initiated by Machiavelli – Lope's king-plays reveal the strong misgiving that the private self does determine how the social role is inhabited, that it is not merely a question of a monarch 'remembering how to seem',[27] of slipping on the garb of regal distance and able rule to hide anger, boredom, deviousness, vice, but of the ethical stature of the individual. One of Lope's central concerns in these plays is the separation of morality from the conduct of kingship and its consequences. In those that concentrate upon the problem of role there is no real resolution because the problem is systemic. To exhort a man to turn into something he is not is an enterprise doomed at least to partial failure – the optimism of theorists that the education of princes could be a sufficient guarantor of effective rule receives very

26 See Graham Holderness, Nick Potter and John Turner, *Shakespeare: The Play of History* (London: Macmillan, 1985), 2.

27 At the end of Alan Bennett's screenplay of his play *The Madness of King George III*, which presents George III as a man who, for all that the world thinks he is crazy, in the things that matter has his wits firmly in place, the king, when asked the secret of his recovery smiles knowingly and answers triumphantly 'I have remembered how to seem.'

lukewarm support from these plays. The ungoverned self compromises the exercise of the role, the prince's two faces are in fact one. Princely inadequacy is so frequently represented in terms of sexual unruliness precisely because it casts the central problem of role versus man in terms that related directly to the social and moral context of every person's life. What did a king and his subjects have more powerfully in common than their sexual desires? The king who fails to govern his own passions is hardly in a position to implement the patriarchy's prohibitions on anti-social outbreaks of desire. Lope's compromised kings are emblematic figures who served as a locus of debate about the Spanish monarchy and Renaissance government in general. The plays narrate a history of human agency against the ideological background of its providential representation. And although each play effectively represents a hopeful victory over absolutism, the intellectual dialectic would seem to remain unresolved – an enduring loyalty to idealizing theory coexisting with a pragmatic acceptance of historical reality, a contradiction which most thinking people presumably lived with. The problem, as Lope seems to have seen it, is that while history showed that kings were not born, which was the very thing that court ceremony and the mystique of majesty were intended to conceal, it also showed that neither could they easily be made.

5

DECIR SIN DECIR: PATTERNS OF COMMUNICATION

> Para donde es menester más prudencia son los auditorios de los reyes. Porque verdaderamente no han de ser reprehendidos en público ellos, ni los prelados, de manera que el pueblo eche de ver sus faltas, porque ellos se irritan, y no quedan aprovechados; y el pueblo les pierde el respeto y se huelga, casi por modo de venganza, que les asienten en el púlpito.[1]

This piece of advice, given by Terrones del Caño in his preaching manual, *Instrucción de predicadores* published in the reign of Philip III (1617), applied no less to the theatre than it did to the pulpit, and for the same reasons, both practical and ideological. Public criticism of kings would have annoyed its targets and therefore been counter-productive as well as dangerous, but it would have been counter-productive too in that it detracted from monarchy rather than enhancing it. At the same time, his last words suggest one interesting explanation for the enduring popularity of plays about princes – that there was a gleeful satisfaction to be derived by audiences from seeing them reduced to human size. Terrones's view of the relationship between people and monarch is far from complacent, and his anxiety speaks volumes about the perceived need for the sort of critical restraint, of self-censorship, that operates in Lope's theatre.

English dramatists were sometimes less cautious, with predictable results: in March, 1608 the Children of Blackfriars attacked the king's Scottish followers and 'presented his majesty as having been drunk for a month and cursing heaven over the way the hawk flew and beating one of his gentlemen

[1] Terrones del Caño, *Instrucción*, 94–5, quoted in Hilary Dansey Smith, *Preaching in the Spanish Golden Age: A Study of some Preachers of the Reign of Philip III* (Oxford: Oxford University Press, 1978), 113. Even preachers could speak (or at least write) their minds, however: in his *Empleo y Exercicio Sancto sobre los Evangelios de las Dominicas de todo el año*, I (Toledo, 1604, 58–9), Fray Diego de la Vega, talking of the exemption of royal and princely houses from the processes of the law, stated 'no ha de entrar alguacil, ni vara de justicia, por ser reservadas: así tampoco la verdad no ha de tener allí entrada'. See Dansey Smith, 115.

for injuring a hunting hound'.[2] James I was so incensed that he ordered the closure of all London theatres, swearing that the players would have to beg their bread in future. In England the use of the theatre for state purposes came much earlier than it did in France and Spain. From the beginning of the seventeenth century onwards, all companies licensed to perform in London and the court were the servants of one of the members of the royal family, and each one had a royal patron. In the 1630s the Lord Chamberlain put the company playing in the Cockpit in Drury Lane in the charge of William Davenant 'to govern and operate in ways that would best serve the King and the Crown'.[3] Nonetheless Samuel Calvert, early in the reign of James I, wrote to Ralph Winwood complaining that 'the players do not forbear to present upon their stage the whole course of the present time, not sparing either Church or King, with such freedom that any would be afraid to hear them'.[4] But they were taking serious risks. Playwrights were imprisoned – Jonson and Chapman for satirizing the king, for example – and, in Kernan's words 'stage censorship showed its teeth year after year' (15). In Spain the situation was substantially different. Lope was not a patronage playwright as Shakespeare was under the new Stuart monarchy and no Spanish acting company enjoyed the status and privilege of the King's Men in England, who had a royal warrant and became grooms of the chamber and servants to James I. Lope's king-plays are an entirely different animal from the political masques of Stuart England which were specifically designed to exalt absolute monarchy and James's claim to divine right, although in Spain the court spectacles under Philip IV would later fulfil a function not far from this. The Spanish theatre, even in the reign of the theatre-loving Philip IV, operated in an altogether freer and less closely supervised way in spite of the regulations that governed its activities and the vigilant eye of the Inquisition. It got into much less trouble, however, partly because Spain's political stability meant there was far less serious dissent for playwrights and players to capitalize on, partly because that stability in a world of instability encouraged Spanish playwrights to write in a less overtly provocative way, and partly because both these circumstances together led the authorities to leave well alone by not reacting to plays with any potential for contemporary application. When a performance of *Richard II* was mounted in 1601 at the request of the Earls of Essex and Southampton it provoked outrage because they were known to be actively conspiring to place James on the throne. The scene of the deposition of Richard II was censored, the company went ahead and performed it anyway, an incensed Elizabeth, acknowledging the implied identification, protested 'Know you not that I am Richard the Second?' and an inquiry was

[2] See Alvin Kernan, *Shakespeare, the King's Playwright: Theatre in the English Court 1603–1613* (New Haven/London: Yale University Press, 1995), 192.

[3] Kernan, *Shakespeare, The King's Playwright*, 14–15.

[4] Kernan, *Shakespeare, The King's Playwright*, 15.

launched.[5] The event took place on the eve of the Essex rebellion and was intended to be provocative, for in England crowns did not sit unchallenged on royal heads. Stuart dramatists too had to proceed with caution. In 1638 Charles I, a passionate reader of plays, objected personally to the title of Massinger's *The King and the Subject* and to a passage describing royal methods of raising money, although the play was set in Spain.[6] In contrast, no Spanish monarch during this period was ever in a situation where implied criticism from the stage could not be loftily ignored – plays after all are fictions in which nothing need be taken as real. As Greenblatt has said:

> the triumphant cunning of the theatre is to make its spectators forget that they are participating in a practical activity, to invent a sphere that seems far removed from the manipulations of the everyday. Shakespeare's theatre is powerful and effective precisely to the extent that the audience believes it to be non useful and hence non practical.[7]

The Spanish theatre no less than the English was a potential arena for subversion – moral, religious, political. This is why it was licensed and censored, this is why it was attacked and opposed. Its popular, commercial identity increased this potential, and with it its danger. In the discussion of sensitive areas strategic evasion was essential. That political anxieties were rarely voiced by the theatre's enemies shows just how successful this evasion was. Even so, the lack of reaction to some of the *privanza* plays, for example, is quite remarkable, and it suggests that a tacit agreement, a kind of unwritten hermeneutical contract, was arrived at between theatre and state along the lines of: 'as long as sufficient decorum is observed you can say these things about monarchs and monarchy and we shall ignore them and pretend that the connection between stage and reality isn't there'.[8] Self-censorship was an ingrained habit of Spanish writers, so they managed extremely well. The possibility of censorship therefore had a hand in determining the shape of drama. In the case of the king-plays, it is how far, short of depicting contemporary kings, the theatre felt able to go, rather than how little distance it travelled,

5 Kernan, *Shakespeare, The King's Playwright*, 9–11.

6 Anne Barton, 'He that plays the king: Ford's *Perkin Warbeck* and the Stuart history play', *Essays, Mainly Shakespearean* (Cambridge: Cambridge University Press, 1994), 234–60, p.256.

7 *Shakespearean Negotiations: The Circulation of Social Energy in Renaissance England* (Oxford: Clarendon Press, 1988), 18–19.

8 Annabel Patterson maintains that this 'cultural bargain', as she calls it, between writers and political leaders was crucial to all writers who aspired to some influence on the shape of their national culture. See *Censorship and Interpretation: The Conditions of Writing and Reading in Early Modern England* (Madison, Wisc.: University of Wisconsin Press, 1984), 7. Of course, risk was not thereby obliterated because circumstances might change, causing problems for revivals.

that is remarkable.[9] No dramatist in Spain was imprisoned for sedition and the only one that can be said to have been harassed was Tirso de Molina.

Lope's response to these circumstances was, as we have seen, to employ a range of enabling stratagems of commentary and interrogation in the construction of a critique of kings and kingship. And the mobilisation of history and legend to his purposes, of course, is one of them. Lacan has identified the process of displacement (*Verschiebung*) which takes place in the veering off of signification, making metonymy one of the major devices employed by the unconscious to elude censorship.[10] Plays about historical or quasi-historical kings functioned very effectively as a form of metonymy (the literal meaning of which, after all, is a changing of name). Adapting the historical models to the requirements of theatrical romance was also to adapt them to the plays' covert purposes. Techniques of distancing and distortion defused criticism but simultaneously allowed it to be made – they empowered as well as protected, they released the playwright's pen to wander at will. And by moving away from the strictly historical profile they universalized the monarch, more actively perhaps inviting comparison between fiction and fact. Play-kings are made to play a protean, multi-purpose role, serving dramatic and political interests at one and the same time. Selection, transposition and fictionalization are common procedures, these techniques of dehistoricization often being aimed at the surreptitious expression of an authorial view or authorial sympathies (even a play probably destined for the court like *El piadoso aragonés* takes a maverick tack), or at releasing the play's relevance to contemporary issues, such as royal youthfulness and favouritism (*La corona merecida*, *La fortuna merecida*). The allied technique of shading, of intensifying certain features of character and allowing others to recede, achieves the same purpose (*El príncipe perfecto*). The handling of such matters, of course, was a delicate matter of judgement – too obvious an identification of a favourite might be unwise – and in *La fortuna merecida*, for example, which must have approached the acceptable limits of contemporary targeting, a technique of deflection is used to avoid overt association with the current favourite: the mature, established adviser of history becomes a young, inexperienced newcomer. In both historically based and novelesque plays Renaissance ideas of kingship are used as a model against which to judge leaders from previous or unspecified ages, the application of the model simultaneously allowing a critique of the contemporary situation. These ideas are expressed by means of both negative and positive example, and very occasionally embodied in model princes, with, in *El príncipe perfecto,* techniques of identification and difference being used to place the reigning monarch in the position of both identifying with the stage-king and realizing that he had a

[9] In England regulations banning the depiction of contemporary members of royalty on stage and screen survived until the 1960s.

[10] *Écrits* (Paris: Éditions du Seuil, 1966), 158.

lot to live up to: the prince who stares back at the royal spectator from the stage's mirror is an ideal self. The effect is intensified by the reverse mirroring of the lesson that is being learnt in the lessons in kingship taking place on stage. Even exemplary kings are carefully denied perfection, however, for his perception of the essentially human identity of princes was absolutely central to Lope's ideas on kingship. Where negative examples are concerned, in historical and fictional princes sexual unruliness, invented where necessary, consistently operates as a paradigm for political unreliability, its depiction becoming a codified critique of princely conduct. In view of the prurience and concern generated even today by this aspect of private behaviour in the public person, it is easy to see that in the context of the narrower official morality of the seventeenth century sexual irresponsibility would have been a powerful theoretical indicator, at least, of the less-than-ideal king. (In the reign of Philip IV Spain had to come to terms as best it could with a problem that had given it little obvious cause for concern over the previous hundred-and-fifty years.) Plots can in their entirety function as broad metaphors or parables, as coded messages to the Crown and any other interested persons (*Las paces de los reyes*, *Querer la propia desdicha*, *La mayor virtud de un rey*), sometimes with characters and dialogue to reinforce their relevance (*El poder en el discreto*). Overt messages and plain speaking, often but by no means always from the mouths of *graciosos*, are commoner than might be thought (*La inocente sangre*, *El rey por semejanza*, *Porfiando vence amor*), but a central form of subversion, which I shall return to, is the protective double-speak which counterbalances criticism with ritual flattery (notably *El servir con mala estrella*), an effective strategy since the critique, explicit or implied, would certainly have attracted attention in a way that the conventional language of obeisance to royalty would not. In *El postrer godo de España* we have seen an altogether subtler process at work – the setting up of what amounts to an entire counter-text which creates a disjunction between what is said and what is seen to be the case, between the characters' expressed perception of events and the play as a whole, and which through this clash of perspectives speaks trenchantly to the nature of kingship.

With these stratagems Lope was effectively exploiting the concern of neo-classical poetics over whether art was mimetic or creative in order to introduce the element of ambiguity needed to address delicate political issues. Ambiguity, of course, is a powerful tool. It protects against hostile readings – Quintilian had given specific advice on this score: 'You can speak as openly against tyrants … as you like, as long as you can be understood differently' (*Institutio oratoria*).[11] But it also encourages speculation, and poetic drama as a form, with its layered weight of meaning, its subtle complexities, readily lends itself to undeclared purposes. Ears attuned to it and to the topics

11 Patterson, *Censorship and Interpretation*, 15, n.15.

of the day were well equipped to read it in a charged way. When they were performed at court, the political dimension of these plays would have forcefully struck spectators whose lives were filled with speculation and gossip about the monarch and his ministers. In the *corrales*, too, in the confines of a relatively small capital dominated by the court, issues involving princes and their *privados* would have been familiar to most and messages would have been received. Lope recognized this and grasped the nettle, albeit with a gloved hand. In writing, performing and witnessing plays about kings and their favourites, playwrights, players and public were participating in the political life of the nation no less than the media and the public do today. The theatre, like the press and television now, was the principle popularizer of ideas circulating at the time, and like the press and television it articulated dissatisfactions and worries, and in the process educated the uninformed in the problems of government. It was effectively the debating chamber of the age. Lope was in the business not only of selling plays but of imparting views and information, and the nature of what he sold and imparted was dictated by his sure knowledge of what would interest his audience. The relevance of what they saw unfolding before their eyes would only have been enhanced in the *corrales* by performance conditions which drew players and spectators together in the one physical space, all wearing contemporary costume and with the stage not even set apart by differential lighting – conditions which create interchange between stage and audience rather than the pretence that the audience is not there. At court, even in the absence of iconographical stage settings to spell out the link, the physical presence of the monarch – the protagonist in the real theatre of attention[12] – sensitized spectators to what was being enacted, making relevance inescapable. Not only would the allusive capacity of historical situations and figures have been instantly recognized, but the auditorium remained illuminated to allow the royal protagonists to remain visible, which again blurred the distinction between the world of the stage and the real world of court and government. The realization that the king himself might slip into his box in the playhouse or that a play written for the playhouse might subsequently be performed in a royal palace obviously inhibited to some extent the pen of a dramatist eager for advancement. However, if political plays can be said to be subversive if they raise awareness of the problems and fictions of royal authority, if it is not the answer but the question that subverts, then Lope's king-plays certainly qualify.[13] They provoke reflection on the possible implications of what they

[12] James I in his handbook on kingship, *Basilikon Doron*, warned his heir that 'A king is as one set on a stage, whose smallest actions and gestures all the people gazing do behold.' See Stephen Orgel, *The Illusion of Power: Political Theatre in the English Renaissance* (Cambridge: Cambridge University Press, 1975), 42–3.

[13] See Margot Heineman, 'Political Drama', *The Cambridge Companion to English Renaissance Drama*, ed. A.R. Braunmuller and Michael Hattaway (Cambridge: Cambridge University Press, 1990), 177.

portray, they stimulate and enlarge the audience's consciousness of the problems inherent in the political system by which they are governed. Their conciliatory endings are a prudent negotiation of the uncomfortable disjunction between the ideal and the real, and to be distracted by them is to overlook the cumulative force of the theatrical experience offered by the plays, which is an experience of personal inadequacy, moral failure and inept government. The plays themselves contain all the evidence necessary for their own interrogation as unthinking advertisements for absolute monarchy.

The technique that Lope repeatedly used to speak his mind from a platform of safety combines subversive intent with ambiguous procedure in a manner at once obviously disingenuous and exactly calculated. The articulated ideology of monarchy in the texts usually strains violently against that ideology made actual in the individual monarch portrayed. The rhetoric of monarchy aims at mediating between king and subject, its epistemological purpose to affect perception of the truth. But a king's behaviour acts as another form of mediation, with its own epistemological function, which sets up an opposition between the two. In other words, there are two parallel discourses of monarchy in the plays – an ideal and a real, a rhetorical discourse and an enacted discourse – and it is the explicit dislocation between the two that constitutes the plays' critique of kingship. The inappropriateness of the one discourse is revealed in the unravelling of the other. The exhortatory treatises on monarchy and the republic written in Europe at the time were in large part a reaction to anxieties about the nature of monarchy created by the emergence of the new nation-states and the political writing this generated, including an only too acute awareness of the strains placed upon providentialist theory by the realities of human nature. In Spain, theorists like Rivadeneyra, Mariana and Saavedra Fajardo guarded against too blatant a collision between ideology and history by refusing, unlike their counterparts elsewhere, to go as far as to claim for monarchs a divine nature or a divine right. Since an institutional schism within Christianity had been avoided in Spain, ambiguous issues which in other parts of Europe became the basis for polarization and the hardening of doctrine were allowed to remain ambiguous.[14] Even so the discrepancy between ideal kingship and kings was a painful reality lived by Spaniards, knowingly by those with any awareness of political life, and it was this discrepancy that Lope exploited in his exploration of the political issues of the day, constructing a dualistic discourse not only to make political points but, in the very process of making those points, to shield himself against criticism. Criticism, even clearly targeted criticism, of royal failings is superficially neutralized by the iteration of ideological constructions of monarchy. At the same time, in the portrayal of individual mon-

14 Cf. Alan Sinfield, *Literature in Protestant England 1560–1660* (London: Croom Helm, 1982), 8.

archs the flattering rhetoric of kingship is skilfully manipulated in order to indicate its inappropriateness to the particular case. It is noticeable that Lope has a tendency to deploy such rhetoric for his most unsuitable kings and to omit it when the monarch in question is doing a reasonable job. What the plays offer is a dynamic view of both the current political ideology and the stresses upon it, their dialogic identity guaranteeing a degree of authorial neutrality which allows the listener to hear whichever point of view he chooses. Audiences participated in the creation of the play-text's meaning by being faced with contradictions and counter-currents which needed in some way to be resolved or absorbed into a way of understanding what they saw and heard. The central paradox dramatized by Lope in the king-plays – that monarchy consistently failed to make demigods of men – invited interrogation of both monarchs and monarchy. The rhetoric of kingship – images of the sun king and the divinity of majesty, rehearsal of the love, loyalty and obedience owed a prince, the sovereign's supreme authority – played its part in this process, setting out the impossible ideal by which individual kings are measured, but it also functioned as protective camouflage for the critical inferences the spectators were being encouraged to draw. Renaissance rhetoric was the study and application of the power of language usage, and Lope was here exploiting rhetoric's capacity for shaping a multiple response.

That Lope uses the rhetoric of kingship at all has been taken as evidence of his self-appointed role as propagandist for absolutism, and it would certainly have done Lope no harm if he had been so perceived at the time. However, it is difficult to believe that those living the political realities of the age were oblivious to the implications of his portrayal of kings in his king-plays, to the fact that the rhetoric is used as a way of constructing absolutism in order to combat it. And it is surely reasonable to take consistency as a process whereby intention becomes discernible in the text. By making unruliness, inadequacy, ineffectiveness normative in his depiction of princes, Lope inevitably conveys his perception of monarchy as a highly problematic institution in practical terms. Indeed cumulatively his princes may readily be seen to reflect a crisis of confidence in the system. Since Lope's king-plays repeatedly make the same critical points about kings and kingship then this repetition may be taken as purposeful, and his apparently contradictory use of the adulatory court rhetoric that became increasingly fashionable in the seventeenth century therefore needs to be considered with care. I have already emphasized its tactical value as a form of protection against censure. A more substantive point to make is one that has in the present context been inexplicably overlooked – dramatic language is used by characters in a play for their own ends. They are interested parties, behaving as what have been called 'intentional agents'.[15] Characters indeed in any literary text speak in charac-

15 Brian Vickers, *Appropriating Shakespeare*, 77.

ter in the context of given situations: what they say must be understood against the situation in which it is said, and whether or not they may be taken as mouthpieces for the author depends on the information provided by the work in its entirety, and even then must remain uncertain. But in a play the context of an utterance is vital in the transmission of both the character's meaning and the work's, because there is no other way in which the playwright can communicate. It is noticeable in the king-plays that those who use such rhetoric are frequently either innocent loyalists who subsequently discover that their confidence in their king is misplaced or self-serving realists compromised by having agendas of their own. Often the rhetoric is part of an ethos of court fawning and flattery which is shown to be damaging to the proper conduct of monarchy.

The interpretive model for the dramatic commentator is there in life itself. That the contextualization of utterance is crucial in matters of meaning, relevance, and intentionality in discourse has been one of the major contributions of linguistics, specifically pragmatics,[16] with discourse analysis and speech-act theory attempting to understand and explain the extremely complex and elusive process of successful communication. The pioneering work of such as Austin and Searle has not failed to generate dissent as well as disciples and continues to be modified and refined, but some of the basic insights of pragmatics are extremely helpful in an attempt to get a grip on the less-than-straightforward way in which Lope's plays make their political points.[17] If a speech-act is generally understood as an utterance in a given situation or context, whose meaning is determined, or largely determined, by that situation or context, then it is possible to see not only dramatic dialogue as constituting a succession of speech acts, but to see an entire play, too, as an utterance within a given context, with the meaning(s) extracted from the play depending on the situation in which it is performed – the particular theatrical tradition, social conditions, political issues, national ethos and aspirations.[18] The structuralist view of linguistic utterance as having both an intersubjective reality for the subjects experiencing it and a social and historical identity shared by the individuals who make up the speech community lends itself to the same perception.[19] A play overflows its text and communicates with its audience in a variety of extra-textual ways, some identifiable, some probably

16 See Laurence R. Horn, 'Pragmatic Theory', *Linguistics: The Cambridge Survey*. Vol. 1, *Linguistic Theory: Foundations* ed. Frederick J. Newmeyer (Cambridge: Cambridge University Press, 1988), 113–45.

17 See J.L. Austin, *How to Do Things with Words*, ed. J.O. Urmson (Oxford: Clarendon Press, 1962); and J. Searle, *Expression and Meaning* (Cambridge: Cambridge University Press, 1979).

18 Cf. M.A.K. Halliday and Ruqaiya Hasan, *Language, Context and Text: Aspects of Language in a Social-Semiotic Perspective* (Oxford: Oxford University Press, 1989).

19 See Simon Clarke, *The Foundations of Structuralism: A Critique of Lévi-Strauss and the Structuralist Movement* (Brighton: Harvester Press, 1981), 176–82.

not. Successful speech acts depend on shared assumptions, understood conventions and accepted procedures – true of the linguistic texture of the dialogue and of the dramatic form of the *comedia* itself. It follows that utterances can be understood in different ways in different situations. A statement within the situation of the play's world can be understood differently within the situation of the world of the theatre public, and in two ways. Firstly, the theatre public will bring to the utterance the context, and its relevancies, of its own time, and extrapolate from the text to non-textual reality. Secondly, it will also bring to the utterance its superior knowledge of the play's action and will accordingly understand it differently, that is, in the way intended by the author but denied the character him or herself. Within the play itself, of course, as happens all the time in everyday life, characters will make utterances which in context will be 'correctly' received rather than taken at face value by the recipients of the utterances, because they will be in possession of the facts which belie the words. In some circumstances it can be irrelevant whether the recipient correctly understands or not, since the utterance may be intended to be taken as a perlocutionary rather than an illocutionary act, that is, the speaker can appear to be invoking the meaning that arises from the words that are actually said and not from the words in context.[20] It is their perlocutionary identity that protects the speaker from the consequences of possible contextual meanings – which is exactly the process at work when Lope resorts to the ritualized rhetoric of kingship in a play which is highly critical of monarchical behaviour. We saw this technique at work in a number of plays in chapters 3 and 4 and we shall see it again in *El Duque de Viseo* in chapter 6.

Austin and Searle regarded their analysis as excluding literary linguistic usage on the grounds that language gains function and meaning though patterns of usage. This has been disputed by Iser, however, and certainly it would seem that dramatic dialogue, which necessarily models itself on conversational patterns and assumptions, 'must have some qualities of the speech acts it imitates and, indeed, only differs from them in its mode of application',[21] even, one might add, in Renaissance verse drama. One of these qualities is intentionality. Wittgenstein's insight that to discover meaning it is essential to examine purpose, the speaker's intention,[22] has been absorbed into subsequent linguistic theory: 'The important point is that meaning and understanding are correlative, and both involve intentionality: the meaning of the utterance necessarily involves the sender's communica-

20 These are Austin's terms, *How to Do Things with Words*, 108ff.

21 Wolfgang Iser, *The Act of Reading: A Theory of Aesthetic Response* (Baltimore/London: Johns Hopkins University Press, 1980), 60.

22 Developed in his *Philosophical Investigation*, 1945 (Oxford: Oxford University Press, 1969).

tive intention.'[23] Meaning is 'an intentional object'.[24] Speech-act theory's demonstration that the receiver needs to recognize the sender's intention to communicate has led to the assertion that a work of literature is the result of 'intentional behaviour . . . directed at some response in the reader' who attributes an intention to the author,[25] and more trenchantly to the insistence that 'Writing, like speech or any language "performed", is inevitably and properly conceived as purposive.'[26] And since a literary text is indeed an utterance whose aim is communication of some sort the logic of this seems sound. Treating both dialogue and play as speech acts therefore leads to the presumption that meaning is fully determined in each case by situation, that meaning is purposefully placed, and that meaning would have been assumed by the audience to be there. This does not imply, of course, that all groups in the audience would have understood the play with the same degree of sophistication, but it does mean that their reading(s) depended on shared sets of circumstances (one within and one outside the play) and the shared expectation that the play had something to say about its subject. In other words, as in an exchange of utterance between two speakers, communication is fully achieved only through the tacit recognition on both sides of all the determinants, internal and external to the play, which identify the meaning intended – events, personalities, hidden feelings and motives, ironies, allusions, imagery, and so on. Just as, in conversation, real meaning is often communicated not by what the words say but by what they imply, half say or do not say (an utterance, of course, can even mean the opposite of what it says), the same is true of the speech act that is a play. Literal-minded interpretations of Lope's treatment of monarchy fail because they take inadequate cognizance of the fact that his plays are communications directed at a knowing audience in circumstances characterized at once by political awareness and by the need for tact.

The linguistic principle of relevance seems to me to be useful here. 'Communicated information comes with a guarantee of relevance . . . the principle of relevance is essential to human communication . . . [it] is enough on its own to account for the interaction of linguistic meaning and contextual factors in utterance interpretation.'[27] Relevance, in other words, is an essential part of information processing. The assumption that a statement made to us in everyday life is relevant, makes thought and intention manifest, is what

23 John Lyons, *Semantics* (Cambridge: Cambridge University Press, 1977), 732–5.

24 E.D. Hirsch, *Validity in Interpretation* (New Haven: Yale University Press, 1967), 38.

25 S.H. Olsen, *The Structure of Literary Understanding* (Cambridge: Cambridge University Press, 1978), 5.

26 Peter Lamarque, 'The Death of the Author: An Analytical Autopsy', *British Journal of Aesthetics* 30 (1990), 391–31, p.330.

27 Dan Sperber and Deirdre Wilson, *Relevance, Communication and Cognition* (Oxford: Basil Blackwell, 1986), vii.

triggers the complex process whereby we instantaneously identify what we think its meaning is. On the basis of this assumption we have traditionally assumed that all forms of linguistic communication, including literary texts, have a hermeneutical identity that involves meaning and relevance, the search for which has been the traditional occupation of the literary commentator. Clearly, if meaning is determined by the contextual then texts will communicate different things in different contexts, although this is not to say that the meaning it communicated to its own time, in so far as this is recuperable, is not primary in so far as it is directly linked to the process of creation. When Arthur Miller's *The Crucible* appeared in 1953, it was seen, as it was meant to be seen, as an ingenious way of commenting on McCarthyism. When the film appeared in 1997, it was taken (as it was meant to be) more directly as a paradigm for the persecution of families by the social services and the law in the UK (Cleveland and the Orkneys) and the US, after evidence of witchcraft practices had supposedly been provided by children. Here we have a striking example of drama representing reality, obliquely when necessary, and of drama, in return, being inevitably 'read' in relation to social experience, the nature of its representational relevance changing with events. It is simply not possible that in a society highly sensitive to monarchical issues Lope's king-plays could have been written or 'read' in isolation from real-life concerns – it has been argued that the most pervasive dimension of the contextual which determines the extraction of meaning is a knowledge of reality.[28] Seventeenth-century Spanish playgoers hearing plays, however unhistorical and improbable, talking to them about the ways of kings and the problems of kingship, at different levels inevitably understood them, made sense of them, in terms of the relevance of their own experience or knowledge of monarchy.[29] And playwrights at the time wrote with this fact in mind.

How they communicated meanings as obliquely as was required has also been more sharply defined for us in recent years by the work of pragmatists, psycholinguists and philosophers of language, who have shown that the ages-old code model of communication, whereby communication is achieved through the encoding and decoding of messages (words or signs forming languages), needs to be supplemented by an inferential model, because verbal communication involves both coding and inferential processes.[30] According

[28] Wendell Harris, *Interpretive Acts: In Search of Meaning* (Oxford: Oxford University Press, 1988), 78.

[29] In October 1998 the Thai government refused permission for a new film of *The King and I* to be filmed on location in Thailand for fear it might diminish the respect in which the country holds the present king.

[30] Paul Grice and David Lewis are the most notable of the proposers of an inferential model; see Grice, 'Logic and Conversation', *Studies in the Way of Words* (Cambridge, Mass./London: Harvard University Press, 1989; and David Lewis, *Philosophical Papers* I (New York: Oxford University Press, 1983). Sperber and Wilson subsequently proposed the combined model in the face of attempts to base a theory of communication on one or

to the inferential model, communication is achieved by providing evidence for an intended inference. Literary texts, it is clear, have always in fact used both processes, and indeed the inferential model was produced because the code model alone does not 'explain how myths and literary works succeed in communicating more than their linguistic meaning, and how rites and customs succeed in communicating at all'.[31] Thus within the larger code of language itself, Calderón, for example, often communicates meaning by means of a highly stylized network of encoded metaphors which he uses as a set of recognized and recognizable signals, but he also provides evidence of many different kinds – amongst them characterization, structure, endings and use of theatrical space, contrasts, parallels, contradictions and ironies – to permit more to be communicated than the surface meaning of words and actions. We saw in the previous two chapters what sorts of evidence Lope provides in the king-plays to stimulate responses that go beyond the surface circumstances of the particular play.

> What a better understanding of myth, literature, ritual. . .has shown is that these cultural phenomena do not in general serve to convey precise and predictable messages. They focus the attention of the audience in certain directions; they help to impose some structure on experience. To that extent, some similarity of representations between the artists or performers and the audience, and hence some degree of communication, is achieved.[32]

Lope did not have to be explicit in his critique of king and kingship. Focusing the attention of his audience and providing the evidence they needed to draw their own conclusions were enough. The processes involved in the interpretation of everyday communication and the similarity of representations between play kings and real kings would automatically have done their work, with the spectators, using non-linguistic information, determining the meaning of what they saw. The significance of the rhetoric used by courtiers to flatter princes would have been understood in each case with reference to time and place, identity of speaker and listener, the intentions of both, and so on. The deployment of the rhetoric of majesty could thus be the most impertinent subversion of all, because proclamation brought into question the very

other model. See *Relevance, Communication and Cognition*, 2–6. Sperber and Wilson define inference and decodification thus: 'An inferential process starts from a set of premises and results in a set of conclusions which follow logically from, or are at least warranted by, the premises.' 'A decoding process starts from a signal and results in the recovery of a message which is associated to the signal by an underlying code' (12–13). It occurs to me, however, that the decoding process could be seen as a specific sort of inference, the code representing a set of premises, and the authors do elsewhere concede that an inferential process can be used as part of the decoding process (14).

31 Sperber and Wilson, *Relevance, Communication and Cognition*, 9.

32 Sperber and Wilson, *Relevance, Communication and Cognition*, 8.

thing proclaimed. Kingship rhetoric, was, of course, itself a form of code in that it was a linguistic convention to which speakers and listeners applied identical decoding rules. But in the plays the shared code is subverted by the inferential evidence that surrounds it, that is through the audience's knowledge (and within the plays often the players' knowledge) of situation, character, intentions, ambitions, and so on. This evidence works incrementally, because as the play proceeds the context of interpretation expands to include the information derived from previous utterances.

If we accept the definition that an inferential process starts from a set of premises and results in a set of conclusions which are warranted by those premises,[33] then on the evidence of the plays it is difficult to see how contemporary audiences could not have made disquieting connections between the worlds of fiction and fact. As has been pointed out, it is one of the cardinal principles of the hermeneutics of censorship 'that the institutionally unspeakable makes itself heard inferentially, in the space between what is written or acted and what the audience, knowing what they know, might expect to read or see'.[34] Lope could certainly rely on his audience (or a substantial part of it, at least) being able to supply the context which allowed such connections to be recovered. 'Reading' speeches, like 'reading' plays, is not just a process of linguistic decoding but also of inferring meaning from the context of the utterance. Since communication is deemed by philosophers of language to be successful not when hearers recognize the linguistic significance of the utterance but when they infer the speaker's true meaning from it, it might be argued that if critics in the past have not read the plays as a political critique, then Lope failed in communicating his purpose. But it is the inferential process which has failed and it has failed precisely because the context of the speech act that is the play, its cognitive environment, has been missing and reconstructed with insufficient sensitivity to all the evidence. In his aim to combine politics with prudence Lope could rely upon the fact that contemporary audiences would automatically supply the premises, assumptions, anxieties which subsequent readers effortfully need to recreate. And although the authorially neutral text of a printed play makes the ascription of intentions even more problematic than is the case with a prose narrative – which is why a play-text lends itself particularly well over time to different critical and stage interpretations – he could also rely upon the fact that on the stage, every dialogic speech act could draw upon emphasis, tone, intonation, facial expression, gesture and movement, and body language generally, to convey meaning to an audience conditioned by circumstances to receive it. The context of utterance is important even in normal communication where the speaker's intentions are clear. In sensitive communication, where the com-

33 Sperber and Wilson, *Relevance, Communication and Cognition*, 12.
34 Patterson, *Censorship and Interpretation*, 63.

municator's intentions are necessarily covert or ambiguous, as is the case with the king-plays, the immediate context of circumstances within the play and the cognitive environment shared by its spectators become all the more crucial

Speech act theory developed in reaction against what was seen as too narrow an emphasis on the informative use of language, and in recognition of the fact that language is embedded in social institutions and can be used to perform actions: to create states of affairs and relationships, for example, to influence the thoughts and actions of others, to create and discharge obligations, to flatter, deceive, protect oneself, misinform.[35] This creative power of speech is possible partly because the meaning and purpose of the utterance can be quite other than the linguistic utterance itself. This is why to take a character's utterance about kingship without considering the circumstances that determine its meaning and intention can be crucially misleading. And this is why Lope could make such an utterance work for him in two ways at once – as a deadpan assertion of a king's identity as a quasi-divine being which guarded against criticism, and as a provocative counterpoint to the realities of royal behaviour within and outside the play. If a necessary condition of a successful irony is that it should express 'a value judgement that is more positive than the circumstances deserve', then the adulation of patently unworthy monarchs in the plays would certainly qualify and the critical implication would have been readily picked up by the audience.[36] Dramatic dialogue is directed not only at the listeners on stage but at those watching, and the meaning conveyed need not be the same in both cases.[37] The absence of the dramatist from his text is, after all, only apparent – he does not address the audience directly, but the play itself is his *langue*. Speech-act theorists have tried to show how indirect or implicit speech-acts are performed, generally in accord with the assumption of Grice (for whom speech involves a constant process of inference and interpretation), that almost any statement can be an implicit or indirect speech-act.[38] Thus 'the door is open' (statement) can convey 'the door shouldn't be open' (accusation, reproof), 'the door should be closed' (request or order), 'who left the door open?' (accusatory, rhetorical or real question). The exact nature of the process of inference is

35 Sperber and Wilson, *Relevance, Communication and Cognition*, 243.

36 The definition is given in D. Perret, 'On Irony', *Pragmatics Microfiche* 1.7: D3, Dept of Linguistics, University of Cambridge, quoted in Penelope Brown and Stephen C. Levinson, *Some Universals in Language Usage* (Cambridge: Cambridge University Press, 1987), 262.

37 For a detailed examination of the workings of dramatic dialogue, see Andrew Kennedy, *Dramatic Dialogue: The Duologue of Personal Encounter* (Cambridge: Cambridge University Press, 1983). The concept of drama as dialogue centred is argued in Peter Szondi, *Theorie des modernen Dramas* (Frankfurt: Suhrkamp, 1959).

38 Sperber and Wilson, *Relevance, Communication and Cognition*, 244. Grice's 'Logic and Conversation' focuses on implicature. The example that follows is mine.

still much debated, although its existence *per se* is undeniable. However, broad acceptance is given to the basic assumption that although different listeners might understand the utterance in different ways, those in command of the circumstances surrounding the utterance will best grasp the intended implication. If the explicit utterance does not fit the situation, then the hearer infers another conclusion from it. The brain appears to rule out alternative interpretations until it – rightly or wrongly – thinks it has hit on the correct one. The parallel with the complex modulations of dramatic dialogue is not necessarily exact, but the example of the open door illustrates at a simple level the indeterminacy of implicature that Lope exploits in his dialogue, in that the implicit meaning has to be supplied by the listener and not all listeners will supply the same implicature. This lends itself to equivocation and to inadequate discrimination, exploitable resources in the communication of possible meanings. Intentional ambiguity is allowed in, and in this way responsibility can be eluded by the writer artfully constructing his text with more than one purpose in mind. What applies to the detail of the play applies, too, to the play as a whole. If a play may be seen as an utterance intended to communicate a meaning determined by its context, that is a speech-act, which 'does' something in that it informs, influences, stimulates thought and reaction, then Lope's king-plays are, to varying degrees, political acts. As such, their ability to communicate by implication rather than by assertion is an integral part not only of their identity as play texts – they are creative fictions not tracts – but of their identity as play texts in a society where political debate was tolerated only as long as its critical edge did not become too obvious or too sharp. Audiences faced with explicit utterance that did not fit the situation – for example, eulogies of kings that bore no resemblance to the facts, kings who spoke one way and acted another, kings whose words and acts betrayed what they should be – would, if the Gricean model for communication holds, have been forced to infer conclusions that did fit, conclusions which logically, since the mismatch was of his making, were the conclusions that Lope wished them to infer. Interpretations are jointly negotiated by speaker and hearer and need not be inferred from a single statement.[39] Both speech-act theory and discourse analysis generally support the view that we seek a consistent interpretation in reading because we take it for granted that we and the author share certain assumptions about the communication of meaning.[40] We must therefore be alert to the role of political utterance (in the broadest sense) within the plays, to its relationship to character and action, to its source, direction and association, as well as to the role it played in Lope's strategy for the containment of risk and the safeguarding, even furtherance, of his career – always bearing in mind that such a strategy is not necessarily

[39] See John J. Gumperz, *Discourse Strategies* (Cambridge: Cambridge University Press, 1982).

[40] See Wendell Harris, *Interpretive Acts*, 70.

always operating fully consciously but becomes to some extent a habit of mind and a practice of expression.

It is obvious that writers have at their disposal forms of expression and representation which allow them to conceal what they are saying or appear to say the opposite of what is being said. The seventeenth-century Spanish theatre was subject not only to formal institutionalized censorship – always there to be rigorously invoked even if often laxly applied – but to the censorship of its own form. The *comedia*'s own identity imposed constraints upon what could be said and how it could be said – not explicit prohibitions or prescriptions but tacit assumptions and expectations which largely determined what was written and performed. But this complicity between playwrights and audience regarding what sort of theatre the *comedia* should be included a recognition that a play could contain a special kind of intention designed to be recognized by its audience, that there were things to be read between the lines as well as in them, that there were signs and signals directed at spectators grown used to interpreting them. The *comedia* is a duplicitous form that could only tackle sensitive or contentious issues by dissimulating, and even to some extent, perhaps, betraying, them.[41] Thus, the reiteration of divine imagery of kingship, whatever its real purpose, inevitably contributes to its inscription within the perception of kingship, and thence, in accordance with the neo-Kantian view that language and representations contribute to the construction of reality, to the practice of kingship itself. Similarly, carefully negotiated endings providing, however superficially, satisfactory resolutions to intractable or unfaceable political dilemmas dilute the strength of the message. Yet it was in that very duplicity that the *comedia*'s effectiveness as political commentary lay. Lope was unashamedly and literally duplicitous in his approach, raising double dealing to a fine art in the way he simultaneously promoted and subverted monarchy, for reasons both strategic and substantial. To see this as toadyism or cravenness is crucially to misunderstand it. Prudence was needed even for the expression of a genuine perplexity over the contradictions embedded in monarchy, and Lope in dealing more often and more explicitly than any other playwright with the problems surrounding kingship recognized that to be effective he had to apply the exact degree of discretion required – no more and no less.

Again, pragmatics offers us an interesting model for the processes at work here. The concept of politeness, among various other areas of social behaviour, is of central interest to pragmatists, and Lope, of course, was certainly a pragmatist in the usual sense, in that he operated within the parameters of what he knew it was possible to get away with. Brown and Levinson have argued that certain precise parallels in language usage in many different lan-

[41] This suggestion is made in general terms by Pierre Bourdieu, 'Censorship and the Imposition of Form', in *Language and Symbolic Power*, ed. John B. Thompson, trans. Gino Raymond and Matthew Adamson (Cambridge: Polity Press, 1991), 137–59, p.158.

guages can be shown to derive from certain assumptions about 'face', or self-esteem:

> Politeness, like formal diplomatic protocol (for which it must surely be the model) presupposes (the) potential for aggression as it seeks to disarm it, and makes possible communication between potentially aggressive parties (1).

The parallel with writers working within a context of possible censorship will immediately be obvious. Lope's procedures for dealing with political issues involving a whole range of sensitivities, including the loss of face, achieve communication with his audience precisely by anticipating censure and disarming it. His duplicity therefore functions in the theatre in the way in which politeness functions in life. Politeness works within the world of the play, in the interaction between the characters which mimics that in the real world, and it works outside the world of the play, in the interaction between stage and audience. Just as a great deal of the mismatch between what is 'said' and what is 'implicated' in everyday speech may be attributed to politeness, to the desire not to offend by being too direct, so too may the mismatch between what Lope's king-plays say overtly and what they say obliquely. Just as in conversation what is implicated is defused by what is said, so in the theatre Lope uses the rhetoric of kingship to 'protect' the less palatable aspects of the plays. He is applying techniques which are essential to social relationships generally. And just as language use in social interaction involves the constant and instant interpretation of a complex set of signals and evidence, so his audience applied their interpretive experience to the complex information offered by the plays.

In arguing that politeness promotes successful communication by saving face, on the grounds that the maintenance of self-esteem is in the mutual interest of all, Brown and Levinson identify three main strategies, relating to the relationship between speaker and addressee and to the potential offensiveness of the message. Positive politeness (the expression of solidarity) and negative politeness (the expression of restraint) in a general sense can both be seen to be at work in Lope's plays – the use of kingship rhetoric is a way of creating an impression of solidarity, while the negotiation of viable endings implicitly places limits on the critique that has gone before. It is the third strategy however, which they call 'going off-record', which best characterizes Lope's overall procedure. This is when there is more than one unambiguously attributable intention, so that the speaker cannot be held to have committed him- or herself to one particular intention. Having it both ways is an effective strategy of evasion, and the linguistic realizations of off-record strategies correspond to the familiar range of weapons that constitute the writer's literary arsenal: metaphor and irony, rhetorical questions, understatement and overstatement, hints and clues with negotiable meanings, contradictions and counter currents, and so on. Clearly, to criticize a king is the ultimate in face-threatening acts, and to criticize his favourite scarcely less so. To minimize the threat while still making the point was patently in the interest of all concerned, playwright, king and nation. In this way, the relationship between speaker and addressee, playwright and audience, and beyond the audience the Crown, was not sacrificed, even if that between playwright and Crown was not exactly enhanced. Seventeenth-century Spain was a society highly, even abnormally, sensitized to the notion of face, there called honour, and to the need to preserve it at all costs. Elaborating on the concept, Brown and Levinson observe:

> Thus face is something that is emotionally invested. . .and must be constantly attended to in interaction. . .normally everyone's face depends on everyone else's being maintained, and since people can be expected to defend their faces if threatened, and in defending their own to threaten other faces, it is in general in every participant's best interest to maintain each other's face (61).[42]

The configurations of honour are instantly recognizable here, although the content of face will obviously differ in different cultures. For Brown and Levinson the aspects of face are basic wants 'which every member [of society] knows every other member desires, and which in general it is in the interest of every member to partially satisfy' (62). Since the monarch symbolized the nation and the state, it was in everybody's interests to satisfy what the monarch needed to maintain face and dignity. Brown and Levinson continue: 'a mere bow to face acts like a diplomatic declaration of good intentions; it is not in general required that an actor fully satisfy another's face wants'. Lope's use of kingship rhetoric functions precisely as the 'mere bow' that disarms antagonism. The positive act of politeness it involves is aimed at enhancing the image the other claims for himself, it 'anoints' the face of the addressee by indicating that in some respects he approves of him, and the potential face threat of an act is thus minimized.[43] Such rhetoric was as invaluable an element of Lope's defensive strategy as was historical displacement, another form of face-saving politeness.

Face is ignored, we are told, in cases of social breakdown, and the breakdown of his relations with his king was the last thing that Lope wanted. Included among the acts which threaten face, or consistency of self-image, are expressions of disapproval, criticism, contempt or ridicule, complaints and reprimands, accusation and insults, irreverence and the raising of dangerously emotional or divisive topics, and blatant non co-operation in some activity – all of which to some extent can be applied to the treatment of kings

[42] Brown and Levinson base their discussion of face on E. Goffman, *Interaction Ritual: Essays on Face to Face Behaviour* (Harmondsworth: Penguin, 1972).

[43] Brown and Levinson, *Some Universals in Language Usage*, 70.

within and by the plays. Included in the acts that lead to self-inflicted damage to face are apologies, self-humiliation, acting foolishly, self-contradiction, admissions of guilt or responsibility, emotional leakage, such as non-control of language, tears or temper – all of which in their turn can be identified in the representation of kings in the plays. The emotional leakage of passion and sexuality, as we have seen, plays a key role in Lope's construction of a critique of kingship. The threat posed by these unflattering portrayals of kings and kingship is minimized by the deployment of stratagems of politeness comparable with those identified as being a universal feature of language usage in social communication. Such stratagems, along with those to which I drew attention earlier, enabled Lope to set up a context of utterance to what is done and said within the plays which persuaded the audience to come to the conclusions he wanted it to come to without undue risk to himself. Juan Luis Vives in the early sixteenth century had been under no illusions about the fraudulence of language, 'porque en el lenguaje hay muchos fraudes, ya que se pliega a capricho del que habla', referring to fraudulent words, words that bend to the speaker's purpose, as 'lenguaje forzado'.[44] The language of the king-plays and the language constituted by the king-plays prove his point well.

The question of intentionality that lies at the heart of the displacements of covert writing is of course ultimately impossible to resolve unless the author is around to say what (s)he meant. Consistency of preoccupation and vision amount to a *prima facie* case rather than proof. Even the use of techniques of containment and evasion do not guarantee it, for in the professional and socio-political context within which Lope operated self-censorship was necessarily a way of life. However, comparing Lope's procedures in the king-plays with the ways in which pragmatists seek to understand how intentionality, relevance, implicature and meaning work in normal conversation produces such close parallels that the conclusions seem inescapable. I take as axiomatic the importance of the connection between context of utterance and inference, the cognitive evidence which would predispose spectators to seek meanings that would make sense of apparent paradoxes and contradictions in the texts, paradoxes and contradictions whose existence *per se* is beyond dispute. A necessary part of this context in its widest sense, both for the public of his day and for us now, must be the recognition that in his work, as in his life, Lope in spite of all the pressures to conform was a rebel. His theatre rejected the conventionally understood aesthetic values of order and restraint, defied the opposition of theorists and moralists alike, and held fast to its own vision of what theatre should be. Lope wilfully went his own way and succeeded against the odds. By the standards of his day in Spain, his very public private life too was characterized by stubborn indiscipline. Such recal-

44 In *De Concordia et Discordia in Humano Genere*, 87.

citrance in matters both private and professional does not sit easily with irreflexive political conformism. The man who rethought the identity and purpose of an entire literary form in the face of fierce establishment hostility, and who was privy, through his patron, to the intrigue and disaffection that characterized court life, is unlikely to have had nothing but piously correct thoughts about the political system in which he lived. As an apologist for monarchy he fails miserably. On the other hand as the author of a radical critique of monarchy, one which goes to the very roots of the contradictions inherent in absolutism, he is cumulatively very effective. It is not a question of the plays necessarily revealing the contradictions inherent in the ideology because the ideology itself was contradictory, as Pierre Macherey would argue[45] – any conscious propagandist worth his salt could cope with that – but of a repeated pattern of dramatic strategies which choose to foreground precisely the problems and limitations and not the strengths of monarchy. The crucial point is that it was not in Lope's interest to be identified as subversive by intention. His technique is to inscribe an alternative viewpoint within a text that lays claim to deference and respect, to query and comply, interrogate and legitimate simultaneously. In a popular, commercial theatre the need for successful communication was paramount and this, I would argue, is a far more productive and appropriate way of viewing Lope's procedures than the reductive and ill-defined subversion and containment model favoured by New Historicists, or even Dollimore's general model of subversive re-inscription whereby containment is seen as being potentially as productive as transgression, although Lope's plays do in fact fit that model very well.[46] However hard Lope dared to push, guarantees had to be built into the play's action and dialogue to prevent it posing a threat, either to the authorities or the audience, because threat would have been counterproductive in commercial and diplomatic terms, and therefore in political terms as well. Like conversations which sustain communication, play-texts both draw on conventions of linguistic (as well as dramatic) discourse and take account of audience expectations. Early Modern Spain was not yet the time nor the place for these conventions and expectations to be overtly overturned even if in England, whose unruly politics made dissent more plausible and therefore more vocal, greater risks were taken and often paid for. Interrogation had to be oblique, diffuse and cumulative, rather than traceable to a readily identifiable set of remarks or events. Its very identity had to be elusive, striking the right balance between self-protection and successful communication. Its presence had to be felt but not forced upon the attention, in order to give the

[45] See Jonathan Dollimore, *Radical Tragedy: Religion, Ideology and Power in the Drama of Shakespeare and his Contemporaries* (London: Harvester Wheatsheaf, 1989), 68.

[46] *Radical Tragedy*, and also *Sexual Dissidence: Augustine to Wilde, Freud to Foucault* (Oxford: Clarendon Press, 1991).

authorities and the spectators the option of choosing to ignore any awkward implications if they so wished. Such a strategy of diplomacy is closely akin to the politeness that has been identified as being essential to sustained and successful communication, with Lope underneath that protective umbrella developing his own techniques of engagement.[47] Lope's advice to his patron Sessa in a letter of early 1630 when relations between the unruly aristocrat and Olivares were strained, probably as a result of a manifesto against the Conde Duque that Sessa was said to have given to the King in June 1629, was 'la mayor discreción es hacer de los enemigos amigos y humillarse como el caldero al pozo para sacar el agua'.[48] For his patron to be out of favour with Olivares would do Lope no good at all and the tone of the letter is earnest, even beseeching. The realization that in politics discretion and diplomacy are essential in those who wish to operate effectively is precisely what stimulates their use in his politically inspired plays.

47 The application of functional linguistics to the study of literary texts is still in its infancy. I was encouraged to discover, when the writing of this chapter was already complete, that the relevance of politeness strategies was beginning to attract the attention of other literary scholars.

48 *Epistolario de Lope de Vega*, IV, no.523, 143.

6

THE POLITICS OF TRAGEDY: ABSOLUTISM AND REASON OF STATE

El Duque de Viseo

There is no more memorable expression of the central paradox of monarchy and no stronger statement of the dangers of absolutism than Lope's greatest political play *El Duque de Viseo*, the tragedy of a man fit to be a king and of a king fit only to be a man. No seventeenth-century Spanish play better deserves to be considered a political act and it therefore warrants extended scrutiny. Inscrutably supportive as always of monarchy itself, it is in every one of its parts a condemnation, and an explicit condemnation at that, of the monarch who misunderstands and abuses his power. Every voice in the play denounces the man, although everyone, including his victims, remains impeccably loyal to the icon – a perfect example of the positive politeness (the expression of solidarity) identified in the previous chapter as promoting the successful communication of unpalatable truths. That the contract between the King and his vassals is betrayed only by the King himself, with disastrous consequences, is an eloquent statement that he has exceeded an authority that is not in its nature boundless. The Duke of Viseo, when he enjoins patience upon fellow nobles who have been high-handedly treated by the King on the grounds that he is 'nuestro dueño absoluto' (Act II, 1088b)[1] has yet to learn the true meaning of absolutism. High on the play's agenda is the concern to show what the real implications of the rhetoric of absolute monarchy are, and Lope is deft in exploiting simultaneously the surface meaning of words (for the containment of risk) and their contextualized implications (for censure and interrogation).

A few years before *El Duque de Viseo* was written – it was published in the *Sexta parte de las comedias de Lope de Vega* in 1615 and Morley and Bruerton have assigned it to 1608–09 – Mariana in his treatise on kingship, while deciding in favour of single government as being the most efficient of the options available, had issued grave warnings both about the dangers of tyranny and about the influence of those granted privileged access to a mon-

[1] Textual references are to *Lope Félix de Vega Carpio. Obras escogidas*, III, *Teatro*, ed. Federico Carlos Sainz de Robles (Madrid: Aguilar, 1974).

arch's ear. He sees the law as an essential restraint upon the necessarily suspect fairness of a single individual, and urges that every ruler should take the advice of the nation's foremost citizens.[2] Lope's play is a powerful and moving dramatization of precisely these views and concerns. Juan II of Portugal, a young, insecure monarch whose harsh, unapproachable manner and concern for the image rather than the substance of kingship earn him no admirers, is an easy target for a Iago-like favourite who seeks revenge on a family of four fellow nobles for a personal slight by persuading the King that they are plotting to place his brother-in-law, the Duke of Viseo, on the throne. Underestimating both his master's tyrannical disposition and his fear of usurpation, don Egas crucially misjudges the outcome of the events he has set in train, and even he is horrified to see his plan spiralling out of control until it ends with the public murder by the King himself of Viseo, an innocent and universally loved and admired man. In fact, the two nobles put to death by the King in the play are the two most explicitly loyal to him, the two most willing to defend his royal immunity in the face of criticism and gossip – a telling indictment of all he is and stands for, but also inevitably an implicit questioning of the value of an obedience which recognizes no fault. He is absolutism incarnate – he disposes of people at will, takes no counsel, has no interest in justice, believes he is above the law: 'Un rey, que a todo excede, pues los reyes/ deshacen y hacen leyes, mucho obliga/ a respeto' (Act II, 1095a), and is impervious to all attempts to restrain him. For Quevedo, the prince's own will had no place in right rule and the ruler who followed his own will was quite simply a tyrant.[3] The difficulty of distinguishing between absolutism and tyranny which prevented contemporary Spanish theorists from endorsing the former is vividly demonstrated here by the use of both terms: in the mouths of the two people in the play who uninhibitedly speak their minds – the Queen and Elvira – Viseo's dutiful 'dueño absoluto' explodes into the outraged truthfulness of 'injusto pecho' and 'Jerjes portugués' (Act III, 1096a–b). Xerxes I, King of Persia, was a byword in the Renaissance for brutality and tyranny, and years later another of Lope's rulers, the Duke of Ferrara in *El castigo sin venganza*, would invoke his name as encouragement to another infamous murder, that of his beloved son. Shortly beforehand, the Queen employs an interesting juxtaposition of words in establishing her impartiality:

> Si de ser al Rey tirano
> el Duque intención tuviera,

2 *Del rey*, chap.II, 45–62.

3 *Política de Dios y gobierno de Cristo*, Primera Parte (1617), *Obras completas*, ed. Felicidad Buendía, I, *Obras en Prosa*, chap.1 (Madrid: Aguilar, 1958), 533a–b.

yo, Elvira, la espada diera
con que su cuello cortara. (Act III, 1096a)

Not only does her syntax, in the process of imagining the possibility of tyranny on the part of the Duke – an unusual application of the word in any case – insert the spectre of tyranny into the body of the play, but it focuses attention on the coupling of 'tirano' with 'rey'. It is not difficult to see the association of ideas in the Queen's mind and that association is effectively communicated to the audience.

When Viseo, tactfully trying to give his king a lesson in kingship, reminds him that even Alexander was accustomed to taking legal advice (Mariana's admonition almost visibly hangs in the air here),

Alejandro Severo, cuyo imperio
fue tenido a misterio, no juzgaba
si no se acompañaba de veinte hombres
de más famosos nombres de letrados,
que estaban celebrados en el mundo. . . (Act II, 1095a)

the King's brutal answer is to reveal the body of the garrotted Duke of Guimaráns – the eldest brother of the four and the one who has all along urged patience and obedience upon his siblings. And his conscience remains impermeable to the end. Don Egas's death at the hands of one of Viseo's loyal peasants affords the King a glimmer of the possibility that his favourite might have been implicated in the whole affair from the start, but the realization that it is his own behaviour which has throughout been at issue does not even cross his mind. For him absolutism clearly does not involve the acceptance of responsibility, and his final 'no tiene más remedio' is as cold and abrupt as is his behaviour at the beginning of the play – no words of regret, let alone of remorse, pass his lips. Leonardo, a noble, discreetly reiterates his sovereign's incomplete view of the truth

Si como prudente y cuerdo
nos quieres oír, sabrás
que este traidor lisonjero
te ha puesto en tantas desdichas (Act III, 1108b)

and this is the final word said on the matter. The King escapes explicit censure – and this is the sort of silence that has been taken as indicating on Lope's part an unquestioning acceptance of a monarch's right to do as he pleased. But to re-enact power is not to legitimate it. Silence can be more telling than words and there is no reason for anyone else to speak when the play itself has spoken. Leonardo is one of four nobles who only a few minutes before have refused point blank to obey the King's order to kill Viseo – a loss of moral authority predicted by Mariana: 'El poder de los príncipes se destruye y se debilita desde el momento en que les falta el apoyo del respeto y del amor en los súbditos.'[4] The King himself, the earthly representative and guarantor of God's justice, has been reduced by their disobedience to slaying with his own hand an innocent man without establishing the truth. Reason, control, the divine-like nature of kingship, all are betrayed at the instigation of a favoured advisor (not for nothing did Quevedo remind his readers that the very first counsellor was Satan himself[5]) in a spectacular abdication of appointed role. No more needs to be said. The play promises no new beginnings – Spain's classical tragedies normally end in desolation not in hope – and there is no sign that the King has acquired either *prudencia* or *cordura*. Not a single spectator could have emerged from the experience of seeing it performed still innocent of the dangers of the political system in which they lived – not just because the entire thrust of the play's plot, the conclusions Lope invited them to infer from events, would have alerted them, but because the conduct of kingship is throughout a live and articulated issue within the dialogue itself.

Indeed the very first scenes of the play constitute an extraordinary dialectic on the nature of kingship, a dialectic which both sets out the issues and in the process of doing so acts as a necessary guarantor of Lope's political good faith. It would be difficult, after all, to conceive of a less flattering portrait of a monarch, without moving into monstrosity and madness, than the one offered by this play, so the device of doublespeak, the diplomatic 'politeness' identified earlier as being central to Lope's interrogation of political issues, is undoubtedly at work in this particularly substantial probing of matters germane to monarchical governance. At the very moment the play opens we are taken straight into the world of court politics as, after an exchange of courtesies, the Condestable, back from leading the Portuguese troops to victory in Africa, and the Duque de Viseo begin to analyse the King's character and compare his qualities with those necessary in a king. The words are circumspect, their implications less so:

Cond. ¿Cómo con su Alteza os va?
Viseo. Ya su condición sabéis.
No dicen que se parece
a don Alonso su padre;
más tiene el rey de su madre.
Cond. ¡Cómo esa plática crece!
Aunque no es malo que sea
grave un rey.
Viseo. En la humildad
luce más la majestad

[4] *Del rey*, chap.VI, 112.
[5] *Política de Dios*, 551.

	que la corona hermosea.	
Cond.	Nunca la mucha blandura	
	fue al imperio provechosa.	
Viseo.	Al ser amado es forzosa,	
	si es con prudencia y cordura.	
Cond.	Los reyes son como nieve,	
	que, tratados, se deshacen.	
	Para ser mirados nacen:	
	nadie a tocarlos se atreve.	
	Conservar esta blancura	
	conviene a la majestad.	
Viseo.	Sí; pero tanta frialdad	
	conservada en tanta altura	
	helará los corazones	
	y el amor de sus vasallos.	
	Bueno me parece honrarlos	
	con obras y con razones.	(Act I, 1074b–5a)[6]

The warrior believes in a little aloofness and harshness, the statesman realizes that to be loved by his subjects a ruler must cultivate a wise humility. The King has been by implication both criticized and defended, and at this stage the Condestable, who will be falsely accused by Egas as plotting against the throne, is the one willing to give his sovereign the benefit of the doubt. His political acumen has, however, a sharp edge consistent with what will become an increasing, and increasingly vocal, dissatisfaction with the King's failings. His devastating statement that kings melt away in the face of close scrutiny and contact is an extremely subversive version of the more usual observation that remoteness enhances the mystique of kingship. Viseo, a simpler and ultimately truer man, takes the words without their cynical implications and goes straight to the political and philosophical heart of the matter – that the image of monarchy is nothing if it does not, through right reason and right actions, carry with it the hearts and minds of the people. His vision of the ideal king is Mariana's virtuous, beloved monarch: 'apacible', 'tratable', 'accesible', possessing 'modestia' and 'a ninguno gravoso'.[7] The short exchange encapsulates whole chapters dedicated by political theorists to trying to balance the rival claims of royal accessibility on the one hand and royal dignity and distance on the other. That they never really succeeded in reconciling the two – establishing them instead as parallel and therefore rival claims upon the practice of kingship – exposes, of course, the paradox at the heart of monarchy, and it is instructive to note how, as the seventeenth century advanced, the balance did tip in favour of the politics of charisma and the need for remoteness to preserve the mystique became perceived to be the

6 *Obras escogidas*, III, *Teatro.*
7 *Del rey*, chap.V, 95–7.

more urgent – in Saavedra Fajardo, for example, as we have seen.[8] Lope, from within the increasingly ritualized court of Philip III, clearly thought otherwise. As for those words 'prudencia' and 'cordura', the conditions that Viseo places upon 'blandura' in the well-loved monarch, they re-emerge at the end of the play from Leonardo's mouth, still wrapped in their unfulfilled conditionality:

Leon. Si como prudente y cuerdo
nos quieres oír, sabrás
que este traidor lisonjero
te ha puesto en tantas desdichas.

(Act III, 1108b)

These key qualities of kingship are inscribed at the start as a condition of Juan II's success and reinscribed at the last as a measure of his failure. The political vision is Viseo's and his murder is a betrayal not only of what he is but of all he stands for.

After the King has entered the scene, greeted the Condestable, the conquering hero, with insulting indifference and ingratitude, and swept off again accompanied by Viseo, the political discussion continues, now between the offended Condestable and his three brothers, the Duke of Guimaráns, the Count of Faro and, the youngest, don Álvaro de Portugal. The siblings are outraged by the lack of recognition accorded their brother's heroism, and Faro and Álvaro are quick to condemn the failure to distinguish between those who serve the nation and those who do not. We are on familiar ground here, of course, for the lack of royal recognition for just desserts, combining as it did the principles of gratitude and justice, was not only a theoretical and practical concern of political philosophers, who saw it as a major feature of negligent and unsuccessful government, but a personal hobby horse of Lope himself. In the conversation that follows, relatively free as is to be expected between brothers, some voices are more guarded than others. Faro says little, the Condestable not much more, although he cannot help his natural scepticism breaking through his cautious attempt to play down the slight he has received lest feelings run too high. It is the oldest and youngest brothers who are the most vociferous. Álvaro declares his loyalty to the King but, his thought processes patently obvious, dares to express the view that it is Viseo who for his personal qualities is worthy of a – he prudently rejects the use of 'the' – kingdom. Shortly afterwards, chided by his eldest brother Guimaráns, in one breath he insists he loves the King, protests that there is no harm in thinking ill of him, and concedes that it is imprudent to talk ill of kings behind their backs. Now clearly nobody in this play loves the King, every-

[8] See chap.2, 25.

body hates the King. What commands their love and loyalty is the idea of the king as the nation incarnate; the man who actually wears the crown repels love. The dilemma is captured by Álvaro's attempt to think in three different directions at once. Guimaráns, however, thinks only in one. His is the voice of total submission to the royal will: 'áspero y tierno, sea ley/ en todo servir al Rey', and again, 'Al Rey serville, y no más' (Act I, 1076a). He urges obedience and silence not only out of concern for the welfare of his family, but out of conviction. The King must be loved, he insists. The problematical nature of the love subjects should bear their king was a matter addressed by political theory, in recognition presumably of the unlovability of many individuals who wore crowns. Early in the period political philosophers like Mariana took the view that a monarch ought through his virtues and deeds to try to make himself worthy of personal devotion, in the feudal manner. By the middle of the seventeenth century, however, commentators like Saavedra Fajardo and Andrés Mendo (in his *Príncipe perfecto y ministros ajustados* of 1662) had realistically settled for a more generalized, abstract sentiment: 'Entre el príncipe y el pueblo suele haber una inclinacion o simpatía natural que le hace amable, sin que sea menester otra diligencia,' an elusive definition that conveys little more than the difficulty of the enterprise.[9] Lope's view here clearly coincides with Mariana's. The point has already been made by Viseo that a king's subjects do not love to order, that their love must be earned. And after the other three brothers have departed the Condestable, left to himself, is unequivocal in his conviction that a king cannot take refuge in the excuse of his own character, that it is imperative that the king born with a less than ideal temperament learn how to woo his people:

> Influya el cielo, influyan los planetas
> (que nacen con los hombres las fortunas)
> las condiciones, y tal vez algunas,
> en sujetos perfetos, imperfetas.
> Las causas, a nosotros tan secretas,
> siendo disculpas, no les den ningunas;
> que en viendo condiciones importunas,
> huyen las voluntades más sujetas.
> Aunque desde este polo al de Calixto
> gobierne un rey, de serlo no se alabe,
> si rey de voluntades no se ha visto.
> ¡Dichoso aquel que con prudencia sabe
> vencer su condición y ser bienquisto,
> que es de la voluntad la mejor llave! (Act I, 1076b)

9 Saavedra Fajardo, *Idea de un príncipe político-cristiano*, II, 123. See Maravall, *La teoría española del estado*, 347–8.

In the scene as a whole, therefore, the circumspect articulation of royal authority and the need for loyalty to it is punctuated by adamant assertions about the need for rule by willing consent and by clear insinuations that love, loyalty and respect cannot be commanded but have to be fully earned. Firmly established as they are right at the very beginning of the play, these signposts trace a path for the audience's response to what subsequently happens. In terms of both length and weight the rhetoric of prescription swamps the rhetoric of absolutism and largely determines the political identity of the play.

Another powerfully affecting element in the deconstruction of absolutist values is the system's ironic consumption of those most supportive of it and its failure generally to safeguard the well-intentioned from harm, from which the audience is invited to draw its own inferences. Guimaráns, absolutism's most assiduous spokesman, is shown to be the archetypal blinkered loyalist who will believe no ill of his king, so convinced is he of his God-given authority. His conviction that 'el Rey acierta en todo' (Act II, 1087b), flying as it does in the face of the already evident truth, betrays a complacency of which the play's entire action is an indictment. Any authority Guimaráns had as a political observer and judge is entirely compromised by his weakness and his lack of confidence in his own judgement when for a crucial time he becomes the focus of the action. Inés, don Egas's betrothed, persuades the Condestable to reveal to her, in confidence and against his better judgement, that Egas is of Moorish descent on his paternal grandmother's side. Inés, in refusing then to marry Egas, betrays the Condestable's confidence and reveals to Egas the source of her information. Guimaráns is so incensed by her dishonourable behaviour and by her obduracy in refusing to change her mind and rescue the situation for his family's reputation that he foolishly strikes her across the face within the precincts of the palace. The brothers now have two implacable enemies – don Egas and Inés – ready to lie to bring them all down. The King with his usual negligent contempt for the well-being of his subjects orders Guimaráns to make amends by marrying the woman who hates him (a solution regarded as inhuman and shaming by both sides) on pain of arraignment for treason. So confounded is Guimaráns by finding himself in such an appalling dilemma that he has to ask his brothers' advice before reacting to the King's command. Egged on by their outrage, he begins at last to show some backbone, but even as the troubled Viseo leaves to inform the King of Guimaráns's refusal, we see that ingrained habits die hard. To Viseo's parting warning that the King is their 'dueño absoluto', Guimaráns responds,

Guim. Viseo, ese honrado fruto
nace de vivir en ley
que nos muestra como a vos
que al rey, en la paz, o guerra,

respetemos en la tierra,
porque está en lugar de Dios.
Los príncipes en el suelo
somos, en toda ocasión,
lo que los ángeles son
delante del Rey del cielo.
Porque de aquel propio modo
se debe, por excelencia,
a cuanto hiciere obediencia
y darle gracias por todo. (Act II, 1088b)

His sense of injustice at the King's decision has driven him into a disobedience entirely at odds with his understanding of monarchy, and after Viseo's departure his courage falters: 'Yo hice lo que los dos/ me aconsejasteis' he reminds his younger brothers. Here is a man temperamentally averse to disloyalty who at every opportunity gives his king the benefit of the doubt. His protestations of fidelity are real, not a form of self-defence, and it will take the unwarranted victimization of his brothers by the King to make him begin to see things as they really are. The news of their banishment wrings from him the admission that his sovereign might after all be fallible, although even now his criticism is couched in a traditional formula of respect (ever since Seneca in his *De Clementia*, written for the sixteen-year-old Nero, had argued that the *princeps* needed also to be a *sapiens*, wisdom had been perceived as an attribute of princes):

Si en él resplandece la justicia,
y hubo en ellos malicia, bien ha hecho,
estando satisfecho de su culpa;
pero si los disculpa todo el mundo
ciego está su profundo entendimiento. (Act II, 1094a)

He can have no conception of how fallible, that his king is a man so fearful and so lacking in moral fibre as to have him killed merely in order to distract his brothers from the thoughts he thinks they have of usurping the throne. As for Viseo, he responds to Guimaráns's comparison of princes before their king with angels before the King of Heaven with a touch of cynicism that suggests that, although he normally keeps such thoughts to himself, he is not as much of a political innocent as he sometimes seems:

Si esta inferior jerarquía
es imitación, señor,
de la esfera superior,
alto pensamiento os guía. (Act II, 1089a)

The text is sown with the conditionals which allow characters to mean more than they seem to say. And care with words is essential – one of the play's persistent motifs is the danger of speech, particularly of Montesquieu's 'paroles indiscrètes': 'Rien ne rend encore le crime de lèse-majesté plus arbitraire que quand des paroles indiscrètes en deviennent la matière' (*De l'esprit des lois*).[10] Criticism of court gossip and intrigue is a common feature of Lope's drama, and of the Golden-Age theatre in general, but no play better demonstrates the problematical nature of *murmuración*. When are facts gossip? When is justified criticism intrigue? Repeated references are made by the characters to the imprudence of being overheard, to the need for silence in order to protect the system, but a political system which muzzles the truth is shown to be a system which breeds gross injustice. The malicious gossip of Egas and Inés spreads its poison, and those of bad faith – Egas, Inés, the King – are shown eavesdropping and spying upon the well-intentioned. What these latter pass amongst themselves – evidently too carelessly – are the justified anxieties of loyalists faced with a profoundly flawed monarch. The cause and the solution of both lies and truth is the King, whose inadequate behaviour creates an atmosphere in which fictions can feed off disaffection. Clearly there is a devil in the plot, but he is there at the King's own instigation. The dangers of the *mal ministro* (synonymous for political theorists with the favourite, itself synonymous with wheedler and flatterer) in the state where the monarch rules without constraints are made as apparent here as they are in the political treatises of the time.

The welfare of the state conveniently demands that don Egas carry the blame for what has happened. But that the responsibility is the King's is never left in any doubt, and his youth – 'Oh malaconsejado rey mancebo' (Act II, 1092a) – is not allowed to dilute it. It is a monarch's business not to be misled by false witness. In playing on the King's fears for his own ends, Egas little thinks that he has set in motion a trajectory from dysfunctionality to tyranny. Horrified to discover that the King is convinced of Viseo's complicity, he repeatedly assures him of Viseo's innocence. The King's jealousy of Viseo's popularity, however, has taken its murderous hold. Towards the end of Act I, when the four brothers still think they have only royal arrogance and ingratitude to complain of, the King is already guilty of not establishing the truth of Egas's accusations, a negligence compounded by his unenquiring acceptance of the corroborating evidence of a woman with an axe to grind. This lack of concern for the truth, this willingness to believe his favourite only when it suits his own fears and prejudices to do so, in short this betrayal of the prime monarchical principle of justice, is the key element in Lope's portrait of a king unfit for rule. When he invokes vengeance for a crime that has not been committed, then conflates vengeance with justice and 'virtud santa' (Act II, 1094b), he reveals himself as a man incapable of thinking as a

10 Quoted in Patterson, *Censorship and Interpretation*, 9.

monarch should. The portrait in its entirety, however, is damning. His weasel words: 'Levanta, amado primo./ Notablemente estimo tu obediencia' (Act II, 1094b), to Viseo, the man he intends to kill, and his arbitrary garotting of Guimaráns, reveal him to be as treacherous as any favourite. The complete collapse of his control over both the situation and himself at the end involve an emotional excess totally inappropriate in a monarch and a consequent loss of face recoverable only through the good will of his courtiers – and this in a monarch who at the start refused a public appearance on a balcony as being inconsistent with his dignity, for fear of appearing 'descompuesto'. And his continuing imperviousness to guilt pronounces him morally bankrupt. The detail of his characterization, too, is clearly meant to contribute to the same unflattering reading. His view of his subjects as pawns to be disposed of at will (by marriage, reallocation of titles, murder); his intemperate decisions; his specious arguments in favour of his actions; his readiness to shrug off responsibility for his actions onto others; his imperviousness to reason: all are cut from the same cloth. His invocation of reason of state as his justification for the idea that he should rid himself of Viseo before any plot to put him on the throne comes to a head is immediately denounced as untenable by Egas himself:

Egas. No quiera Dios que por razón de estado
(que muchas veces el demonio inventa)
el inculpable Duque tu cuñado
pierda la vida, o dalle alguna afrenta.
Castigar la justicia al que es culpado
es imitar a Dios; no cuando intenta
por las razones de futuros daños,
verter la sangre en propios y en extraños.
Rey. ¿No debe conservar el Rey su vida?
Egas. Debe, mas no quitarla al inocente.
Rey. ¿Y si éste da la causa a que atrevida
le opone al cetro la plebeya gente?
Egas. Si su virtud la tiene tan rendida
¿es bien, señor, que un rey cristiano intente
matar al virtuoso porque es bueno,
y está de gracias y virtudes lleno?
Rey. Este punto es sutil.
Egas. No hay sutileza
contra la ley de Dios.
Rey. En esto veo,
don Egas, tu verdad y tu nobleza,
y que condenas justamente al reo;
pues viendo que amenaza tu cabeza,
abogas por el duque de Viseo. (Act I, 1081a–b)

Egas's genuine attempt to protect Viseo places him in greater danger.

Convinced already by jealousy of Viseo's guilt, the King chooses to regard Egas's defence of him as the sign of a gallantry which merely gives added credence to his earlier accusations against the Condestable and his brothers. Since lies are taken for truth, truth is seen as lies. The King's chooses to believe Egas only when what he says accords with the promptings of his own fears. The fact that the liar is here arguing the just cause works in two contrary ways. For those in command of all the circumstances (the spectators) don Egas's earlier deception of the King actually lends force to his argument: if a favourite capable of maliciously provoking a calamity dares to argue selflessly against his King in defence of an innocent man then at this moment he must have right on his side. For the King, however, who knows little more than he has been told and chooses to believe, Egas's words are special pleading born of generosity. He is offered ethics and sees only casuistry. Subjectivity and situation, as usual in interchange as we saw in the previous chapter, determine the inference of meaning. The King's nimble step sideways when faced with the implacable logic of Egas's argument against reason of state is a pivotal moment in the action, because it is effectively the King's moral Rubicon in his descent into tyranny. Not a few who saw this play would have remembered the consequences of a real royal favourite pressing the opposite policy upon his king at the time of the Escobedo affair and felt the added force of Egas's words. Malice and treachery are not normally associated with virtuous principles, but Egas's is a complex, nuanced character and no simple medieval devil figure.

Indeed, the only thoroughly demonized person in the play is the King himself. He is deliberately deceived certainly, but he is excused neither for his willingness to be so nor for the way he conducts himself thereafter. We are never sorry for him as we are even for don Egas, whose happiness and reputation are casually destroyed by indiscretion and prejudice. Since the King seems to feel nothing himself we do not feel for him. We are not invited, indeed we are not allowed, to take even his youth and insecurity as warranting sympathy, so determined is Lope to paint the unflattering face of absolutism. He even utilizes sexual unruliness again, if somewhat sketchily, as a sign of the politically dysfunctional. The King is not at all well disposed to his new queen who 'es por quien él hace menos' (Act II, 1085a), perhaps because she is too clear-sighted about his shortcomings, but he is very well disposed indeed towards Viseo's beloved Elvira. From a conversation between her and Viseo in which Viseo is trying to persuade her to intervene on Guimaráns's behalf, we learn that the King is something of a ladies' man and has been paying her court, that only for her does his manner ever soften. When she approaches the King his manner is gallant but his response and its motives are in fact disingenuous and provocative. He claims to respect the process of law, to have no power to disregard Guimaráns's insult to Inés. When Elvira explains she is asking for compassion not pardon, for something that will make peace between the two people involved (Act II, 1086a), the

King then promises for her sake a 'medio piadoso'. He is interested, however, in neither peace nor due process and the 'medio piadoso' turns out to be the enforced marriage of Guimaráns to Inés, a maliciously cruel solution which Elvira and Egas both feel unable to question. With Egas out of the room, the King tells Elvira that, if she asks him to, he will allow power to trample reason and set Guimaráns free. He is of course both placing the responsibility for Guimaráns's fate unfairly on Elvira's shoulders and rhetorically loading the dice one way. Elvira reacts as he must hope she will – she is not the woman to fly in the face of reason and the justice of the aggrieved, she will not ask for Guimaráns to go scot-free. The King is a fragmented, devious man, always seeming to act in accord with some not entirely visible agenda, his motives elusive and unstable. His offer to Elvira is difficult to read, but only readable in a light unflattering to himself. Either he is prepared, for the sake of a pretty face, to abandon his duty to see that justice is done, or he is intent both on getting his way and shrugging off blame. There is more evidence for the second explanation than the first. Later on, when Inés begs him to punish Guimaráns for his insult to her by simply banishing him from court, he will claim, absurdly, that he has no power to do this – Elvira wants the marriage to take place, he says, and he has to respect her wishes. Power without responsibility is what he desires throughout the play, which is why the disobedience of his nobles at the end is such a hugely significant act – he is forced to become the instrument of his own iniquity and kill Viseo himself if he wants him killed. His insistence earlier on that Guimaráns marry Inés is an act of mean-spirited vengeance masquerading first as duty, then crassly as courtly compulsion, which mocks both grievance and justice with a punishment more painful to the victim of the crime than the blow that dishonoured her. Juan is vicious as well as dysfunctional.

The case mounted by behaviour, dialogue and events against the King and the absolutist cast of monarchy he represents is a damning one. But so that there may be no possible doubt in the spectators' minds that this vision of kingship is a nightmare, Lope goes so far as to harness the supernatural to his cause. Banished from the court by the King, Viseo returns under cover of night to see Elvira. As he walks back through the deserted and pitch-black streets looking for a light by which to read the letter Elvira has given him, a letter which will reveal that the King is to give her to don Egas to spite Viseo, 'por darle enojos' (Act III, 1101b), he makes out a cross at a street corner with a flickering lantern. Moved by the sight of it he protests his innocence and his devotion to the King; 'Por el divino Señor/ que en vos sus espaldas puso,/ que adoro al Rey' (Act III, 1103b).[11] As if the very expression of his

11 The Aguilar text reads 'adora al Rey', which is clearly wrong. Francisco Ruiz Ramón in his somewhat earlier reader's edition of the play (Alianza Editorial: Madrid, 1966, 178) also corrects to 'adoro'.

loyalty has been the trigger, suddenly the noise of chains and a harsh trumpet rend the air, and a voice begins to sing:

> Don Juan, Rey de Portugal,
> ese que llaman el Bravo,
> quejoso vive en Lisboa
> de sus deudos y vasallos.
> Con su fuerte condición
> piensa que quieren matarlo
> los portugueses famosos,
> cuatro inocentes hermanos.
> Al Condestable destierra,
> también al conde de Faro,
> y a don Álvaro, el menor;
> que la envidia puede tanto.
> . . .
> Al duque de Guimaráns
> mandó en público teatro
> cortar la honrada cabeza,
> digna de roble y lauro.
> . . .
> Del buen duque de Viseo,
> mancebo fuerte y gallardo,
> tiene mil quejas el Rey,
> con ser su primo y cuñado.
> Guárdate, Duque inocente;
> guárdate, Abel desdichado,
> que malas informaciones
> ensangrientan nobles manos.
> Viseo. ¿Que me guarde yo? ¿Por qué?
> ¿Por qué he de guardarme, estando
> inocente como estoy? (Act III, 1103b–4a)

The information about Guimaráns and his brothers is in factual terms superfluous because everybody on stage and in the audience is already aware of what has happened. But it has a purpose both dramatic and theatrical, a function within the world of the play and within the shared world of play and playhouse. It reminds Viseo of the injustices committed by the King, and adds weight to the warning the voice then issues. It recapitulates events for the audience, re-emphasizing the innocence and honourableness of the victims, and the harshness of the King's character, and with the reference to the 'público teatro' the identities of fictional and real worlds momentarily merge to jolt the audience into forgetting the separation between the two. Misinformation immediately afterwards receives a notable mention, but don Egas's name is never uttered and the weight of responsibility is explicitly placed with the King. Even the reference to envy, usually associated in the *comedia* with intrigue amongst courtiers, accords with the King's character and motives rather than with Egas's. Egas's motives are rejection, hatred and the desire for revenge. The King is vulnerable to his machinations because he recognizes in Viseo the qualities and the popularity that make him a convincing rival. Viseo agrees with the voice about the power of envy, 'envidias pueden/ hacer un hombre pedazos/ desde los cercos del sol/ hasta el mar de sus agravios', and it is the King, rather than Egas, who through envy and jealousy disintegrates into villainy on the grand scale. The play's last words will conjure up the spectre of envy a second time, reminding the audience at the very last moment of the nature of the King's involvement.

The voice's warning to Viseo even more emotively combines praise for the victim with implied censure of the King – Viseo's innocence and his family relationship with the King, both stressed, signify that if he is Abel then the King is Cain, the world's first murderer who through jealousy killed his brother. Dramatic tension and tragic inevitability demand that the warning be heard but not heeded, it is a promise of disaster rather than a guard against it. Viseo's reaction is a combination of indignation, disbelief and naïveté, it is also a sure indication that avoidance of his fate is not something he can contemplate. His *de facto* innocence gives him a sense of invulnerability – essential in every tragic protagonist – which reveals his political innocence. He cannot believe that he can be in any real danger from his King. He has, after all done nothing wrong: unlike Elvira he has not guessed that Guimaráns died not for slapping Inés and then refusing to marry her but for supposedly plotting to place Viseo on the throne (Act III, 1103a). Thus when recalled by the King to the court, like the loyal subject he is he obeys. The assumptions he makes about the way a king behaves mark him out as a man fit to be one, but they also precipitate his death. He has crucially overlooked the fact that the 'dueño absoluto' is bound by nothing other than his own will. Even a second warning fails. No sooner has he protested his innocence than the corpse of Guimaráns in a white cloak with the red cross of the Order of Christ passes before his astonished eyes and admonishes:

Guim. Duque . . .
Viseo. ¡Ay, cielos soberanos!
Guim. Duque . . .
Viseo. ¿Qué es esto que veo?
Guim. Duque . . .
Viseo. Todo estoy temblando.
Guim. Guárdate del Rey.
Viseo. ¿Qué dices?
Guim. Que te guardes. (*Desaparécese*)

Viseo knows that 'las visiones/ son sombra que hace el pensamiento', although he is so overcome that he collapses to the ground, and perhaps it is this rational self-reassurance too which diverts him from caution. The dramatic impact of the apparition is enormous. The corpse itself, the triple attempt to fix the Duke's attention, the stark directness of the warning, its repetition, the spareness of the entire exchange, all sear the moment and its message into our attention, locating danger unequivocally in the King. Beware of the King – the concept is a blasphemy within the framework of Renaissance belief that God had entrusted his people to the care of princes. The cross appears twice in association with the warning, twice Christ is invoked in association with the victimization of the innocent – the very Christ whom Quevedo holds up in his *Política de Dios y gobierno de Cristo* as the model for the earthly king. The scene is the ultimate condemnation of a rule in which the shepherd has become the wolf.

Menéndez y Pelayo was scathing about Lope's distortion of history in this play, but the very extent of the distortion indicates that Lope had a decided agenda of his own.[12] To turn two conspirators against the crown – the Dukes of Braganza and Viseu – into the innocent victims Guimaráns and Viseo, to turn a harsh but admired King regarded as a role model for princes (and used as one by Lope himself in *El príncipe perfecto*) into a weak and morally bankrupt tyrant, indicates that he was interested in the dynamics of royal power and had something to say about them. Those had been unruly times politically in Portugal, and there as elsewhere in Europe in the sixteenth century internecine jostling for royal power had been rife. In the intrigue that surrounded thrones, it is now often hard to distinguish right from wrong, and heroism and villainy are a matter of interpretation rather than fact. Within Spain's stable monarchy legitimacy was not an issue, but the nature and management of monarchy were, and in contemplating the events of these years as they are set out in Ruy de Pina's *Crónica del rey don Juan II* Lope evidently saw in them the stuff not only of tragedy but of an issue that had by the time he was writing become the compelling subject of political debate – the meaning of kingship. How should a king govern and by what principles should he govern? What happens if a king 'goes bad'? Can one man rule alone and what are the consequences of his doing so? What are the consequences of the king's not ruling alone, what happens then to the power vested in the crown? All these were questions already in play at the end of the sixteenth century in Spain, but made more pressing, as we have seen, by the succession of a young, weak monarch interested only in his God and his own amusement, and eager to hand over the government of his realm to a chosen favourite and *his* chosen favourites. The development of European monarchies along absolutist lines as the seventeenth century got under way only gave pause for harder thought on these issues, and provoked excited and prolonged anxiety about the shadow of tyranny and what to do about it. The

[12] *Estudios sobre el teatro de Lope de Vega* (Madrid: Consejo Superior de Investigaciones Científicas, 1949), V, 128–47.

advent of the rule of favourites in an increasingly absolutist age – the combination even more problematical than its separate parts – is clearly the moving force behind Lope's manipulation of the historical sources of his play. If Morley and Bruerton's dating is correct, when Lope was writing it Rodrigo Calderón enjoyed complete ascendancy over a favourite who in turn had complete ascendancy over Philip III. Perceived, like Antonio Pérez before him, as manipulative and deceitful, although it would be some years before he was suspected, then accused, of poisoning both the Queen and Luis de Aliaga – Inquisitor General, royal confessor and major court plotter – Calderón could easily have been the inspiration for don Egas. No two monarchs could have been more different than Lope's Juan and the 'pallid, anonymous creature, whose only virtue appeared to reside in a total absence of vice', in John Elliott's memorable words, who occupied the Spanish throne,[13] but, whether power is in the hands of vice or negative virtue, the problem of how much there is, and who uses it and in what way, remains the same.

A favourite seeking vengeance for a destructive personal affront mobilizes for his own ends a king's authority and a king's fear. Events, coincidences, good intentions, viewed through the eyes of insecurity and jealousy, then conspire to sign Viseo's death warrant. The tender nonsense of courtship and the play of rustics are misconstrued by a willing ear as evidence of treason and consign him to a fate from which there is no escape once the seeds of suspicion are sown. Obedience, loyalty, patience, right thinking are rendered meaningless by a ruler who refuses to recognize them; reason, persuasion, even constructive flattery, fail in the face of a monarch intent solely on the execution of his own will. And here, of course, lies the burden of the play. Absolutism offers the subject no guarantees. Rivadeneyra had rejected absolutism – 'ningún rey es absoluto, ni independiente, ni proprietario' (I, 475), as being inconsistent with the monarch's relationship to the divine. One of Rivadeneyra's self-appointed tasks was to safeguard the authority and independence of the Church from the power of secular princes: 'Guardas son de la ley de Dios, mas no intérpretes' (I, 485), and he firmly states that the monarch is God's lieutenant and subject to God's law. Mariana, much more radical, took it for granted that power ultimately resided with the people (chap. 6, 123), although since his abiding concern is with stability his judgement is that a legitimate monarch must be tolerated 'mientras no llegue a despreciar públicamente todas las leyes de la honestidad y del pudor que debe observar' (chap. 6, 126). And this, of course, is the philosophy which implicitly underpins Lope's critique of kingship in his theatre. At the highest level reason of state is a compelling pressure because political instability does not promote justice. For Spain's seventeenth-century theorists the spectre of tyranny was equalled only by the spectre of tyrannicide, the almost certain

13 *Imperial Spain*, 295.

promoter of civil strife. The play's last scene is heavy with symbolism and insinuation and leaves us in no doubt as to its judgement of the King and what he stands for. The emblematic juxtaposition of Viseo's bloody corpse with the crown and sceptre on a pillow at his side is meant by the King as a warning to the nobles that the Crown's power is absolute. Given Viseo's innocence and personal qualities, however, its effect is at once to condemn the tyranny of absolutism and to suggest that the truer king is the man who has been murdered. The Queen underwrites this suggestion when she scathingly addresses her husband as don Juan, 'Dadme licencia, don Juan,/ para no mirarle', a slight not lost on the King, who brushes it aside with sarcastic indifference, '. . .Pienso/ que no me llamaste Rey/ por ver ya difunto el vuestro' (1107b). For all this, Juan's behaviour is at the last tolerated with silence by his nobles. But it is the silence not of consent but of political realism – any alternative was more problematical than the *status quo*. It must be borne in mind that the idea of the state, rather than the monarch or the monarch in parliament, as the bearer of sovereignty had not yet entered European political thought.[14] Just as Mariana's central preoccupation is with tyranny, however, so *El Duque de Viseo* shows that it is absolutism that allows tyranny in. Under absolutism the people are always subject to the possibility of tyranny, because tyranny is the form that absolutism takes when it falls into the wrong hands. Rule by the will of one individual depends for its quality on the nature and good will of that individual alone, and absolutism effectively cedes to the monarch the coercive power of the law. Where no distinction is made between the law and the will of the monarch, liberty is perpetually at risk. Juan flagrantly ignores the basic provisions both of the rule of law and of natural justice – he fails to establish the truth, his victims are ignorant of their alleged crime of *lèse-majesté*, and they are not given the opportunity to defend themselves. That the innocent men who are sacrificed are the very nobles who throughout have shown themselves with their uncritical loyalty to be most seduced by the idea of absolutist rule is an irony not merely tragic but pointedly telling. In the context of the political beliefs and thinking of its time the play is a bold investigation of the implications and risks of absolutism. My investigation has been able to do little justice to the qualities of the play as theatre, as tragedy, because this has not been my brief, but of course in performance these carry the emotional force that drives home the political message. It is our sense of outrage over what happens to Viseo that hones our sensitivity to the political values that have shaped his fate. As so often in Spain's classical tragedies the play offers no sense of catharsis, the problem

14 See Quentin Skinner, *Liberty Before Liberalism* (Cambridge: Cambridge University Press, 1997). The application of the word 'state' to Early Modern European monarchies is of course in itself not unproblematical, but for the purposes of this book I have used it as the most convenient way of referring to the largely centrally organized sovereign political power with the monarch (or other hereditary ruler) at its head.

has not gone away (crucially because the problematical figure is not the one dead at the close of the action) and the ending, with the King's blank imperviousness to blame, provokes rather than appeases. We have seen that it is weakness, not strength, that leads to tyranny and the King is an unchanged man. Viseo, therefore, is no Girardian scapegoat whose death will purge the realm of violence. Under absolutism there are no guarantees. Like so many other of Lope's history plays, *El Duque de Viseo* presents a view of history where agency is all rather than one which encourages a providentialist interpretation of events, but it shows that where agency is located within the ruler who harnesses power to his own will then that too spawns its own, malign, version of inevitability.

El castigo sin venganza

The tragedy commonly regarded as Lope's greatest play lies for the most part outside the parameters of this discussion. However, since it problematizes the issue of political power it does have its contribution to make, for all that the peculiar circumstances of the plot place it in a category of its own. Here the ruler is the protagonist in a domestic crisis with political ramifications where the victims of power are actually guilty not innocent. The taboo sin of incest committed by illegitimate son and young stepmother who become lovers is a crime against the state because questions of authority, loss of face and inheritance are involved, and the problematical issue is how a father and husband who is also the head of state copes with this intractable situation. The Duke of Ferrara cares little for his wife Casandra, whom he has married by proxy sight unseen, her sole purpose being to bear him a legitimate heir to safeguard the state from civil strife after his own death. He cares a great deal about his son Federico, however, whose very existence is a living testimony to his dissolute youth and to his earlier neglect of his responsibility to secure the legitimate inheritance of his line. The crime and his own duty to the state require he take action, but a trial that makes public the cuckoldry of the head of state by his own son will only compound the damage. Contemporary political philosophers such as Pedro Portocarrero y Guzmán in his *Theatro monárquico de España*[15] and Juan Alfonso Rodríguez de Lancina in his *Comentarios políticos a los Anales de Cayo Vero Cornelio Tácito*[16] argued that power was the guarantee of liberty through the operation of justice, and the problematical nature of the interaction of power and justice in these very special circumstances comes under scrutiny in this play. It is apparently in the interest of the state that the Duke proceed as he does and

15 (Madrid: García Infanzón, 1700), 166.
16 (Madrid: Melchor Alvárez, 1687), 2.

justice is in a sense done – although they ostensibly die for different reasons, the couple pay with their lives for the crime they have committed, which would almost certainly have been the outcome had their case come to public trial. There is, however, a terrible wrongness about the Duke's solution as well as a terrible rightness, and this deeply problematical conjunction encapsulates the tragic force of the entire play.

The play is based on a historical incident involving the Marquis Nicholas of Ferrara in 1425, although Lope probably took the story from Bandello's novella *Il Marchese Niccoló Terzo*, either directly or from a Spanish translation of a French version of Bandello's tale published in 1603. Lope introduced several changes into the narrative, but the only one of significance here affects the ending. In Bandello's original, and in the subsequent French and Spanish versions, the young couple are executed in public, rendering unequivocal that their deaths indeed constituted punishment and not vengeance. It was Lope himself who made the Duke's motives so deeply ambiguous and his solution so Machiavellian, thereby transforming a cautionary tale into an infinitely complex work of art. The innately problematical nature of the situation was admirably captured by Edward Gibbon in his account (pub. 1814) of the historical event in his *Antiquities of the House of Brunswick*:

> Under the reign of Nicholas III Ferrara was polluted with a domestic tragedy. By the testimony of a maid and his own observation the Marquis of Este discovered the incestuous loves of his wife, Parisina, and Hugo his bastard son, a beautiful and valiant youth. They were beheaded in the castle by the sentence of a husband and a father, who published his shame and survived their execution. He was unfortunate if they were guilty; if they were innocent he was still more unfortunate; nor is there any possible situation in which I can sincerely approve the last act of the justice of a parent.

Gibbon's beautifully judged and compassionate words themselves point to the infinitely increased complexity that results from Lope's shifting of the source of ambiguity. In *El castigo sin venganza* the ambiguity lies not in the question of whether or not the taboo sin and crime of incest has been committed (we know it has), but in the nature of the Duke's motivation in killing the guilty pair secretly – an area fraught with psychological and linguistic subtleties. Where Lope anticipates Gibbon is in his appraisal of the incident as a deeply unfortunate situation from which no one emerges the winner, and in his sense that there is something gravely amiss in the manner in which justice is applied.

There are three observations in Gibbon's account which are particularly relevant to Lope's play. First is the use of the uncompromising word 'pollution'. In fact and fiction what has happened is, for the reign and for the realm, a grave crisis which confronts the shamed ruler with the severest test. Saavedra Fajardo was under no illusions about the importance of honour to successful rule:

> Es el honor uno de los principales instrumentos de reinar: si no fuera hijo de lo honesto y glorioso le tuviera por invención política. Firmeza es de los imperios. Ninguno se puede sustentar sin él. Si faltare en el príncipe, faltará la guarda de sus virtudes, el estímulo de su fama y el vínculo con que se hace amar y respetar (*Empresa* VIII).

In using the term 'honor' Saavedra is, of course, referring not only to the public perception of the ruler (his *honra*) but the integrity on which that perception should based (*honor*), and it is precisely the separation of the two in his own life that has produced the Duke of Ferrara's dilemma. Here and elsewhere, however, Saavedra does not underestimate the absolute political importance of image: 'los imperios se conservan con su misma autoridad y reputación'.[17] In Ferrara action, therefore, has to be taken; the stain must be eradicated and the reputation of ruler and state restored. However, what makes the situation so serious – that the head of state has been cuckolded by his own son – is precisely what makes it so difficult to deal with. Now clearly common sense and natural justice dictate that in each case the ruler/husband/father should distance himself and hand over the case to the representatives of the law. But these rulers incorporate the law, have *de facto* power of life and death over their subjects, and have a strong vested interest both as rulers and as individuals in the outcome. At this point Marquis and Duke part company. Whereas the Duke decides to try and maintain secrecy and have the lovers killed in private, the Marquis 'published his shame'. Both sentence the lovers to death, but the Marquis then behaves as an independent judge would do by not seeking to suppress the truth. His motive might well have been strategy rather than principle, but that Gibbon thought he was taking a huge risk is evident from his 'and survived the execution'. The phrase also indicates that the Marquis's gamble paid off – presumably because he was seen as a decisive ruler capable of taking action even against his own family, the display of power and resolution amply compensating for the shame suffered. The Duke's manoeuvres, on the other hand, turn out to be counterproductive – his cuckoldry is not a secret and his behaviour is villainous, a form of refined cruelty almost calculated to ruin his reputation rather than rescue it. It is true that although the Marquis wins in the public relations stakes, they both emerge ethically compromised, albeit to differing degrees. Gibbon sees an essential incompatibility in 'the justice of a parent', in the idea of a parent sitting in judgement on a child; that Lope does too is obvious from the Duke's tormented monologue in Act III, where schizoid word pairing – *rigor/templanza, padre/marido, castigo/venganza* – betray the gropings and tearings of an anguished mind, and where the language of the processes of law is deployed by the Duke both to make the thought of his son's death

17 For the rest of this quotation, see chap.2, 18.

bearable to him and to keep under some degree of face-saving control the urge for revenge that confuses his understanding of his public duty. But that the Marquis conducted himself more suitably given the circumstances there can be no doubt from the outcome. The Duke reacts to the crisis like a private individual – he behaves like an avenging Calderonian husband – and not like a ruler, and with every action he forfeits his right to our respect if not our sympathy. What we see throughout his handling of the situation is the operation not of the law, but of the Duke's own will. It does not matter that the end result is the same, because the means by which the end is achieved are the crucial measure both of the Duke's own ethical stature and of the extent to which his subjects have some guarantee of liberty. The cloud that stubbornly hangs over his motivation at the end of the play – has he really played the reluctant statesman or has he played the avenging husband? – together with the tortured self-knowledge that contemplates the killing of a beloved son and the end of hope, creates the inevitable impression that both for himself and for the state the solution was the wrong one. The Duke in his long monologue before the final scene rejects the idea of vengeance upon a beloved son as unthinkable and convinces himself that the terrible course he has taken constitutes punishment underpinned by reason of state. But this messy tangle of motivation itself speaks loudly to the unacceptability of the victim's acting as judge upon those who have offended against him. Where the ruler's will has the force of law there is no insurance against injustice.

It is the infamous deviousness of the Duke's handling of the couple's punishment which above all confuses our responses to the play. If we consider the situation counterfactually we can concede that Casandra's reputation is secured and that both are spared the anticipation and humiliation of a public execution. But Federico dies an alleged double murderer (the Duke claims he murdered his stepmother because she was with child) rather than as a lover, and there is something irreduceably repellent about a man's being ordered to kill unknowingly the woman he loves and then being killed himself for a crime he committed on the order of his judge and executioner. A mockery is made of justice and the law, of truth, and on this rock the dukedom of Ferrara stands at the end of the play. The furies the Duke unleashed many years ago with his irresponsible behaviour will descend upon Ferrara when he dies, and so rotten is the state – for the Duke is the state – that we can scarcely regret the fact. In trying too late to save the state from harm he has precipitated a situation that will not only eventually bring about the very calamity he sought to avoid, but has dragged himself, Federico and Ferrara down into the mire of infamy and dishonour – there are too many people who know what has transpired for the reputation of father, son or state to be saved. The circumstances of the crisis conspire to place reason of state under the severest pressure. The principle itself is not invalidated. It was after all by not marrying at the right time, as reason of state demanded, that the Duke years before sowed the seeds of disaster. This inability to make the right discriminations between self and role characterizes his life and his actions throughout the play. When he does his duty by marrying he is doing too little too late, and his continuing philandering drives Casandra into Federico's arms. The conversion he believes he has undergone, when it comes, again comes too late, the harm is already done, and his conviction that he is now a reformed man, that duty rather than indulgence will in future regulate his life, makes the discovery of his son's relationship with his wife all the more sickening. This lack of control over the pressures that shape his life becomes most evident when he is anguishing over his own motivation in executing the young couple. He may convince himself that their deaths are punishment not vengeance, sufficiently at least to make the unthinkable thinkable, but he does not entirely succeed in convincing us. The reason of state argument that determines the manner of their deaths, that publicity would undermine the Duke's reputation and therefore the state's, leads to a scene of such horror and moral bankruptcy as to gravely discredit the principle itself. If in contemporary political thought the only acceptable justification for an unjust act was the preservation of the possibility of justice – the tyrant is killed to prevent tyranny, war is waged to guarantee peace – then the Duke's action does not qualify. The spectators' realization that the argument of necessity does not even achieve its end of secrecy, finally, reveals it to be strategically as well as ethically an extremely unreliable basis for action, a bitter lesson learnt by Philip II at the time of the Escobedo affair. And in the space between how the Duke behaves and how he might be expected to behave implication and inference do their work.

The sight of a ruler so confused as to who he is and what he is doing when he chooses how to dispose of his wife and his much loved son, is eloquent advocacy for the view that the prince should not be *legibus solutus*, free from anterior legal constraints, and a chilling reminder that a will unconstrained can make tyrants of rulers. If there is any possibility at the end of the play – as there must be – that the Duke is acting not as the instrument of divine justice and the law of the state, as he claims, but as the aggrieved husband and father, then his two gruesome acts of execution unequivocally become acts of murder and the Duke forfeits all legitimacy. This brutal conflation of domestic and political worlds – ideologically interconnected in that the husband and father is *in loco regis* within the family – is a paradigm for those very pressures within and upon the individual who represents the state which make it absolutely imperative that his will be not law. The play's political reach extends well beyond its implied reference through the Duke's whoring activities at the beginning of the work to the young Philip IV's sexual adventures under the tutelage of Olivares in the capital a decade before. But this invocation of the earliest scandal of Olivares's *privanza* might well be Lope's way of releasing the work's political charge – by no means dominant in this extremely complex and subtle play, but strongly present nonetheless. Olivares, 'whose reverence' in Elliott's words, 'for the mystery of Spanish kingship was almost overwhelming',[18] dedicated himself to the exaltation of a monarch who, as the Planet King, came nearer to being perceived as an absoute ruler than any other monarch in Spanish history. Not all his subjects by any means gave unthinking credence to this exalted image, though few were as bold as don Fernando de Acevedo, President of the Council of Castile, who on one occasion, when the young Philip tried to dispose arbitrarily of a position at court, caused him to blush by rebuking him thus: 'No, sire, Your Majesty is not able to do everything you want in your kingdom. You would do well to remember that you can alienate nothing in it – not even this post, however insignificant, because it has been agreed by compact with the realm' – a timely lesson, as Elliott observes, in constitutionalism. Court theatre and court poetry lavishly employed and propagated the values and language of absolutism, and a glittering court life, orchestrated by Olivares, provided an aura of brilliance calculated to glorify the figure at its centre. As the years went by, however, criticism of Olivares and by extension of Philip for allowing him his head grew, and by the early thirties – Lope's play was written in 1631 – enough had happened in Lope's life, or rather not enough had happened, as we have already seen, to give him a decidedly jaundiced view of all-powerful, all-giving, God-like kings. *El castigo sin venganza*, is, like *El Duque de Viseo*, a reminder that rulers can behave so badly that the Roman jurist Ulpian's famous maxim that 'quod principi placuit legis habet vicem' – the ruler's will has force of law – is not a sound basis for successful government.

La estrella de Sevilla (?)

El Duque de Viseo and *El castigo sin venganza* both show that there is a boundary between reason of state and the ethically unacceptable which must not be crossed. At the same time *El Duque de Viseo* overtly and *El castigo sin venganza* by implication constitute a devastating critique of the unaccountable ruler. There is in the *comedia* canon another greatly admired tragedy which constitutes a memorable dissection of both reason of state and absolutism – *La estrella de Sevilla*.[19] The text has survived in two different version, a shorter one published under Lope's name as a *suelta* in the mid-seventeenth century and a longer one attributed to 'Cardenio' which appeared in a printed collection of plays in the 1630s. Traditionally the play has been assumed to have been written by Lope. From the end of the nineteenth century, however,

[18] *The Count-Duke of Olivares: The Statesman in an Age of Decline* (New Haven/London: Yale University Press, 1986), 171.

[19] An earlier version of what follows appears in *Heavenly Bodies: The Realms of 'La estrella de Sevilla'*, ed. Frederick A. de Armas (Lewisburg: Bucknell University Press, 1996), 76–91.

doubts began to be expressed about the integrity of the text and its authorship and the debate still continues. In 1931 S.E. Leavitt proposed a little-known playwright by the name of Andrés de Claramonte as the author; in the 1980s Alfredo Rodríguez López-Vázquez argued Claramonte's case more forcefully and in 1991 he published an edition of the play under Claramonte's name. Other contenders for authorship have been Tirso de Molina, Ruiz de Alarcón and Vélez de Guevara. None of the arguments in favour of any of these dramatists has been conclusive and even now none commands general assent amongst *comedia* specialists, but substantial doubts have been sown in the minds of most about the safety of continuing to think that Lope did indeed write the play. I am an agnostic in the matter. The play's metrical pattern persuaded Morley and Bruerton that the play was not Lope's,[20] and it is difficult to believe that Lope was responsible for the play in the form in which it has come down to us. It is characterized by a superbly compelling story, by an extremely well-developed feel for the telling dramatic scene, and by a magnificent sense of tragedy that exactly establishes the fine balance between sympathy, outrage and reluctant acceptance which is necessary to tragedy's emotional complexity – all features of Lope's theatre, as *El Duque de Viseo* and *El castigo sin venganza* illustrate. But the verse is at times wretched, the dialogue repetitive, the seaming clumsy – sins of which Lope, great poet and dramatic craftsman that he was, would have been incapable, certainly after his earliest years as a playwright. This does not mean, however, that he might not have written an original version of the play. Many Golden-Age plays have survived in a corrupt state, many were reworked, many were even pirated by being recreated from memory after a performance. Lope constantly complained that his work was being stolen and reused or recast. What is absolutely clear is that whoever conceived the play was no third-rate dramatist. What is also perfectly clear to me is that there is nothing about the content of the play which suggests it could not have been written by him. López-Vázquez, in discussing in relation to the play's authorship the relative merits of Claramonte and Vélez de Guevara, mentions 'the vigorous construction of the plot and the potent sense of tragedy and of political denunciation in the work',[21] which in his view place them very close; he then rules against Vélez on the grounds that he was the better versifier. But as we have just seen, particularly perhaps in *El Duque de Viseo*, Lope meets not only the first two of López-Vázquez's criteria – constructive vigour and tragic power

20 *The Chronology of Lope de Vega's 'Comedias'*, 284–5.

21 'The Analysis of Authorship: A Methodology', *Heavenly Bodies. The Realms of 'La estrella de Sevilla'*, 195–205. López-Vázquez here argues in favour of Claramonte's authorship on the basis of a classical citation index which compares the frequency of specific classical allusions in the text with their rate of occurrence in representative works by other contenders. He does not submit any plays by Lope to the test because he does not consider him to be in the running.

– but the third – trenchant political criticism – as well. The political matters the play explores and the political points it argues are entirely of a piece with the concerns and judgements that we have seen at work in plays indisputably written by him, and the techniques of criticism used are consistent with those he favoured. This, therefore, is my justification for discussing it here, in spite of the question mark that hangs over it: its political identity argues for rather than against its traditional attribution to Lope de Vega, or at least for Lope's possible authorship of an original on which the play as we now know it was based.

For all its medieval setting, the dramatic business of *La estrella de Sevilla* places it at the heart of the two great and interconnected political issues of the Early Modern period that I have been considering. Whereas the nature of events and the character of the king in *El Duque de Viseo* bring absolutism into sharper focus, *La estrella de Sevilla* reserves its closest scrutiny for the larger and even more controversial matter of the relationship between the political and the ethical spheres, a question forced upon the new national monarchies of Europe by the views on political expediency expressed by Machiavelli in his enormously influential treatise *Il principe*, of 1513.[22] It is worth, therefore, at this juncture, looking a little more closely at how the idea of reason of state fared in Spain. Machiavelli's argument was that the virtues could legitimately yield to the best interests of the ruler or the community, that a morally reprehensible course of action could be justifiably undertaken for political ends – a view vehemently rejected by Erasmus in *The Education of a Christian Prince*, which insisted that justice must never be sacrificed even to life, realm or religion. In Spain as elsewhere in the sixteenth century, Machiavelli's privileging of politics at the expense of ethics and what was seen as his demotion of religion to the status of instrument of state earned him the reputation of devil incarnate and his philosophy the opprobrium of full-blown atheism. Spanish humanists and Jesuits condemned his godlessness, which ensured his works a place on the papal Index of prohibited books of 1557, and Counter-Reformation theorists in general then attacked reason of state and its defenders, coupling Luther and Machiavelli as the two founding fathers of the impious modern state.[23] In 1595 in his *Tratado de la religión y virtudes que debe tener el príncipe cristiano* Rivadeneyra launched Spain's first full-scale attack on Machiavellianism and reason of state, to be followed by, among others, Mariana (1599), Márquez (1612), Santa María (1615), López Bravo (1616), Claudio Clemente with his tellingly named

22 See the edition by Quentin Skinner and Russell Price (Cambridge: Cambridge University Press, 1988); chapters 14–21 were those that attracted most attention, chapter 18, 'How Rulers Should Keep their Promises', being the most notorious.

23 See Quentin Skinner, *The Foundations of Modern Political Thought*, 2 vols, vol.2, *The Age of Reformation* (Cambridge: Cambridge University Press, 1978), 143.

Maquiavelo degollado (1628),[24] Salvador de Mallea (1646) and Blázquez Mayoralgo (1646), not to forget Quevedo's virulent onslaught in his *Política de Dios y gobierno de Cristo* (1615, pub.1635).[25] In *El Duque de Viseo*, written in the early years of the seventeenth century, reason of state is referred to by don Egas, as we saw, as something 'que muchas veces el demonio inventa'. Full-blown Machiavellianism never did acquire any self-confessed converts in Spain, as one might expect, although a few commentators such as Antonio Pérez and Arias Montano are sometimes regarded as almost openly Machiavellian.[26] Even in Spain, however, the uncomfortable conviction gradually grew that the simple equivalences of the past could no longer cope with the political complexities of the modern world. Christian virtue was essential in a prince, but it was now perceived to be no longer enough.

As interest in the concept of statecraft grew, therefore, the idea of reason of state began to slough its association with the Italian anti-Christ and to acquire a more acceptable image. Many purportedly anti-Machiavellian tracts are themselves testimony to the inroads Machiavelli had made on political thinking. The simulations and fraud that Spain connected with Machiavelli and with what became known as false reason of state were still unequivocally refuted – the sphere of the political could and should never function independently of morality – but their place was taken by an ethical version of reason of state connected with the convenient notion of strategic concealment or dissimulation, a stance considered entirely suited to the awe-inspiring remoteness of majesty increasingly cultivated by the Spanish Crown. Those searching for such a compromise solution drew authoritative support from the contemporary intellectual enthusiasm – which in Spain went back to Luis Vives – for the classical historian Tacitus, who was regarded by foes and followers alike as weaving into his writings the very essence of statecraft. They established in Spain the seam of thought known as Tacitism, *tacitismo*, which enshrined history along with nature and psychology – the influence upon historical events of the individual character – as a flexible and pragmatic model

24 The original Latin text, *Machiavelisimus Jugulatus*, was published in 1628, the Spanish translation in 1637.

25 See the edition by J.O. Crosby (Madrid: Castalia, 1966), 173.

26 For Machiavelli, see, for example, Skinner, *The Foundations of Modern Political Thought*; and more specifically Sydney Anglo, *Machiavelli: A Dissection* (London: Victor Gollanz, 1969). For Machiavellianism in Spain, see Recaredo F. de Velasco, *Referencias y transcripciones para la historia de la literatura política en España* (Madrid: Editorial Reus, 1925); Maravall, *La teoría española del estado* and *Estudios de historia del pensamiento español*; Abellán, *Historia crítica del pensamiento español*, vol.2, *La edad de Oro (Siglo XVI)*, and vol.3, *Del Barroco a la Ilustración (Siglos XVII y XVIII)*; and J.A. Fernández-Santamaría, *Reason of State and Statecraft in Spanish Political Thought, 1595–1640* (Lanham, Md.: University Press of America, 1982).

for the political life of the nation.[27] Tacitism naturally did not go uncriticized by the religious ethicists – it took its authority after all from a pagan and did not privilege moral exemplariness at all, let alone Christian principle. Many of its opponents did not bother to differentiate between Machiavelli and the *políticos* on the one hand and the *tacitistas* on the other[28] – Salas y Barbadillo mentions Tacitus, Machiavelli and Bodin all in the same breath in his *Coronas del Parnaso*, 1635. But by 1640 the Christian ideal of the prince had ineluctably become a politico-Christian ideal, as the title of Saavedra Fajardo's treatise *Idea de un príncipe político-cristiano*, as has been observed earlier, shows. The *aprobación* by Fray Pedro Cuenca y Cárdenas, which praises the erudition with which 'la razón de estado se adorna' in the treatise, is a vivid indication that the concept of reason of state had been sanitized and that even in Spain entrenched thinking had moved on. In the forty-five years between Rivadeneyra's *Príncipe cristiano*, with its reference to 'la falsa y perniciosa razón de estado' and Saavedra Fajardo's *Príncipe político-cristiano* the idea that the good governance of the state required more than the application of Christian principle had been assimilated into Spanish thought.

La estrella de Sevilla's nineteenth-century critics, or rather the critics of the *refundición* of the play by Cándido María Trigueros, *Sancho Ortiz de las Roelas*, were reduced to moral outrage by the behaviour of don Sancho, the man who undertakes to kill on the order of his king without knowing whom or exactly why (a situation similar to the one Federico is placed in at the end of *El castigo sin venganza*). One of them, Alberto Lista, observed: 'Para hacer interesante a Ortiz sería necesario que su manera de sentir fuese conforme a la razón o los afectos comunes de los hombres o, por lo menos, una preocupación propia de la época a que se refiere la acción del drama.'[29] It is not clear why Lista considered the concerns of the thirteenth century, in which the action is ostensibly set although it has no obvious historical source,

27 For *tacitismo* see Maravall, *La teoría española del estado* and *Estudios de historia del pensamiento español*; Francisco Sanmartín Boncompte, *Tácito en España* (Barcelona: Consejo Superior de Investigaciones Científicas, 1951); E. Tierno Galván, 'El tacitismo en las doctrinas políticas del Siglo de Oro español', *Escritos 1950–60* (Madrid: Ed. Tecnos, 1971); André Joucl-Ruau, *Le Tacitisme de Saavedra Fajardo*; Fernández-Santamaría, *Reason of State and Statecraft in Spanish Political Thought*; Abellán, *Historia crítica del pensamiento español,* vol.3, *Del Barroco a la Ilustración*. Blázquez Mayoralgo called Tacitus the father of the *políticos* and Machiavelli their captain (Fernández-Santamaría, 77 n.23). Among the *tacitistas* (open and closet) are normally included Álamos de Barrientos, Narbona, Setanti, Ceballos, Ramírez de Prado, Mártir Rizo, Antonio de Herrera, Antonio de Fuertes y Biota, Saavedra Fajardo and Gracián.

28 *Políticos* was the name given political commentators thought to be influenced by the political atheism of Machiavelli; *estadistas* was the neutral term normally used for those versed in the theory of state.

29 See Menéndez y Pelayo's *Observaciones preliminares* to the play in *Obras de Lope de Vega*, Real Academia Española, IX (Madrid, 1899), liii.

more interesting or valid than seventeenth-century concerns – it is an example, perhaps, of the anti-imperialist sentiment the Golden-Age theatre fell foul of in the later nineteenth century – but of course the *comedia* was not in the business of dramatizing the historical problems of the distant past, except in so far as they had any bearing upon the present. As we have seen, it habitually projected seventeenth-century preoccupations about kingship upon the Middle Ages. Medieval dynastic leaders were judged against Renaissance ideas of the king as the embodiment of the state and found wanting. But the comparison produced in the process a critique of contemporary monarchy as well: as we repeatedly saw in chapters 3 and 4, the superimposition of contemporary ideals upon a previous age was an enabling stratagem that allowed misgiving about contemporary realities to be aired.

In the context of traditional perceptions of kingship *La estrella de Sevilla* can be seen, and no doubt was seen by the politically unaware in the audience, in terms of personal loyalty and obedience to the monarch, honour, keeping the faith, and so on. But in the context of contemporary Spain and Europe the play takes on a much wider political dimension – not merely the question of absolutism, of the king's will being paramount whatever the circumstances, but of the ethical problems created by giving priority to the principle of political necessity. The state, that is the king – for the theory of state was at the time inseparable from the figure of the prince – comes before all else. To neglect this dimension of the play is to miss the hard thrust of its contemporary relevance and to misconceive, as did Lista and other nineteenth-century critics, the full nature of its dramatic impact and reception. Trigueros himself put his finger on the powerful appeal exerted by the work when he placed Sancho's dilemma at the heart of the suspense it generates: '¿Executará Sancho Ortiz su encargo? ¿Cuál será su suerte?' The dilemma is precisely that created by the opposing values of loyalty to the sovereign – invoked here in the name of political necessity – and individual conscience, between the interests of the republic and Christian ethics. It is the idea of *lèse-majesté*, an offence against the king as the embodiment of the state, which instantly overcomes Sancho's reluctance to kill an unknown man and which is deliberately invoked by the King in the knowledge that it will have this effect.

The story of the play is a brutally simple formulation of the dilemma posed by the role of ethics in politics, but herein lies its impact and its lasting grip on our imagination. For the pull of opposing allegiances is one we all instinctively recognize. The claims made upon human loyalty by nation or leader have traditionally made of spying, treason, military desertion, draft evasion and cowardice in battle, heinous crimes or at least shameful acts and have created appalling dilemmas for individuals caught in the crossfire of their loyalty to the nation and their loyalty to their own conscience or to those they love. The fact that the state wields punitive powers is a complication that inevitably reinforces its claims, but of course society in complicity with the state employs no less effective psychological weapons such as shame, humiliation, dishonour. Kings have always exerted a special influence upon the behaviour of the individual, as the anthropologist Julian Pitt-Rivers pointed out: 'The respect felt for the monarch possesses something of the same power to render sacred as the reverence for the Divine: in paying this respect, we abnegate our right to question and bind ourselves to accept what might otherwise appear to us wrong. The arbitrary nature of sacred power extends beyond the frontiers of religion.'[30] This special feeling is precisely what is at work in *La estrella de Sevilla*, what the King shamelessly and cynically exploits in order to conceal, in the name of political necessity, behaviour inappropriate in a prince. That this special feeling is ruptured in *El Duque de Viseo* to the extent that four noblemen refuse point blank to do the King's bidding when he orders each of them in turn to kill Viseo, is the play's most trenchant single statement on what he represents.

In *La estrella de Sevilla* the use of *force majeure* and the privileging of reason of state lead, as they do in *El Duque de Viseo,* to a human tragedy that offends against natural law – man's instinctive, God-given sense of what is reasonable and just. The ending here too, overturning as it does *comedia* convention and normal audience expectation – love as we know is supposed to conquer all – may be taken as an invitation to dissent. Its very title, rather than perversely suggesting a thematic bias towards Estrella that is at odds with the centrality of Sancho's dilemma, as Trigueros thought – which is why he suppressed Act I and part of Act II and renamed the play in his *refundición* – images the way in which the play concentrates the political and moral tensions to maximize their tragic effect. For it is in Estrella that the clash between the two opposing sets of values achieves full human impact – her lover kills her brother and she as a consequence loses both. Hers is arguably the most poignant situation of all: Busto is killed, Sancho kills on the order of his king, but it is she who renounces an impossible happiness, to be haunted the rest of her life by the ghost of what might have been.[31] Yet the handling of this issue in the play is not without its complexities. Like *El Duque de Viseo* and *El castigo sin venganza* it reflects at once the convictions and uncertainties of contemporary Spanish thought on the matter of how the reason-of-state argument related to Christian ideas of good and evil. The threat to the throne in *El Duque de Viseo* may be a figment of two men's imagination, but the question of obedience to an unjust monarch troubles the minds of every other character in the play.

Central to *La estrella de Sevilla*'s formulation of the problem is the matter

30 *The Fate of Shechem or The Politics of Sex: Essays in the Anthropology of the Mediterranean* (Cambridge: Cambridge University Press, 1977), 15.

31 She is sacrificed on the altar of political expediency no less than Inés in that other deeply tragic dramatization of the reason of state principle, Vélez de Guevara's *Reinar después de morir*.

of the prince's two identities: not, as has been explained earlier, the contemporary conception of the monarch as being human by nature and divine by grace – which was not an idea promoted by Spanish political philosophy – nor the somewhat bizarre English concept of the king's two bodies, the body natural and the body politic, but the play between the private and public person based upon the perception that the king was human by nature but suprahuman by role. King Sancho el Bravo presents the familiar figure of a redoubtable leader and warrior whose lack of other virtues necessary to kingship is revealed in his sexual misconduct. The conversation he initiates with his despicable side kick don Arias, which reviews Seville's pretty women as if they were mares at a horse fair, sets the tone of his behaviour at the very beginning of the play, creating expectations of unkingliness only too soon confirmed by the way in which he distorts justice, judgement, liberality and prudence in his campaign to suborn and dishonour a loyal and worthy subject. This behaviour reaches the very nadir of cynicism when, about to buy his way into Estrella's bed, he declares 'Divina cosa es reinar' (II, 929)[32] – it is an emblematic moment in which the blasphemous misapplication of the rhetoric of kingship inevitably leads to the total withdrawal of our respect. The real problem posed by *La estrella de Sevilla*, however, is rather knottier than the dichotomy presented by the private person within the public persona. It is whether in the last analysis it is actually possible to distinguish in a king between the personal and the public, between the individual and the state he embodies. The Duke of Ferrara in *El castigo sin venganza*, faced with this very conundrum, spectacularly fails to solve it.

The play at first sight seems to argue a strong and convincing case against reason of state and for morality. It does this by exposing reason of state as the all too convenient instrument of vice. The King trades on the loyalty Sancho owes him, a proper act only if he himself were behaving as a king should. But of course it is the King himself who puts the interests of the state at risk in the first place. In his passion for Estrella he scorns all thought of reputation (Act I, 47–34). He invokes the principle of political necessity initially in order to legitimate behaviour aimed not at protecting the realm from some danger beyond his control, but at concealing his own sexual unruliness and exacting revenge upon the man who dared thwart him (Act II, 1103–4). He has lost sight of the fact that power must be subject to voluntary restraints if tyranny is to be avoided, as Sancho points out:

> Que si un brazo poderoso
> no se vence en lo que puede,
> siempre será riguroso. (Act II, 1492–4)

[32] Textual references are to the edition of the play in *Diez comedias del Siglo de Oro*, ed. José Martel and Hymen Alpern, revised by Leonard Mades (New York: Harper & Row, 1968, second edn).

To Busto's observation that the King's law ought not to trample on justice, Sancho realistically and prophetically replies:

> Si el rey la quiere torcer
> ¿quién fuerza le podrá hacer,
> aviendo interés o gusto? (Act I, 648–50)

The assumption here of a coincidence of public authority and private will is buttressed by the conventional notion that a king can never give offense – a notion that largely determines the play-king's behaviour. Mariana and other theorists of the day, however, pointing to the realities of history, warned princes against the legitimate anger of the people, an anger we see at work, of course, in Busto Tabera.[33] Saavedra Fajardo (*Empresa* VIII), approaching the same problem by a different route, advised kings never to revenge offences directed at them personally rather than at the throne, so that they would not incite hatred by invoking the enormous power at their disposal in order to deal with them – which is exactly what our play-king does. The fact that the word *ley* is used in the play to denote now the King's will, now the idea of codified rules of government, is in itself an interesting indicator of the fusion of man and role in the minds of the characters (Act II, 1751–4, for example). The confusion within the King himself between his two identities is encapsulated very neatly in the confrontation scene with Busto, but it lies at the heart of the entire play and is indeed articulated by the King himself at one point:

> y aunque más me resistí,
> las naturales acciones
> con que hombre nací
> del decoro me sacaron
> que pide mi Majestad. (Act II, 1172–6)

Busto is fully conscious of the respect owed a king: when the King bids him rise he remarks,

> Bien estoy ansí
> que, si el Rey se ha de tratar
> como a santo en el altar
> digno lugar escogí. (Act I, 289–92)

Lope's familiar technique of politeness, of diplomatic double-speak, will be instantly recognizable. Here and elsewhere the playwright anticipates the possibility of giving offence by dressing criticism in the verbal paraphernalia of devotion – rhetoric guards against risk. Here too, as in *El Duque de Viseo*,

[33] *Del rey*, I, 6, 112.

the weight of that 'si', conditional rather than assumptive, is determined by the vivid contrast between the idea and the reality. This is one of many references to kings and kingship in the play – from Busto, Sancho, Estrella, the *alcaldes* and Clarindo – which provide the ideological context in which a specific king's actions are to be judged. A particularly notable example is the confrontation in Act II between the King and Busto in Busto's house which the King has entered in pursuit of Estrella – an extremely delicate situation for Busto to deal with as guardian of the family honour. Busto reprimands the King by pretending not to have recognized him and maintaining he cannot be the King (as the intruder maintains to save his skin) because kings just do not behave in this way. The scene and the particularly literal application of the strategy of *decir sin decir* are both highly reminiscent of that in Lope's *El servir con mala estrella* where Tello too surprises the King secretly visiting his sister. The King, as we saw, 'freezes', whereupon Tello takes his cue and pretends that what he is looking at is a portrait. He nonetheless observes, as if to the air, that it would have been more suitable had the King had himself painted as a warrior rather than as a gallant visiting a lady's house. In both plays, respect is observed, danger is skirted, but what needs to be said is said. Intertextual borrowing was rife in the *comedia*, so it would be unwise to make too much of the similarity, but the overlap of the two titles, which is more likely, one would have thought, to have triggered the same author's memory rather than a different one's, makes of it an interesting coincidence. Sancho the man is confronted with the idea and reality of Sancho the king (Act II, 1061–4), and at one point in the scene Busto adopts the *tú* form of address to hammer his point home (a man who conducts himself thus cannot be a king) before reverting to *vos* out of respect for the intruder's real station. Once the King has infringed upon Busto's sphere of responsibility – 'En mi casa estoy/ y en ella yo he de mandar' (Act II, 999–1000) – Busto at least is in no doubt as to the absolute necessity to oppose vice even in a monarch. In order to send him the message that Seville will not tolerate tyrants, he is prepared to place the King's reputation at risk, publicizing his disreputable behaviour by means of poor Natilde the suborned maid's hanged corpse with the royal warrant in its grasp – an act the King fears might incite a rebellion against him.

The reason of state argument essentially comes into play on two crucial occasions. First, Busto Tabera must be killed and killed secretly in order to keep the whole affair quiet and protect the King's reputation. The King is explicit on this point. In the light of the King's subsequent worries about an uprising in Seville, to this motive is then by implication added the need to guarantee public order. The argument is not so very different from the Duke's in *El castigo sin venganza*. Relevant to the second reason is the problematical matter of whether Busto's rash act really does put the state at risk, that is whether it constitutes *lèse-majesté* as the King maintains, or whether this is merely another piece of cynical manipulation on the King's part. The technical point is probably arguable, but dramatically the King's responsibility for all that has thus far happened, his petty impulse to revenge (which ends up conflating the ideas of dishonour and *lèse-majesté*) for what he considers Busto's impertinent resistance to his sexual depredations, and his intention to deceive Estrella's lover Sancho, all undoubtedly affect the audience's perception of the situation and make death seem a punishment inappropriate to the crime. It is not insignificant, however, as we shall see, that once Sancho is apprised of the supposed nature of the crime, his automatic acceptance of the idea of a secret execution is entirely logical – if the crime is treason, then the King's dishonour would only compound it. So reasons the Duke of Ferrara as well.

Later on, and for the same reasons, the King cannot keep his word and own up to his responsibility for Busto's murder in order to save Sancho from being punished for the crime. This time the King spells out the possible consequences should his behaviour become known: he would be denounced as a tyrant by his deposed father, Alfonso X (condemning himself out of his own mouth by conceding that his behaviour has been tyrannical) and lose the Pope's support in his struggle to contest his young nephew's claim to the throne. The ill-considered behaviour that has dragged the king from the start into a bog of dishonesty, cunning and evasion thus culminates in the worst sin of all – not the murder, which can be rationalized as execution, but the unwillingness to keep faith. Just as Sancho is bound by his word to kill Busto, even when he knows who his target is, so the King – who regards his word as law – is all the more committed to come to Sancho's aid. It was his belief in the word of a king that caused Sancho earlier on to refuse to accept from the King a deed accepting responsibility for Busto's death should Sancho ever need to exonerate himself, an eventuality clearly considered by the King to be extremely remote. Keeping faith is more important than a man's life. Even the repellent don Arias, in Machiavellian terms the fox to King Sancho's lion,[34] who urges him on to crime, draws the line at reneguing on a solemn promise (Act III, 2660–81). The King's reluctance to grasp this nettle, the revelation that he made a promise he had little thought of keeping, his shabby opportunistic attempts to the very last to achieve the same end by other means, serve finally to render contemptible an already disreputable royal character. Little wonder that in restoration France the first performance of Pierre Lebrun's *Le Cid d'Andalousie*, which was partly based on *La estrella de Sevilla*, was delayed because the French authorities objected to its portrayal of royal misbehaviour.[35] In seventeenth-century Spain such portrayals were only too familiar.

Morality and honour, of course, prescribe very different behaviour from

[34] The qualities of the fox and the lion were seen by Machiavelli as being esssential to the effective prince (*Il principe*, chap.18).

[35] See Menendez y Pelayo's *Observaciones preliminares*, lxvii.

reason of state. They rule out in the first place the aggressive sexual behaviour that knowingly insults the integrity and jeopardizes the reputation and happiness of two scions of a noble family. But even allowing for the fact that kings are men and make mistakes, they subsequently proscribe the murder of an innocent man, the deceitful manoeuvres and subterfuges adopted to cover it up, and the blatant evasion of responsibility that puts another man's life at risk – all actions taken in the name of political necessity.

This ignoble behaviour and the blighted lives of the three young people caught up in it strongly signal the dangers inherent in a political principle which ignores morality and which may be too readily invoked to justify wrong-doing. The play's resolution convinces us that good ends do not justify evil means, that 'no se ha de hacer lo injusto/ porque fue razón de estado', as the Count points out to the King in Lope's *La inocente sangre*. There is, however, one intractable element in this conclusion. The King is eventually forced by circumstances to admit that the order to kill Busto came from him. And in the event the step he found so difficult to take has absolutely no consequences for himself. Why? Because it is automatically assumed by Farfán de Ribera and seemingly all other uninformed recipients of the news that, if the King ordered Busto's execution, it must have been with good cause. No questions are asked and Busto, like Federico in *El castigo sin venganza*, goes to his grave branded as at worst a traitor, at best a criminal. Sancho's confident assertion to the King – 'y gana más el que muere/ a traición que el que le mata' (Act II, 1578–9) – may be a telling epitaph for the play, but within the action it is sadly not true. Only the King himself, don Arias, Estrella, don Sancho and the audience are left in possession of the fact that Busto was killed for doing what heads of households were required to do, trying to protect his family and their reputation. His misfortune was in having in his King an adversary who would or could brook no opposition. Is this another of the play's poignant dimensions? Is it a further subversion of absolutism? Or is it, in addition perhaps to both these two, the manifestation of a genuine hesitation over the problem of identifying the point where personal responsibility ends and the public good begins, where morality necessarily gives way to political necessity? The King has finally revealed enough to keep his word, free Sancho and satisfy his subjects. To reveal more would have exonerated Busto, but only at the price of tarnishing the King's own reputation.

The crucial question is whether the reputation of a king constitutes a reason of state sufficiently pressing to justify the death and disgrace of an innocent man (and possibly two innocent men), or at least to excuse the deed once it is done. The text seems to be trying to establish a discrimination here. One of the points made by this tragedy as well as by Lope's king-plays is that the private person cannot ultimately be dissociated from the public – the private has to reflect the public role precisely because the public is affected by the private. The truth of this is still being lived and pondered by princes and presidents today. The fact that the King himself has put his reputation at risk is not only deeply reprehensible but damaging to the state; once that act has been committed, however, the protection of his reputation can only be in the interests of the state. The King has been revealed to be unworthy of rule, absolutism has been shown to threaten the freedom of the subject to act responsibly and morally, but the stage of damage limitation has been reached. The nobles at the end of *El Duque de Viseo* also acknowledge this, with their silence. We must not underestimate what is at issue here. As we saw in chapter 1 the idea of reputation had become a key factor in seventeenth-century political thought and, by the measure of Saavedra Fajardo's statement that 'Los imperios se conservan con su misma autoridad y reputación',[36] the sacrifice of Busto's reputation is a sacrifice well made. On 22 May 1508 Ferdinand the Catholic wrote a letter to his nephew the Conde de Ribagorza, then Viceroy of Naples, reprimanding him for not responding to a papal brief that infringed upon his royal authority by hanging the clerk who delivered it. 113 years later, the self-same Quevedo who in his *Política de Dios* inveighs so violently against reason of state and its founder, and denounces Tacitus as a *bellaco*, makes the following observation in an apologia to the letter: 'La conservación de la jurisdicción y reputación ni ha de considerar dudas, ni tener respetos, ni detenerse en elegir medios.'[37] Such would seem to be the unpalatable logic of the play's final unravelling. Since the king embodies the sovereignty of the state, the protection of his image – whatever the reality – necessarily constitutes reason of state, and this is precisely why Rivadeneyra and others so distrusted it. Leave ethics out of politics and there are no constraints on behaviour inappropriate to either man or king. Busto's death was not only unnecessary – it was not the only way out consistent with the good of the realm – but against justice, the foundation stone of all successful government, 'la madre y ama de los imperios' in López Bravo's words (*Del rey*, 114), and the first duty of those responsible for it, as Farfán sternly points out (Act III, 2906–14). Whether Busto's attempt to publicize the King's behaviour consitutes treason or not, the decision to have him killed is taken by the King at don Arias's instigation before the sight of Natilde's corpse incites the King to fury. The murder itself and the deceitful measures taken to conceal the King's responsibility, therefore, on the evidence of the text and the response it invites, pass beyond the bounds of morality and honourable behaviour into the terrain of what was considered false reason of state. The King's economy with the truth at the end, on the other hand, would seem to constitute no more than the silence, the

36 *Empresa* XXI, 81. The fully elaborated point will be found in chapter 2. One has only to think of the way in which modern money markets respond to the slightest indication of a withdrawal of confidence to understand his reasoning.

37 'Advertencias disculpando los desabrimientos desta carta', *Del Rey don Fernando el Católico al Primer Virrey de Nápoles*, *Obras completas I: Obras en prosa* (Madrid: Aguilar, 1958), 704a.

dissimulation, that came in the seventeenth century to be regarded as expedient in the handling of political matters. The King's exhortation to Sancho, 'obrad, y callemos' (Act II, 1606), before the event may not be acceptable, but secrecy after the event is. In *El Duque de Viseo* the silence which closes the play is the silence of resignation, here it is the silence of concealment. Like Lope de Vega, the author of *La estrella de Sevilla* condemns evil committed in the name of reason of state but seems to acknowledge that it then has a claim in the containment of the damage that has been caused. As for the Maravallian assertion that the play (assumed to be Lope's) promotes absolute rule, however tyrannical and unjust – 'Lope en *La estrella de Sevilla* o en *El Duque de Viseo* desarrolla doctrinalmente la misma concepción de la cruel grandeza del absolutismo monárquico que, como observa Vossler, no permite ninguna rebeldía, ni la menor protesta de la libertad contra la injusta acción del rey' – Sancho's words when he is taken off to prison make nonsense of it:[38]

Yo, si atropello
mi gusto, guardo la ley:
esto, señor, es ser Rey [i.e. what ought to happen]
y esto, señor, es no serlo. [i.e. what is happening]
(Act II, 1871–4)

We too must make discriminations. The play is the story of the clash, played out within the parameters of individual lives, between two opposing value systems held in tension by the need to sustain the social and political system. That absolutism breeds opposition, that reason of state misapplied leads to injustice and tragedy, that a kingdom cannot be properly ruled by the will of its sovereign alone, that virtue and integrity must form the basis of just and effective government, that blind obedience to a ruler's will is dangerous – all these are as amply demonstrated here as they are in *El Duque de Viseo*. But so too is the recognition that political necessity dictates when the interests of the state at the highest level require it to do so. History, political belief and realism, as well as diplomacy, conspire to ensure that monarchy is re-inscribed and kings continue to rule at the end of such plays – playwrights such as Lope and the author of *La estrella de Sevilla* were, like their counterparts elsewhere in Europe, in the business of critiquing hereditary monarchy not suggesting that it should be abolished. In Spain the argument of necessity when it was applied was made to work for inherited legitimacy rather than against it – as it could do, of course, in the face of tyranny – not least because that system had provided Spain with a degree of political stability, as well as

38 See the section ascribed to Maravall, Blecua and Salomon in *Historia y crítica de la literatura española*, ed. Francisco Rico, III, *Siglos de Oro*: Barroco, ed. Bruce W. Wardropper (Barcelona: Editorial Crítica, 1983), 270.

power, unmatched in Europe. As we shall see in the next chapter, visions of alternative political systems were a strong incitement to opting for reform rather than revolution.

La estrella de Sevilla has generally been held to have been written in 1623, on the basis of an allusion to a sumptuary decree involving the wearing of ruffs published in that year.[39] López-Vázquez, in the conviction that the author was Claramonte, has suggested the earlier date of 1617 with a longer, updated version in 1623. The fact that the play seems not to have been performed or printed with any frequency and was not mentioned critically has given rise to the supposition that it reflects some political mystery involving Philip IV and was therefore discreetly forgotten. This is, of course, entirely possible, but it must be borne in mind that these circumstances apply to hundreds of Golden-Age plays because records are so patchy and so much information has been lost. That it is now considered a great play is irrelevant. Such judgements are subjective and in any case the conditions of production and preservation of *comedias* were no respecters of quality or even popularity. Autograph manuscripts of play-texts were often cut up to produce actors' copies. Only the most successful plays ran for as long as a fortnight, and which of them subsequently got published was a fairly arbitrary matter. Many were not published in their author's lifetime and even those published collections overseen by their authors were not always comprehensive. There was no copyright as such, playwrights handed over their manuscripts to actor-managers and often themselves lost track of what they had written. It seems unlikely, if there had been a prolonged conspiracy of silence, that the play would have been published in the 1630s. In general terms the play could have been written in the reign of either Philip III or Philip IV. Both régimes for obvious reasons spawned plays about kingship, favourites, the conduct of government, and the major political issues of absolutism and reason of state. Don Arias in *La estrella de Sevilla* could as easily be an attack on Rodrigo de Calderón as it could on Olivares. The arrival of a new reign could plausibly have been the invitation to write another dramatic mirror for princes but they were written throughout the old reign, and although Philip IV did share a fondness for women with King Sancho, we have seen that sexual unruliness was used time and again by Lope as an indicator of royal dysfunctionality during the reign of Philip III, whose conduct in that regard seems to have been beyond reproach. However, if we accept that the play was probably written in 1623, then its points of relevance and resemblance to the new reign are obvious, including the Arias-like role taken by Olivares in furthering his young sovereign's sexual adventures. Frederick de Armas has pointed out, furthermore, that both kings are the fourth of their name and that Arias's

39 See Ruth Lee Kennedy, 'La estrella de Sevilla, Reinterpreted', *Revista de Archivos, Bibliotecas y Museos* 78 (1975), 385–408.

ingratiating references to the King in terms of Jason and Hercules chime with the appropriation of these mythical heroes by the new régime in order to exalt and burnish the image of the king. The association between Hercules and Spanish kings was not a new one, but it was revived and extensively cultivated largely thanks to the efforts of Olivares. As for Jason, the association was an obvious one because Philip was born under the sign of Aries the ram and the Hapsburg monarchs of Europe all belonged to the Order of the Golden Fleece. In 1622 Lope de Vega, commissioned to write a celebratory work for the king's birthday had written a mythological play called *El vellocino de oro*.[40] There is a reinforcing link, too, between the reference in the play to Atlas and the association of Atlas with Olivares, the minister who carried the real burden of government on his shoulders. De Armas postulates that the political mystery that inspired the play was in fact the murder in that year of the Count of Villamediana, the flamboyant court poet, satirist and wit who wilfully lived on the edge of notoriety and had been expelled from court on several occasions during the previous reign. Rumour had it the king was implicated, variously because Villamediana was in love with the queen or because Villamediana in a court play he himself wrote for the same celebration, *La gloria de Niquea*, praises Philip by alluding indirectly to his love affair with one of the ladies of the court, Francisca de Tabara (note the close similarity to Estrella's surname Tabera), who took the part of Europa, abducted by Jupiter in the form of a bull.[41] It is difficult to believe that Philip would have had Villamediana murdered for such a reason, and in any case it is now generally accepted by historians that Villamediana's death was the result of a homosexual intrigue.[42] However there may well be a less sensational truth in the claim of a connection between incident and play. Rumour can be as fertile a source of play plots as fact, and the gossip that Philip's affair with Francisca de Tabara had led to the murder of the man who dared refer to it in public might readily have provided the point of departure for a play where a king's passion for an Estrella Tabera leads to the murder of the man who seeks to publicize his monarch's misbehaviour. The finished work's political reach, however, extends far beyond the specific historical moment, and its tragic power is generated by far more complex an approach to contemporary political tensions than the pointing of an accusatory finger. At this level, like *El Duque de Viseo,* it is best and most reliably understood as an attempt to come to terms with those conflictive values and realities

40 'The Mysteries of Canonicity', *Heavenly Bodies: The Realms of 'La estrella de Sevilla'*, 15–28, pp.19–20.

41 'The Mysteries of Canonicity', 20.

42 See J.H. Elliott, 'Philip IV of Spain: Prisoner of Ceremony', *The Courts of Europe: Politics, Patronage and Royalty, 1400–1800*, ed. A.G. Dickens (London: Thames and Hudson, 1977), 169–89, p.176; and R.A. Stradling, *Philip IV and the Government of Spain*, 51–2.

external to itself which, in uneasy combination, determined the way in which seventeenth-century monarchies adapted to changing circumstances and conducted their affairs.

7

POLITICAL ANTINOMIES: REBELS WITHIN THE SYSTEM

The Peasant Honour Trilogy

The plays which have dominated perception of Lope's political thinking are those that constitute the famous peasant honour trilogy, a label often dismissed as misleading, but convenient and meaningful nonetheless. The works in question – *Peribáñez y el Comendador de Ocaña*, *Fuenteovejuna*, and *El mejor alcalde el rey* – do not form a narrative triad nor are they the constituent parts of a single dramatic structure or vision. They are strikingly different dramatic and poetic creations. But they are related in that they represent a continuing preoccupation over some eighteen years with the same set of interconnected issues – rank, power and individual worth – dramatically activated and elaborated through recourse to the *comedia* staples of love and honour, in a rural setting where the stark contrasts and certainties of a feudal culture are shown beginning to yield to a more complex and nuanced view of human society. Although set at different times in Spanish history, the political ethos they present is essentially the turbulent transitional ethos of the Early Modern period, with old allegiances and unquestioned assumptions challenged though not yet displaced by different ways of seeing and understanding. And although at the end of each play disruption is averted and dissent neutralized – and here is where the iconic person of the monarch appropriates the action – such is the potency of the plot and the writing that the sense of a world now substantially and forever different from the old is unmistakable. This difference has little if anything, I think, to do with any anachronistic application of modern perspectives, although historical hindsight inevitably lends sharper definition to implications carried by the texts, and everything to do with a recognition of that sense of combined gain and loss with which human beings in all periods tend to experience great change. The necessary end to feudal tyranny is also the end of the rural idyll. The hierarchical structures seen by Church fathers and most Renaissance political theorists alike as legitimated by God, nature and necessity are admitted to be as flawed as those who control them. To suffer rape, to be driven to kill do violence to an innocence that can never be regained. Peribáñez and Casilda are separated, albeit temporarily, at the end by vindication and preferment, and will never quite recuperate the world they have lost.

Revisionist interpretation of the three works could clearly be foolishly anachronistic. Lope is preaching neither revolution nor mob rule; in order for *Fuenteovejuna* to be performed as a revolutionary play in the Soviet Union in the 1930s its ending had to be suppressed, thereby violating the essential identity of the work. On the other hand, it is in fact no less anachronistic to judge them by the simplistic application of the socio-political values and standards of the present day. To read these plays merely as formulaic reaffirmations of a political system perceived as unproblematical provided that small local difficulties are swept away, is to overlook the sensitivities of the time in which they were written and to ignore the shadings of both dramatic text and historical context. It stems from too ready an application of a Renaissance ideology deemed to be monolithic and all-pervasive by such as Tillyard, but now realized to represent only a very partial picture of the realities of Early Modern thought and values.

It is the ruptures and dissonances in the expected patterns of representation and signification which are of interest, not the expected patterns themselves; excoriating seventeenth-century playwrights for not thinking like twentieth-century liberals is a sterile exercise at best. In these texts the monarch unequivocally, if not always unproblematically, assumes at the last his ideal role as 'locus and source of power and as master signifier',[1] as arbiter and judge, as guarantor of harmony and peace. But there are nonetheless severe limitations to this vision: we see that there is no reward without loss (*Peribáñez*), that there is no justice without violence (*Fuenteovejuna*, *El mejor alcalde*), that violence itself is endemic in life and is only controlled by being harnessed to the cause of order. The plays appear to ratify the established order, but their endings are curiously troubled, marked by ironies, violence, torture, the lingering spectre of revolt, of unruliness both at the bottom and near the top of society. Rebellion is overlooked, if not validated or even pardoned, peasants are ennobled and nobles are put to death, formerly decent men have paid for their crimes with their lives, in two cases only by breaking the law do the oppressed gain justice. Even in a world of romance where true love wins through and heroes and heroines ultimately assert themselves over what threatens their happiness, the cumulative reckoning here is far from romantic or ideal. Order in the world of the plays is a necessary compromise rather than an organizing principle, and harmony seems an elusive goal. Repression is seen to release energies which contain the potential for social upheaval, and significant battles are won in what conceivably at some future time might become a war.

All three plays, therefore, contribute to a process of political sensitization. All three, indeed, are in a very real sense political plays, a fact too often

[1] Francis Barker, *The Tremulous Private Body: Essays on Subjection* (London/New York: Methuen, 1984), 31.

obscured by their designation as plays about peasant honour.[2] They pose crucial questions about power and its abuse, about the relationship between power on the one hand and class relations and the good order of society on the other. They pose questions about individual freedoms and human dignity, about cultural values and different ways of perceiving the world and its operations, about the right of men and women to a life free of oppression by their social superiors, about how to cope with lawlessness when the feudal lord of law and order breaks the social contract and turns criminal. All three function as paradigmatic reminders that the past is over, that the unruly militancy and despotism of the medieval aristocracy cannot survive in the seventeenth century.

They can also be read as marking the age's growing realization that it could not afford to disregard the power of the *demos* – events such as the revolt against the Spanish Crown in Flanders and the royal assassinations in France sowed seeds of alarm which bear dramatic fruit in plays such as Calderón's *La vida es sueño*, with its vision of civil strife, and, less explicitly, in Lope's own *El castigo sin venganza*, where a prince lives in fear of both civil war and the judgement of his subjects. The three peasant plays argue that good order depends not on force, but on the contractual relationship between governors and governed. When lawlessness undermines the social hierarchy, disorder results and only the law, incarnate in the monarch, has the authority to impose solutions. The hierarchy is endangered by the inability to recognize that it depends on the consent of willing participants, that this consent depends in its turn both on the social contract's being observed and on the vigilance of the Crown itself and the proper exercise of its own power. Honour, of course, plays its part. Honour was a concept which constituted man as a social being located within a particular social stratum, although its articulation in these three plays challenges purely social definitions of honour and its exclusivist association with rank. It inevitably had a political dimension in that its operating model was the patriarchal model of monarchy itself, with the monarch as both epitome and protector of the honour of the state.[3] Here in these plays we see the model at risk of collapse, leading in *Fuenteovejuna* to peasant revolt, in *El mejor alcalde el rey* to aristocratic insubordination, in *Peribáñez* to individual rebellion across class barriers – all

2 The political dimension of *Fuenteovejuna,* of course, containing as it does a popular uprising, has for some time now been acknowledged and discussed, notably by Javier Herrero, 'The New Monarchy: A Structural Interpretation of *Fuenteovejuna*', *Revista Hispánica Moderna* 36 (1970–71), 173–85; Robin Carter, '*Fuenteovejuna* and Tyranny: Some Problems of Linking Drama with Political Theory', *Forum for Modern Language Studies* 23 (1977), 313–36; and William R. Blue, 'The Politics of Lope's *Fuenteovejuna*', *Hispanic Review* 59 (1991), 293–313.

3 McKendrick, 'Calderón and the Politics of Honour', *The 'Comedia' in the Age of Calderón: Studies in Honour of Albert Sloman, Bulletin of Hispanic Studies* 70 (1993), 135–46.

suggestive of a radical questioning of entrenched and complacent political assumptions, albeit within the framework of a traditional system which should and can – at least within the world of the plays – ultimately guarantee justice of sorts. The monarchical system as it is envisaged here contains within it a commitment to individual claims and freedoms. In the wisely governed state, Lope implies, all would indeed be content to play the part allotted them by Providence.

At the same time there is a recognition – in *Peribáñez* and *El mejor alcalde el rey* – that this hierarchy does not have to be entirely static, is not in its constitution and nature fixed and unchanging, that it is permeable to men of character, integrity and energy. If blood will out (*El mejor alcalde*), then so should worth (*Peribáñez*). As a man intensely desirous of official recognition for himself, Lope was not a natural enemy of social mobility. In *Peribáñez* and *El mejor alcalde el rey* the configurations of resistance (to duty) and confrontation (with *force majeure*) are fictional, but in all three plays the scenes of royal intervention are cameo presentations of the need for the firm, aware, informed application of monarchical authority. The message to the Crown is that the royal magus in the *corral* is not merely a dramatic convenience but a required reality of government. Kings, if they will, can make things happen. King Enrique in *Peribáñez* is an interesting case because here we see the monarch, under the gentle direction of his queen, having to suppress his instinctive caste reactions in order to assume the mantle of dispassionate wisdom appropriate in a sovereign – the man consciously yielding to the role. Emerging from the symbolic as well as the historical realities of monarchy, the plays offer a dramatic model of how royal leadership ought to work.

The plays approach on different fronts the problems of power as they affect the ordering and functioning of the state. *Peribáñez* confronts the importance to the social hierarchy of a sense of self-hood and dignity, of the individual's inviolable place in the scheme of things; *Fuenteovejuna* presents the troubling vision of a justified popular uprising; *El mejor alcalde* contemplates a crisis of royal authority. Although not a major player in terms of the plot, the monarch in each play is absolutely central to the metatext. The probing of some of the fundamental assumptions in which society and state are grounded reveals the flaws and consequential dangers in the system, and the effective as well as the symbolic importance of the monarch to it – what he signifies, what his authority should achieve. The protagonists who trespass across the boundaries of their social identities do so in the name of values higher than that of social role and in the process inevitably suggest that rank is an organizational convenience and not a given. The ease with which Peribáñez and Sancho assume and fit themselves to their elevated positions, so often seen as evidence of Lope's instinctive conservatism – ennoblement rendering their superiority understandable and their behaviour acceptable – merely reinforces this. Even temporary and provisional disruption articulates the feasibility of re-signification. The insistence in these plays on the fabricated nature of social roles and power systems cannot and could not but draw attention to the possibility of alternative systems of definition and organization.

The very iteration and reiteration of the ideal prescription for monarchy necessarily implicate the likelihood of failure or non-compliance. Far from being ideological propaganda for a natural, benign order based on hierarchical principles, the plays confront the reality of disharmony and disunity in political and social life, admit the existence of contradiction and difference within the established system. Order is restored – which of the characters would wish for anything else? – but disorder is shown by the plays to be in certain circumstances justified even though it is not condoned by the representatives of law and order within the plays. The law cannot condone what it proscribes. If plays really were written, as Thomas Heywood in his *An Apology for Actors* (1612) maintains, 'to teach their subjects obedience to their kings, to show the people the untimely ends of such as have moved tumults, commotions and insurrections, to present them with the flourishing estate of those that live in obedience',[4] then *Peribáñez* and *Fuenteovejuna* certainly do not comply. The didactic purpose of drama was a common argument used in defence of the theatre in the Early Modern period, of course, and Heyword's words, aimed at Puritan hostility to the theatre in England, have all the ring of pious rationalization. Although Lope stops wisely short of explicitly endorsing the idea of justified insubordination, he nonetheless makes it absolutely clear where natural justice and social welfare lie. And the very invocation of the notion of a just resistance irresistibly opens up vistas of alternative values and orderings.

That *Fuenteovejuna* and even *Peribáñez* contain subversive potential, at least, there can be little doubt. They have been seen and convincingly performed by disinterested late twentieth-century companies as subversive and it is not really possible to bend a dramatic text in directions it refuses to go. That potential is blocked but not erased by the plays' endings, which close off the more disturbing vistas that begin to open up in the plays. They retreat from subversion as if in alarm at the possibilities that have been unleashed. In *El mejor alcalde el rey* a more comfortable and less threatening route for justice is discovered, a route whereby the state itself becomes the guarantor of right. Even here, however, the lingering implications are disturbing, in that the state finally acts because its own authority has been ignored and not because a peasant woman has been raped – it reacts to *lèse-majesté*, not to wrong-doing. Don Tello loses his head not over a woman, but for being a negligent vassal to his king.

4 Thomas Heywood, *An Apology for Actors*, reprinted for the Shakespeare Society (London, 1841), 53.

Lope replaces the lid on Pandora's box, it may be assumed, partly because he is only too aware of the possibilities it contains, partly because he sensibly preferred to let sleeping censors lie (in the case of *Fuenteovejuna*, of course, historical sources conveniently coincide with the dictates of caution). While the Spanish authorities were not nearly as exercised by the spectre of sedition as were the authorities who policed the English theatre – they had nothing like as much cause to be after all – an unrestricted vision of disorder would not have been tolerable. As its opponents, who certainly saw it as socially subversive, knew only too well, the theatre encouraged the imagination to fly free. In Spain, as elsewhere in Europe, the authorities were much warier about the theatre's influence than about that of the printed text. Not only was the visual image considered more powerful than the word on the page, but the theatre-going public was less well educated than the reading public, and more impressionable when assembled together, it was thought, than the solitary reader. On this score, Francis Bacon agreed with the Spanish moralists who deprecated the influence of the *comedia*: 'The minds of men are more open to impressions and affections when many are gathered together than when they are alone' (*De augmentis scientiarum*, 1623).[5] Certainly the live performance had at its disposal for the conveyance of meaning the whole range of techniques central to theatre – facial expression, tone of voice and emphasis, gesture and movement, complicity with the audience, and so on. The popular identity of the audience undoubtedly placed upon Lope social and political responsibilities that he would not have wanted, for more than one reason, to shirk, and in these plays he contrives, as he so often does, both to have and eat his cake. The interests of individual and monarch are seen to be one. Thus the ending of *Fuenteovejuna* marks the reconciliation of hierarchical and representative modes of authority necessary to good order. But this vision of a consensual reciprocal relationship is directed as much at the Crown as at the people themselves. The full oppositional implications of what happens in the action – a peasant community in revolt against their overlord – so obvious now in a post-revolutionary world, are not followed through because they would have transgressed the bounds of the acceptable let alone the desirable. Lope's instincts might have been populist but his intellectual loyalties were firmly monarchist, for all his preoccupation with the inadequacy of monarchs. When peasants rebel, they rebel against their feudal lord and not against their monarch. The feudal lord who himself rejects his monarch's authority – in *El mejor alcalde el rey* – is executed. There is no question of marriage alone serving as atonement for his crime of abduction and rape, as happens in many Golden-Age plays – his death both serves as a punishment for himself and as the guarantee of the freedom and happiness of his victims.

5 Quoted in Janet Clare, *Art Made Tongue-Tied*, xii.

Legitimate authority is triumphantly reinscribed in all three plays by means of a negotiation between the interests of individual and state.

It is not, I think, in Lope's case a question of the deliberate application of the Bakhtinian safety-valve principle, of a cynical strategy of containment, as New Historicists argue of Renaissance drama in general, but a genuine attempt to reconcile the claims of legitimacy with the rights of the republic on which that legitimacy, according to the political theory of the day in Spain, was based. In the king-plays Lope, as we have seen, focuses on the tension between man and majesty. Here Lope's interest is caught by the wider political role of monarchy itself, rather than by the shortcomings of the human beings who fill that role. Yet the nostalgic, anachronistic vision of monarchy the plays offer may be read not only symbolically, as an essentialist narrative paradigm of the role and function of monarchy, but more analogically as a suggestion that the Hapsburg monarchs had lost their way by becoming too remote, too detached from government and people, too hedged around with courtiers and court rituals, a situation contemporary political theorists constantly warned against, by their very anxiety about what should not happen revealing their conviction that it had.

Self-interest and self-censorship precluded a more directed criticism of the Crown in the king-plays, and in the peasant trilogy, too, tact as well as ideology demanded negotiated endings. In the seventeenth century, including in stable Spain, depicting popular resistance, even revolt, on the stage of a national, popular theatre was an enterprise not unattended by diplomatic pitfalls. Yet the final accomodations dictated by the prudence of politeness (as defined in chapter 5), as well as by political conviction, by no means neutralize the political dialogue activated by the plays. Dollimore, speaking of masque and anti-masque, says:

> Sometimes a kind of poetic justice emerges from the dramatic 'antic' masque, but only as a perfunctory closure – that is, a *formal* restoration of providentialist/political orthodoxy, a compliance with its letter after having destroyed its spirit. In such ways does Jacobean tragedy ironically inscribe a subordinate viewpoint within a dominant one. A sub-literal encoding which bypasses the perfunctory surveillance of the censor, it cannot help but be reactivated in performance.[6]

The inscription of a subordinate within a dominant viewpoint is certainly recorded by the Spanish plays. The spectator's experience of any play is progressive and linear, moving from beginning to end in an orderly and meaningful way, but it is also cumulative. What has gone before is not superseded by what comes after; nothing is left behind, everything feeds into and becomes part of the final product. Anyone who has seen a performance of

6 Jonathan Dollimore, *Radical Tragedy*, 28.

Fuenteovejuna, with its monarchist ending, can testify to the abiding revolutionary spirit of that play. Its democratic energy is powerfully present and felt, an inalienable part of the play's theatrical identity and not something teased out of a conformist text by overly zealous literary critics. Not just here but in all three of Lope's texts, poetic justice – administered, ironically, by monarchs – actually operates in favour of the subordinate rather than the dominant viewpoint. What would the audience have concluded from the success of these peasant heroes? Certainly not that resistance to the misuse of power pays off – they would not have been naïve enough to believe that. However, it is difficult to see how they could not have concluded either that it ought to pay off or that it should not be necessary in the first place. Either way this is not a conservative political message. The social contract in which the established order is theoretically rooted is patently revealed to be perilously unreliable in its operation. Obedience and passivity bring misery, abuse, shame, whereas resistance ends in reintegration and well-being – the message is scarcely encoded at all. Through the mediation of monarchs who find it possible to reconcile the interests of individuals with those of the state by identifying the maverick nobles as the real anti-social elements, the working of poetic justice by implication paradoxically validates resistance. The difficulty experienced by the peasants in coming to terms with what they do is powerfully conveyed. Peribáñez suffers a momentary paralysis of speech and movement before he kills the Comendador; the villagers of Fuenteovejuna cannot initially wrap their minds round the concept of armed revolt against their lord (Barrildo: '¡Contra el señor las armas en la mano!' Act III, 1699)[7] and have to be shamed into doing so by their women; Sancho is so cautious in his response to the threat of violence as to give don Tello time to rape Elvira. If we now, in our substantially changed world, can register both the dilemma of these peasants and the boldness of the solutions they adopt, it does not require much imagination to judge the impact on contemporary audiences of peasants resisting tyranny, of nobles cast as villains and peasants cast as heroes – the same sort of melting down of traditional divisions that disturbed Suárez de Figueroa when he complained in *El pasajero* of the way in which plays habitually depicted lackeys speaking familiarly to their masters.[8] Reaction no doubt ran the gamut from outrage through unease to scarcely suppressed satisfaction. The crimes that precipitate the nobles' deaths are not even, by the cynical standards of the worldly in traditional society, heinous crimes – the unwanted attentions of gentlemen have been the expected lot of peasant women and working girls from time immemorial, and whatever the law, have in practice figured very low down on the scale of male transgression. For subordinates to kill a dominant male for seduction or

[7] Quotations are from the edition by Francisco Ruiz Ramón (Salamanca: Publicaciones del Colegio de España, 1980).

[8] Alivio III, ed. Mª López Bascuñana (Barcelona: PPU, 1998).

rape of a subordinate female was by any standards daring fare, rendered acceptable only by the neutralizing contribution of the figure at the apex of the social pyramid himself.

In *Peribáñez* and *Fuenteovejuna* violence is a strategy of desperation resorted to by peasants temporarily alienated from the system by nobles who endanger the vested interests they exploit. Lope's source for *Fuenteovejuna*, Francisco de Rades y Andrada's *Crónica de las tres órdenes de caballería de Santiago, Calatrava y Alcántara (1572)*, is very explicit on this score:

> Estando las cosas desta Orden en el estado dicho ya, dõ Fernã Gomez de Guzman Comendador mayor de Calatraua, que residia en Fuenteouejuna villa de su Encomienda, hizo tantos y tan grandes agrauios alos vezinos de aquel pueblo, que no pudiendo ya suffrirlos ni dissimularlos, determinaron todos de vn consentimiento y voluntad alçarse contra el y matarle.[9]

And in the play Estéban, Laurencia's father, minces no words either when he speaks to the King and Queen of the Comendador's 'sobrada tiranía' and 'insufrible rigor' (Act III, 2394–5), robustly conveying the message that there is inevitably a limit to the passivity of even the most loyal subjects. Lope might well have chosen an alternative, fifteenth-century source, the *Crónica de Palencia*, written by Alonso de Palencia (1423–90),[10] which idealizes the Comendador and vilifies the villagers, but his interest clearly lay elsewhere. It is inconceivable that he would not have consulted Mariana's *Historia de España* (1592–1605), the Castilian translation of which was published in 1610, to see what Spain's leading historian and most radical political philosopher, whose work he admired and knew well, had to say about the incident. The passage is an interesting one, in that it strikes the same sort of equilibrium that Lope does between disapproval of sedition and understanding, at least, for its cause, and is equally clear that violence begets violence:

> En muchos lugares a un mismo tiempo andaba la guerra y se hacía sin quedar parte alguna del todo libre destos males, de que resultaba, como suele acontecer, muchedumbre de malhechores y gran libertad en las maldades, en particular los de Fuenteovejuna una noche del mes de abril, se apellidaron para dar la muerte a Fernán Gómez de Guzmán, comendador mayor de Calatrava; extraño caso, que se le empleó bien por sus tiranías y agravios que hacía a la gente por sí y por medio de los soldados que tenía allí por orden de su Maestre, y el pueblo por el rey de Portugal. La constancia del pueblo fue tal, que magüer atormentaron muchos, y entre ellos mozos y

9 The relevant section of the *Crónica* is reproduced in an appendix in Ruiz Ramón, 181–6.

10 For a study of the range of possible sources, see Teresa J. Kirschner, *El protagonista colectivo en 'Fuenteovejuna'* (Salamanca: Universidad de Salamanca, 1979). Clearly there is no way of knowing which of these sources Lope may have seen and discarded.

> mujeres, no les pudieron hacer confesar más de que Fuenteovejuna cometió el caso y no más. Por toda la provincia andaban soldados descarriados, por las ciudades, pueblos y campos hacían muertes y robos, ensuciábanlo todo con fuerzas y deshonestidades, prestos para cualquier mal. Los jueces prestaban poco y eran poca parte para atajar estos daños.[11]

The vision of anarchy and mayhem so vividly captured here must have appeared to Lope, as he read, a powerful argument for the consensual rule of law and order within the centralized state. *Fuenteovejuna* and *Peribáñez*, set one in the public domain the other in the private, reveal in their distinct ways the inadequacies of a socio-political system where there is no realistic appeal against the depredations of an overlord who represents the law within his own lands. At the end social reintegration is essential for both individuals and society – hence the function of the monarch. *El mejor alcalde el rey* offers the blueprint of how the system should work – recourse to the law, incarnate in the monarch, is the proper, constructive response that should be available to the aggrieved, and violence is institutionalized in the state – only the state inflicts punishment. It is when the state fails the individual that order breaks down and the state itself is threatened. The duty of the sovereign is to safeguard the rights of all within the system. In these three plays the king is the agent (albeit reluctant in two cases) of poetic justice and providential concern. His role is predominantly symbolic although it is also partly functional, and in *Peribáñez*, as we saw, there is more than a hint of the differentiated characterization – unpredictability, wilfulness, barely controlled temper – with which we are familiar from other plays. These other plays uncover the problems inherent in Renaissance theory on monarchy. Renaissance rhetoric may purport to present a king as a perfect man, but the information given the spectators in the course of the king-plays by a succession of signifiers invited them to build up a very different picture. What we learn there as well as in *Peribáñez* is that the royal icon is not a perfect man but the idea of a perfect man, a man of damask and velvet. One of Lope's self-appointed tasks was the communication of this truth: the conditions for royal perfection are always readable in the plays but never realized. In *Peribáñez*, however, the doctrine has ultimately to be seen to work in order to be illustrative and prescriptive.

How perfunctory, therefore, are the endings? They are, of course, perfunctory in the formal sense. They belong to a Renaissance tradition of perfunctory resolutions which contemporary audiences were content to read as the dramatic convention and convenience they were. But how perfunctory is their espousal of the solution they provide to the issues developed in the action that has gone before? Are they serenely confident reaffirmations of the

[11] *Historia de España*, chap. XI, *Obras del Padre Juan de Mariana*: Biblioteca de Autores Españoles, 30 and 31, vol.31 (Madrid: M. Rivadeneyra, 1872), 193a.

political system and providential order, or are they a dishonest evasion of the plays' own implications? Or are they something at once more complex, less complacent and less cynical? There can be no doubt that in part they do constitute a strategy of political containment, an attempt to contain within acceptable limits the possibilities knowingly created in the body of the play. There can be no doubt, either, that they offer the ideal of a just and effective monarchy. But at the same time there can be no shadow of a doubt that if these endings are simply devised as propaganda for the system, then they are remarkably ineffective – at most, decidedly partial and strongly prescriptive validations of a patently flawed political structure. They are, in the grammatical sense, imperfect rather than perfect endings; they lack finitude in that they raise more questions than they answer, even about kings. How secure is the recovery of order and well-being? How reliable the protection of the state? How provisional the resolutions? What has the cost been? The plays' final vision of a just and harmonious order is a vision heavily undercut by irony that offers guarantees of absolutely nothing. It is not, I think, that Lope was, complacently or cynically, just going through the motions, but that he found himself occupying that uncomfortable place between the allure of belief and the proddings of doubt.

The endings, of course, are where realism (the realities of peasant existence and the possibilities of peasant revolt in a feudal environment) moves towards romance and symbolism, in the interests of considerations no doubt part political, part diplomatic and part commercial – although in *Fuenteovejuna,* where triumphalism comes only after torture, romance is appropriately tempered by the grim realities of historical witness. But the plays themselves, for all their undoubted glamourization of certain aspects of rural life, may be recognized as realistic in the Brechtian sense, in that they show how things really were, what the reality of class relationships was behind the complacent theorizing about hierarchical order.[12] Not that all nobles sexually harassed their tenants – though many surely did. The action is a particular, and particularly effective and emotive, representation of the realities of class hierarchy, of power and its abuse, the nature of this representation being determined in part by the evidence of real life, in part by theatrical imperatives. And the ending in two of the plays (*Peribáñez* and *El mejor alcalde*) occupies an uneasy space between romance and the material realism of social advancement and wealth acquisition, the fairy-tale rewards of status and riches robbed of their traditional innocence by the decidedly social orientation of the plays.

The immediately obvious target of the plays' attention is not the system but those who play it. The nobleman in each case represents rotten wood in the social tree, the diseased arm of the body of the state, in the metaphorical

12 *Bertold Brecht. Brecht on Theatre*, ed. John Willett (London: Methuen 1964).

terms favoured by political theorists at the time. Those who rebel against their superiors are paradoxically rebelling in the name of family and social order and harmony – they rebel on behalf of the system. This is why the peasants are ideologically the natural allies of the monarch, the system incarnate. Implicit in the three plays is a unitary vision of the polity as an ethical and socio-political union that served the common good. This, however, places an apparently irreduceable tension at the heart of the action, because the system itself is also necessarily implicated. Its pattern of power is shown to breed corruption and constant vigilance is needed at the top to guarantee its integrity and survival. The unitary vision, in its intentions good, is therefore revealed as flawed and fragile, and this revelation necessarily destabilizes the view of it as natural and consequently right. Those rebels who resort to violence are therefore both right and wrong; their rebellion is both desirable and undesirable. And it is the monarch alone – the embodiment of justice as well as law – who is capable of resolving the tension, by both punishing, or waiving punishment (either way the appropriateness of punishment is inscribed), and by rewarding. Only the rebel who resorts to an authority higher than either social rank or violence is praised and rewarded accordingly (Sancho).

To believe in a political system and yet be critical of the way it works is a central reality of human life, even in a modern democracy. In an age when there were no real, and scarcely any conceivable, alternatives, the dichotomy was all the more acute. In Europe in general, Spain by and large excepted, monarchy was in perpetual crisis during most of the period in question, yet the system still proved extraordinarily difficult to dislodge. What kept monarchy in political play was primarily the symbolic value accorded the monarch himself. The king was the locus where supreme power, national pride, cultural identity and the highest ideals and values simultaneously found their centre and most exalted expression; he represented both people and God and therefore possessed an inherent sacredness which could survive even breaks in the hereditary line. The charisma was the role's and not the man's, which is why Lope's remorseless stripping away of the monarch's ceremonial and symbolic identity in the king-plays in effect constitutes a form of literary *lèse-majesté*. To remove the mystique was to bring into question the very ideology of kingship. As Stephen Greenblatt has said,

> At some level we know perfectly well that the power of the prince is largely a collective invention, the symbolic embodiment of the desire, pleasure and violence of thousands of subjects, the instrumental expression of complex networks of dependency and fear, the agent rather than the maker of the social will.[13]

13 *Shakespearean Negotiations*, 4.

What Lope does in those plays is effectively to deconstruct the symbol, to show that behind it there is a man like others whose heart beats and whose blood flows. In the peasant trilogy, on the contrary, it serves Lope's dramatic and political purposes to emphasize the king's symbolic identity, so tellingly captured in Peribáñez when Casilda (ingenuously or disingenuously – either is possible) claims she had always thought that kings were made of damask or velvet:

Casilda.	¿Que son	
	los reyes de carne y hueso?	
Costanza.	Pues ¿de qué pensabas tú?	
Casilda.	De damasco o terciopelo.	(Act I, 986–9)[14]

The only too human nature of her king is at the end amply demonstrated, not merely by the tender family intimacies between himself and the Queen (on the face of it, disproportionately extended) and by his choleric reaction to Peribáñez's presence, but by his ready admission that he had forgotten for a moment how to do his job. The Queen has to remind him:

Reina.	Bien dice. Oílde, señor.	
Rey.	Bien decís; no me acordaba	
	que las partes se han de oír,	
	y más cuando son tan flacas.	(Act III, 3028–30)

But even he ultimately plays his appointed role as arbiter of justice and consequentially engineer of the dramatic resolution. The monarch's function in these plays is to represent the will of the nation.

If the monarch's multiple and contradictory identity – man yet more than man, head of the republic yet in some mystic sense the republic itself, the law and yet not above the law, the pinnacle of the hierarchy and yet above/outside the hierarchy – helped guarantee the survival of the system, in the three plays it has the effect of making Lope seem at once radical and conservative. Greenblatt gives the following definition of a totalizing society:

> One that posits an occult network linking all human, natural, and cosmic powers and that claims on behalf of its ruling elite a privileged place in this network. Such a society generates vivid dreams of access to the linked powers and vests control of this access in a religious and state bureaucracy at whose pinnacle is the symbolic figure of the monarch.[15]

In our three plays Lope conjures up precisely this vision of unity, showing it

14 Quotations are taken from the edition by J.M. Ruano and J.E. Varey (London: Tamesis Texts, 1980).

15 *Shakespearean Negotiations*, 2.

fractured and then, through the monarch, restored to health. Greenblatt goes on to say that Elizabethan and Jacobean visions of hidden unity began to him to seem,

> like anxious rhetorical attempts to conceal cracks, conflicts and disarray. I had tried to organise the mixed motives of Tudor and Stuart culture under the rubric *power*, but that term implied a structural unity and stability of command belied by much of what I actually knew about the exercise of authority and force in the period (2).

Lope, however, makes no attempt to conceal the cracks. The very *re*-imposition of a vision of harmony allows, demands, the depiction of tensions and disarray. And once depicted, they permanently inhabit the text, or as Dollimore puts it:

> We may feel that such closure was a kind of condition for subversive thought to be foregrounded at all. But we should recognize too that such a condition cannot control what it permits: closure could never retrospectively guarantee ideological erasure of what, for a while, existed prior to and so independently of it.[16]

The strains in the system are irreversibly discovered and the cure is placed in the hands of one man. The fragility of such a political solution is written into the ending, heavily spiked with irony, of *Peribáñez* where King Enrique, like his counterparts in the king-plays, is shown to be a fractured icon. At best this vision for health and harmony is a conflictive one – a centralized monarchy that guarantees unity and therefore greatness, yet which conducts itself along the lines of the smaller more intimate monarchies of a past age. In reality, the thorough exercise of authority and force was simply no longer within the reach of a single individual.

The discrepancies that Lope opens up between socio-political theory and socio-political practice threaten, therefore, to resist the reassurance of their hopeful resolution. The plays are, in the language of Cultural Materialism and New Historicism 'sites of institutional and ideological contestation',[17] in other words there is more going on in them than meets the eye. *Fuenteovejuna*, with its fleeting glimpse of an alternative political system that would have been recognized, if at all, only with horror by contemporary onlookers, is particularly interesting in the way its revolutionary spirit is at odds with its apparent purpose – to celebrate the unique role of monarchy. This tension is only eased by identifying the cause of monarch so closely with the cause of the people as to put the play's vision of monarchy itself at odds with the

16 *Radical Tragedy*, 60–1.

17 Greenblatt, *Shakespearean Negotiations*, 2.

political realities of the *ancien régime*. When Lope nostalgically evokes an age when kings championed the cause of the people, he offers, and knew full well that he offered, an ideal of government that had little in common with the political configurations and alignments of contemporary Spain.

The ideological function of the *deus ex machina* king is presumably to foster a sense of confidence and hope in a divine design that guaranteed order and justice, in the face of a self-evidently very different reality. But that function is imperfectly achieved in *Fuenteovejuna* with its vision of justice only through communal mayhem, and also in *Peribáñez* with its vision of justice via a combination of murder and, once in the royal palace, something suspiciously akin to arbitrariness and muddle. The plays strongly create the impression of wistfully projecting solutions and worlds that do not convince the playwright himself. It is a promise of a totalizing wholeness shot through with palpable anxiety. In *Fuenteovejuna* that anxiety reaches extreme proportions when the peasants' assumption of control is emblematized by the physical disintegration of their overlord's body. In *Discipline and Punish*,[18] Foucault draws attention to the importance given public executions at a time when social controls were otherwise minimal – no police forces, no standing armies. Renaissance power characteristically operated through display (state entries, royal progresses, religious processions, *autos de fe*) and public displays of punishment were a terrible emblem of the power of the state over the bodies of its subjects.[19] Lope presents his seventeenth-century audience with a harrowing image of this very power in the torture scene at the play's end, a scene whose effectiveness is doubled by the on-stage commentary upon the off-stage responses and screams of old men, women and children on the rack. The detached professionalism of the anonymous judge, the resigned attitude of the villagers to the whole process, and then the judge's disinterested praise for their courage and his matter-of-fact advice to the King and Queen – all serve to intensify rather than to dilute the impact of state machinery in motion. The sight and sound of peasants contributing through suffering in this way to the definition of what it is to be human constituted a potent theatrical offering. As for the Comendador, his murder and dismemberment is carnival misrule gone wrong, become real and out of control – because a peasantry reluctant to take the law into their own hands has just been pushed too far. *El mejor alcalde el rey* illustrates the more orderly and desirable solution that should be offered by the state. It is the play that comes nearest to a

18 Trans. Alan Sheridan (New York: Vintage, 1979), 51.

19 It is not, however, easy to connect the rise of the theatre in Spain with a monarchical display of power in the way Leonard Tannenhouse does in his *Power on Display: The Politics of Shakespeare's Genres* (New York/London, Methuen, 1986), 104–7, for the simple reason that in Spain the rise of the theatre coincided with the reign of that very private and austere monarch Philip II. The court theatre of Philip IV, of course, was a different matter.

confident appropriation of the promise of monarchy as envisaged by the Spanish political theorists of the day. But even so it ends with the promise of a ritual beheading and, as we saw, what in the event actually galvanizes the monarch into action is not so much concern for justice as for the preservation of his own authority – the two are, within the Renaissance ideology of monarchy, in practical terms interconnected, of course, since authority presents itself as the guarantor of justice, but ethically justice should be the higher concern of the two. Even when depicting the rule of law at work within a highly romanticized dramatic action, Lope seems unable to hold scepticism entirely at bay.

I have argued that all three plays may be considered to have a strong political identity. In political terms their chronology, however, traces an expanding horizon of concern. In each case the main focus of dramatic conflict and tension is a crisis rooted in an abuse of power and social responsibility – first a marital crisis (*Peribáñez*), then a crisis of community rights (*Fuenteovejuna*) and then, *with El mejor alcalde el rey*, as with the king-plays, a crisis of royal authority. Here the very authority of the King is called into question by one of his nobles in such a way as to engage the play explicitly with the issue of authority within the state as well as with questions of class and feudal rights and responsibilities. The date suggested for the play – 1620–23 – coincides with a restless period at the Spanish court. The late years of the lax reign of Philip III were riven by aristocratic factionalism as different groupings vied for political power, and the succession of the young Philip IV in 1621 merely intensified the jockeying for position. The new régime promptly set about prosecuting old enemies from the Lerma régime and a Junta de Reformación was created to raise the standard of public morality – 'to uproot vices and abuses and bribery', which amongst other things meant an investigation into the corrupt practices of the previous government.[20] Then, in 1622, enormous bad feeling was created by the murder by an unknown assassin in August of that year of the Count of Villamediana. Although, as was mentioned earlier, the murder is now generally assumed to have been the result of a homosexual intrigue, it was widely thought at the time that the new king, under the influence of Olivares, must have suppressed investigation into the affair for political reasons.[21] Two months later, in October, Madrid was abuzz once more, this time with conjecture about the sudden demise at the early age of forty-six of the apparently healthy Count of Lemos, son-in-law of the ousted favourite the Duke of Lerma, whose faction was still trying to maintain influence at court. Lemos, a distinguished diplomat who had spent six successful years as viceroy of Naples, had the previous year been ordered by the king to stay away from Madrid, but was now

[20] See Elliott, *The Count-Duke of Olivares*, 104–5.
[21] See chap.6, 165.

given permission to visit his sick mother in the capital. He stayed on after her death and died suddenly two months later. There is no mention in Lope's correspondence of the death of Villamediana, rather surprisingly perhaps in view of the scandal and the fact that Villamediana had on several occasions targeted Lope and his amorous entanglements in his satirical verse. It suggests that Lope, who in his communications to his patron the Duke of Sessa consistently adopted a policy of cautious reticence with regard to public matters,[22] although his words are often sly and knowing, felt that the issue was sensitive enough to make silence the prudent option. He does, however, mention the mysterious death of Lemos, whose secretary he had been for two years from 1598 to 1600 and for whom he clearly still held warm feelings. They had been in touch the year before Lemos's exile, when Lemos commissioned a play from Lope for the Feast of the Rosario in May 1620. The letter to Sessa, which is assumed to have been written in October 1622, is extremely brief but heavy with shock and insinuation:

> Duque mi Señor, yo no sabía nada del Conde que Dios tiene, y prometo a Vex.[a] que me ha dado tal pesadunbre qual en my vida la he tenido; por aora haze un año que le suçedio la primera desgraçia; para la que es tan grande no ay consuelo, y más hauiendo caydo en onbre tan bien quisto; mucho ay que hablar y que no es para papel: yo aguardo a Vex.[a], a quien me guarde Dios, como yo he menester.[23]

Whatever the truth of the matter in either case, the significant point here is that the king, even in what one might have expected to be the honeymoon period of his reign, was not considered to be immune to criticism or suspicion, even scandal. As Stradling points out, his sexual adventures in the backstreets of Madrid became so notorious soon after he reached the throne in 1621 that the Archbishop of Granada complained about the matter that same year to Olivares, who was known to accompany the king on his expeditions.[24] Within a few years, as Olivares's popularity began to wane, the king's conduct and actions generally caused sufficient unease for rumours to spread that Olivares exerted some unnatural power over him.

So – too little authority, too much authority, too little judgement and justice, the wrong advice and influences – such matters were in the air that Lope breathed. The spectre of aristocratic insubordination in *El mejor*

22 In an undated letter to the Duke Lope is quite explicit about this: 'Ya sabe V. Ex[a] mi cobardia y mis respetos, que aun lo que un onbre habla no esta seguro en el ayre, quanto mas lo que escrive en el papel que embia.' Cayetano Alberto de La Barrera, *Nueva Biografía de Lope de Vega*, 2 vols, Biblioteca de Autores Españoles 262 and 263, vol.2 (Madrid: Atlas, 1974), 138.

23 *Epistolario*, ed. Agustín González de Amezúa, Vol.IV, 76, no.460.

24 *Philip IV and the Government of Spain*, 52.

alcalde el rey would certainly seem to correspond to anxieties about the monarchy and the attitudes and behaviour of Spain's political barons during these sensitive years, and the trenchant display of royal authority and justice with which the plot ends could readily have been seen as containing a message directed at monarch, favourites and nobles alike.[25] The uncompromising words uttered by the King,

> Divinas y humanas letras
> dan ejemplos: es traidor
> todo hombre que no respeta
> a su rey, y que habla mal
> de su persona en su ausencia. . . (Act III, 500b)[26]

carry an explicit emphasis that seems to transcend the boards and speak directly to the contemporary audience in a capital awash with gossip. But the King's physical intervention speaks silent words to Philip himself as well. Lope's patron Sessa, who had had a chequered political career, was an opponent of Olivares and would have preferred the king to govern by himself with the help of a group of advisers. Lope, although always eager not to lose Olivares's favour, or anybody else's for that matter, seems on the evidence of his plays to have been sympathetic to this view of royal governance. In this regard, in *El mejor alcalde el rey*, the device of the King's disguise as a judge and the highly charged discovery of his true identity are not just good theatre but carry a very significant symbolic weight. Anne Barton has drawn attention to the considerable number of kings who adopt disguise in the English history plays between 1587 and 1600, some out of political necessity, but most as 'a caprice, for reasons that are fundamentally exploratory and quixotic'.[27] The undoubtedly much larger number of disguised kings in Lope's theatre would fall into the two same rough categories, *El mejor alcalde el rey* into the first in so far as the disguise is, if not exactly necessary, then unquestionably politically motivated and purposeful.[28] The King is a living icon in relation to which authority, power and justice instantly acquire meaning and value. The mere idea of the law, of majesty, is not in itself powerful enough to reduce don Tello to obedience (and in *Peribáñez* and *Fuenteovejuna* too, of course, the law incarnate has a crucial role), neither is the King's own

[25] The play has been read as a possible attack on a single minister. See Bernard Bentley's 'El mejor alcalde el rey y la responsabilidad política', *Lope de Vega y los orígenes del teatro español, Actas del Primer Congreso Internacional sobre Lope de Vega*, ed. Manuel Criado de Val (Madrid: Edi-6, S.A., 1981), 415–24.

[26] Quotations are from Lope Félix de Vega Carpio, *Obras escogidas*, vol.1.

[27] 'The King Disguised: Shakespeare's *Henry V* and the Comical History', *Essays, Mainly Shakespearean*, 207–33, p.207.

[28] The Duke of Ferrara in *El castigo sin venganza* is a good example of the second category.

written word and signature, nor the Crown's representative. However, as soon as the judge reveals his true identity, the play's political business reorganizes itself around him as the state asserts its authority over nobles and peasants alike. In the interests of justice and the polis the monarch in person takes charge, unruliness is punished and yields to reinstatement and restoration. In an age trying to come to terms with the problems inherent in conceiving of and communicating the idea of one man as the incarnation of the state without an extended political infrastructure to support it, royal image, visibility and presentation were all-important – the panoply and iconography of Renaissance festivities, triumphal entries, and royal progresses were directed to this very end. The King's commanding appearance on the Comendador's own territory in *El mejor alcalde el rey* is a declaration of right and of intent – the right to exert authority within that territory and the intention of doing so.[29] It is an affirmation at once of sovereignty and the rule of law, and the nearest Lope came to identifying the physical body of the king with the power of the state. The synergy of authority and law is captured by the King's metonymical play with the two concepts of might and justice:

Rey.	Pues ¿qué diferencia tiene del rey quien en nombre viene suyo?	
Don Tello.	Mucha contra mí. Y vos, ¿adónde traéis la vara?	
Rey.	En la vaina está, de donde presto saldrá, y lo que pasa veréis.	
Don Tello.	¿Vara en la vaina? ¡Oh, qué bien!	(Act III, 499a)

When needs must, justice's rod mimics the sword. At the same time, the sword within the sheath must be the sword of justice. The conceit of the sheathed rod of office is the King's way of conveying the dual nature of his authority.

Anne Barton sees Shakespeare in *Henry V* as rejecting as attractive but untrue the idea of a personal engagement of the king with his subject (215), on the grounds that Henry V is only effective when functioning as king. The vast majority of Lope's kings are dysfunctional both as kings and as human beings. If we search through his plays for kings who represent a viable ideal of monarchy we find precious few. Rarely does his representation of princes confine itself to iterating and elaborating upon the symbolic role of the monarch of convention, rarely does it fail to probe and problematize its

[29] Cf. Thomas Hobbes 'the right of doing any action is called authority', *Leviathan*, Book I, chap.16.

subject. Even here in the three peasant plays, where kings fulfil a narrowly delineated and iconic function, disquiet about the problematical operation of power and authority within the monarchical system as a whole seeps through. Kings may be made of 'carne y hueso', as Casilda sees and Peribáñez almost to his cost discovers, but they still have power of life and death. Even a royal reward can be a poisoned chalice – as a result of the hasty decision of a hasty temperament, the honour of fighting for king and faith brings with it separation from a beloved wife, from the source of wealth, even possibly from life itself. At the same time the war against Granada could equally be perceived as an overriding sacred obligation, not lost on audiences in 1607 when anti-*morisco* feeling was building up to the expulsion of the *morisco* population in early 1609.[30] Lope offers more than one way of reading even these endings, where monarchs do do more or less what is required and expected of them. The portrayal of an incompetent king at the end of *Peribáñez* is immediately preceded by a vision of a loving royal family, father, mother and son, which not only links the present with the past in the legitimacy of the line, but manages in the process to suggest its legitimation by another, higher reality as well:

Rey. ¿Cómo queda don Juan?
Reina. Por veros llora.
Rey. Guárdele Dios, que es un divino espejo
donde se ven agora retratados,
mejor que los presentes, los pasados.
Reina. El príncipe don Juan es hijo vuestro;
con esto sólo encarecido queda. (Act III, 2936–41)

The effects Lope achieves are rarely straightforward. His considered strategy of covering his back by offsetting the unflattering with the flattering, subversion with support, criticism with praise, might have been a transparent, even blatant one, to the public, or sections of the public, of the day, but it had all the strength of simplicity and allowed him a licence it would have been well nigh impossible to challenge. The monarchist endings of these three plays neither erase nor contradict the political scrutiny that precedes them – they merely serve to reinforce the discovery of an acutely political Lope, beset by anxieties and doubts, a man with more hope than confidence in the political system in which he lived, a man who saw the need for change but feared the price that might have to be paid. The three plays have always been recognized in their different ways as great plays – what must be added to that

30 The play has recently been redated to 1607 (from 1608) on the basis of an allusion to the convening of the Cortes that year and of another to the second birthday of the young prince, Philip. See Françoise and Roland Labarve, 'Sobre la fecha de *Peribáñez y el Comendador de Ocaña*', *Criticón* (Toulouse) 54 (1992), 123–26.

evaluation is a recognition of their power surreptitiously and effortlessly to use history, poetry and romance to create a fictional world so closely in touch with the political and social realities of a world in flux.

El villano en su rincón

No attempt to assess Lope de Vega's attitude to monarchy and his handling of the issues it raises can ignore another, very different, play where a king is confronted by a peasant, for here the confrontation constitutes the guiding idea behind the work. *El villano en su rincón* is a curious, seemingly rather pointless play, about a French peasant who has vowed, for no very convincing reason, never to set eyes on his king and a king sufficiently irritated by this impertinence to seek the peasant out. There is little action, conflict or tension and the work has all the sedate, ritual feel of a court entertainment. The central character, Juan Labrador, was probably inspired by a well-known epitaph for a folkloric figure of the same name (in the play, Juan Labrador has prepared the same epitaph for his own death) and the plot owes much to narrative traditions of romance, novella and fairy tale.[31] The king who goes in disguise to see the peasant, the royal demand first for money and then for the peasant's children, the feast with masked retainers at the end, the symbolism of sceptre, sword and mirror, the cross-class marriages and symbolic changes of apparel, the siblings' social elevation – the play is a collage of familiar resonances, and one might even be tempted to categorize it as a dramatic parable if it were only clearer what the moral of the parable was supposed to be. Often described as an emblematic text, it lacks the allegorical certitude of emblem and it might be best described rather as a meditation on the mystique of kingship and the charisma of the court in the context of enduring values. It was written almost certainly to mark the marriage alliances that had been contracted in 1612 between the royal houses of Spain and France. The two young queens, Anne of Austria and Elizabeth of Bourbon, were exchanged at the frontier in November 1615 in a ceremony of great splendour, and amongst the Spanish aristocrats who accompanied the Infanta to the border was the Duke of Sessa, accompanied by his secretary Lope de Vega.[32] It is a play, therefore, to celebrate an interlude of Franco-Spanish accord, to flatter the monarch and amuse his courtiers and their ladies. Along the way, however, it engages with some interesting issues and

[31] The tale of a French king who when lost while hunting dines with a prosperous and dignified charcoal burner is found in Antonio de Torquemada's *Coloquios satíricos*, written in the middle of the sixteenth century.

[32] See Marcel Bataillon, 'El villano en su rincón', *Varia lección de clásicos españoles* (Madrid: Editorial Gredos, 1964), 329–72, which contains a detailed discussion of the play's sources.

makes some substantial points. It is, furthermore, cut through with touches of irony, caricature, parody and criticism. The iconized king is shown to be a man with faults and with something to learn, but so is the iconized peasant.

The work's operating principle is the tension between two value-systems, that represented by urban life and the court on the one hand, that represented by the simple sufficiencies of rural life on the other. The tension constitutes an ancient and familiar topos in literature and thought, and this *Beatus ille* theme had undergone a lively revival in the sixteenth century in Europe, partly as a result of the revival of interest in classical antiquity and the prelapsarian myth, partly in response to the rapidly changing circumstances of social and economic life. The best-known essay on the topic in Spain was Antonio de Guevara's *Menosprecio de corte y alabanza de aldea*, published in 1539. In Lope's play, as elsewhere in Renaissance writing, the vision of life in the bosom of nature is a good deal further removed from pragmatic reality than the portrayal of life at court. The work offers, however, no simple victory for the rural idyll. The two strains of thought pull neither quite together nor quite apart: court and country life are simultaneously presented as both desirable and lacking, social climbing is at once parodied and endorsed, the king is both idealized and humanized, and Juan Labrador is admired and at the same time made to toe the line. The play is therefore something of a conundrum, curious most of all for its reluctance to display its hand and take sides. The great French Hispanist, Marcel Bataillon, after searching for the meaning he presumed the play must have, gave up on it – 'El tema fundamental resiste'[33] – and since a brief flurry of interest in the work in the early seventies relatively little further commentary has been ventured.

Centrally implicated in the play's apparent ambivalence is Juan's attitude to kingship. His long speech of homage to monarchy in Act I ('¿Qué es ver al rey?')[34] is strongly interleaved with assertions of his own personal sovereignty and self-sufficiency, dutiful and defiant by turn. The result is a seemingly truculent but essentially very intelligent balancing act between political piety and anarchic self-assertion. He acknowledges the monarch's centrality in the life of the state, but seeks to deny him any place in his own psyche and well-being. Any notion of dependence and subservience, indeed of inferiority, is missing in Juan Labrador's perception of what it means to be king of one's own castle. A king may be a political necessity, a fact of life, the heartbeat at the centre of national life who must command and receive all loyalty and homage, but 'los que viven…del trabajo de su mano' (1178a) are also kings – that is, of course, by implication most men. Juan Labrador sees himself as a sovereign individual, as one who gives unconditional loyalty

33 In his *Varia lección de clásicos españoles*, 368.

34 *Obras escogidas, I Teatro*, 1178.

only because he chooses to do so. But unlike his impressionable, socially ambitious son, Feliciano, he is not seduced by the glamour and panoply surrounding the throne. The speech is therefore simultaneously deferential and defiant. It encapsulates both Lope's own ambivalence regarding monarchy in practice and his double-handed way – censure with minimum risk – of dealing with it. But it also reaches further than that. It is a Pedro Crespo-type speech; Juan is prepared to give his wealth to the king but not his soul. The king may be God's viceroy on earth, but his own *rincón* on earth is 'divino': 'Ay mi divino rincón,/ donde soy rey de mis pajas' (Act I, 1178b). The appropriation of the vocabulary of the rhetoric of majesty here is meaningful and deliberate. And it is, effectively, an appropriation of the concept of sovereignty for the common man in a transitional period suspended between the medieval world and modernity, when ideas about the subject and subjectivity were in the process of reformulation. Juan Labrador, as a man fully conscious of his own worth and achievements, is not seeking to undermine the King, but to define himself in relation to him, in relation, that is, to traditional, hierarchical structures of social organization.

The play indeed is centrally concerned with identity and self-definition. Juan's daughter, Lisarda, is a socially ambiguous creature, completely open in her determination to marry out of her class. When Otón takes her to be a 'señora de gran calidad' (Act I, 1174a) whose 'talle y habla es celestial' (Act I, 1173a), Marín, the lackey, reads the signs more accurately (she is without coach or chair and has only one *escudero* with her), but this detracts not one whit from her very real capacity to play the lady. Subsequently her gift of a diamond ring to Marín confuses the discovery that she is a *villana* (*villanas* do not give such gifts) and Marín is dazzled by the beauty of this hybrid creature ('que en una aldea/ se ha humanado un serafín', Act I, 1176b). Wealth and personal attributes blur her social category, the signifiers send conflicting messages. Her gloves are not those of a peasant girl ('No es de escardido ni hoz/ el guante desta doncella', Act I, 1183b), neither is her speech. She can write, dance and do everything else a noble court lady can (Act II, 1187b), and neither the village men nor her brother can think of a local suitor good enough for her. She does indeed end up marrying her courtier. Her brother, Feliciano, for his part, also seeks to reconstruct himself as a person of gentle birth. He yearns to live within the ambit of majesty, to wear fine clothes, to lose his rustic identity and escape (his word: 'cuando me puedo escapar', Act I, 1179a) to a new life. If the King could only see him 'tan cortesano y pulido' he would become something different, distinct, special, such is the power of the royal gaze, the source not only of social approbation but of social transformation. The clothes – the outer signifiers of breeding and class – for him are crucial:

voy a París con vestido
tan cortesano y pulido
que el rey me puede mirar. (Act I, 1179a)

Visibility, the royal validation essential to the enterprise, is not possible without them. Felicano's ambitions are touched with naïveté and couched in frankness, but he is nonetheless a lightly parodied figure. He represents the gullibility of callow youth, seduced by outer display, impatient with his father's sterling values. Lisarda's determination to marry above her and her contempt for rural life and rural men, her conviction that 'Para Corte me crié' (Act I, 1180a), reveal her for her part as a rather vain and silly young woman, in spite of her superior qualities. Neither brother nor sister is a human being with views worthy of much respect, so what they say and stand for cannot readily be what the audience is intended to admire. Yet ambition is rewarded and the social climbers achieve their desires.

Juan Labrador, on the other hand, is a man of industry, frugality, integrity and Christian charity ('porque a los pobres/ reparte la más parte de su hacienda', Act I, 1182a) – a role model if ever there was one. He is also a man of inordinate complacency, smugness and lack of curiosity, whose undoubted contentment and sense of fulfilment find expression in an irrational vow never to clap eyes on the King, as if the very act would threaten his existence.[35] This then becomes a self-fulfilling prophecy. His deep-seated mistrust of court life and his attempt to assert his sense of self by reference to the King and his court is presented as worthy of admiration yet ultimately compromised, if not rendered void, and again the audience is given no clear signals to suggest how they might respond. All in the play, in one way or another, succumb to the mystique of centralized monarchy and its social reverberations, however foolishly, whatever the cost, and perhaps this is the rueful observation which Lope is making and which Juan Labrador has to learn. The play depicts not only individuals but an entire society in the process of redefinition, in a flux of social mobility (the desire to move nearer the apex) and urban expansion (the desire to move nearer the centre) which of course reflects the realities of Spain at the time. As for the figure at the pinnacle and stable centre of this vertical and horizontal flow, the King is candid about his reactions to the old man (nobody is subtle in this play), but these seem either puerile (pique at Juan's attitude) or predictable (envy of his life). Neither reaction is dramatically explored, or made to seem particularly coherent. The King is merely a cipher manifesting the responses that might be deemed to follow from his position. He represents authority that is used to

[35] Dian Fox in her lively reading of the play in *Refiguring the Hero: From Peasant to Noble in Lope de Vega and Calderón* (University Park, Pa.: Pennsylvania State University Press, 1991) sees Juan Labrador's flaws as rendering him unfit for heroism, but Lope's heroes are rarely monochrome creations.

being revered, to being the cynosure of all eyes, the locus of all that is superlative and desirable. What troubles, even alarms him, is the threat to his and others' view of his place in the scheme of things. He is irritated by a peasant's imperviousness to the charisma of majesty but at the same time feels the envy kings are occasionally expected to feel for the serene fulfilment supposedly achieved by the simple man at the opposite end of the social scale (Act II, 1184–5a). It is because Juan Labrador represents a threat to the dominant value system that he must be brought to heel. The King feels demeaned by Juan's attitude: 'que de tus venturas siento/ desprecios de mi valor' (Act II, 1190a), and wants to understand his thinking: 'yo veré, Juan Labrador,/ despacio tu pensamiento' (Act II, 1190a). It is significant that for the King the knowledge of Juan's loyalty and devotion is not enough – proximity and obeisance are necessary, because a king, to be a king, must be seen to be a king and must be served as king: 'para que vea que es justo/ ver rey y servir señor' (Act II, 1190a). To put such words in the King's own mouth is not an obvious dramatic strategy, and it is difficult to imagine an actor delivering such lines without appearing pompous or vapid or both. But while it might not seem very plausible that a monarch would say such things about himself, these reactions are of course rooted in a conception and practice of majesty where royal visibility and attendance at court were of supreme importance. The development of court life during the reign of Philip III depended on the greater visibility of the monarch after the death of the reclusive Philip II, and its deliberate elaboration and ritualization during the reign of Philip IV was perceived as making an essential contribution to the dignity and grandeur of the state. While remoteness was essential to majesty, the aura of majesty had to be palpable and experienced in order to exist; in turn that aura touched and illuminated the lives of those who experienced it. By denying the need for this exchange, Juan Labrador, in spite of his royalist sentiments, denies monarchy part of its power and its *raison d'être*, in a sense even its very existence. How can a monarch be a mirror to his subjects if they refuse to look at him? This is why he is made to yield. The play scrutinizes both Feliciano's impressionability and gullibility where the pomp of power is concerned and the anthropologically undeniable mystique of its physical presence.

The king in this play serves literally as the voice of monarchy. The scene with the masked retainers at the end is a rehearsal of the basic tenets of Renaissance monarchy and the King resorts explicitly to the familiar images:

> Este espejo es el segundo
> porque es el rey el espejo
> en que el reino se compone
> para salir bien compuesto.
> Vasallo que no se mira
> en el rey, esté muy cierto
> que sin concierto ha vivido,

y que vive descompuesto.
Mira al rey, Juan Labrador;
que no hay rincón tan pequeño
adonde no alcance el sol.
Rey es el sol. (Act III, 1206a)

It is not difficult to imagine such passages being performed and received with appropriate solemnity in the court itself, but neither is it difficult to imagine a somewhat less respectful treatment in the public playhouses. In view of the character constructed for him, Juan's response to the above homily, 'Al sol tiemblo', is, like the King's own speeches, a gift to irreverence. Little if anything in this text is free from elusiveness of tone.

The King's final elevation of Juan to *mayordomo del rey* is a crude choice of victory heavy with dramatic irony, for it forces the old peasant to exchange a life that the King himself admires for a court existence that is severely criticized in the course of the play. The legitimacy of the play's ending is thus inevitably undermined by what has gone before; its very illogicality – it is not necessary after all to destroy the idyll in order to secure Juan's capitulation – is an invitation to question the wisdom of the King's action. He is, of course, a *mancebo*, young in the ways of kingship, which is presumably why he needs to keep articulating the premises on which these are based. When he goes to meet Juan 'a cuerpo', that is, dressed as a courtier and without his royal robes, he is determined to establish whether Juan has found the key to a power greater than his own. He does indeed discover that Juan has access to riches denied him – time, solitude, choice of lifestyle, freedom from cares. It is not a reconstruction of peasant life that many at the time would have recognized, of course, but that is not the issue in a fictional world fashioned by opposing ethoses. When it comes to Juan Labrador's lack of desire to see the king, the King misses the point. He produces the traditional arguments in favour of monarchy (the principle being that Nature sets the example), failing to see that Juan is a monarchist, but one immune to the glamour of the paraphernalia of monarchy (Act II, 1192b), that he is a man who is satisfied with his lot, does not need the excitement of the court to give life meaning, and understands and defines himself accordingly. The King is an impetuous youth of inadequate judgement – as full of himself as Felicano. He asks for Lisarda's hand as soon as he sets eyes on her, and tries in vain to detain three village girls in turn at night in his quarters when he visits the village – sexual behaviour which, as we have seen, is used by Lope as an indicator of a lack of royal judgement but which is also a dig, perhaps, at the looseness of the court in contrast to the solid virtues and common sense of country life. Is this the mirror, one wonders, in which his subjects are intended to see themselves? His retention of Juan at court is as ill judged as his sexual behaviour, and his astonishing vision of social equality,

que es el mariscal [Otón, Lisarda's suitor]
hombre bien intencionado,
y el labrador tan honrado,
que en nada es desigual. . . (Act III, 1197b)

however laudable, owes more to enthusiasm than reality. Both his admiration and his envy, it transpires, have their realistic limits: 'a no ser rey de Francia/ tuviera por más ganancia/ que fuera Juan Labrador' (Act III, 1198b). For all the caveats surrounding the King's character and behaviour, however, his endorsement of the values Juan Labrador stands for remains undiluted, which is why his action at the end seems to do such violence to it. Juan's reward for being the man he is is the removal of that very identity.

If the play's representation of monarchy may appear mildly mischievous at times, there can be little doubt that, for all its recognition of the importance of the court, it is critical of court life. Indeed, in terms of its *menosprecio de corte y alabanza de aldea* structure it contains much more overt *menosprecio* than *alabanza*, openly attacking the ambition, envy and ingratitude that fuels court activity. The second of Juan's hymns to self-sufficiency and rural contentment in Act I is larded with familiar references both to the lack of reward at court: '¿Hame de dar encomienda/ ni plaza de consejero?' (Act I, 1178b) and to the tribulations of those who achieve it:

¡Dura ambición! ¿Qué trabajas
haciendo al aire edificios,
pues los más altos oficios
no llevan más de mortajas? (Act I, 1179b)

Two voices may readily be detected here – the character's and his creator's. Juan Labrador's disillusionment is the articulation of Lope's own; the '¿Qué es ver al rey?' speech is a dialogue that each of them is having with himself. The term 'cortesano', it emerges, is used in the countryside as a term of contempt and abuse (in like vein, aristocrats are referred to as 'judíos'), and Feliciano's swift acclimatization to the ways of the court is signalled by his plan, once he is suitably attired, to take on two lackeys and six pages – prompting his fellow villager, Fileto, clearly no ignoramus where Spain's demographic changes were concerned, to observe tartly,

Si no hubieran los señores
los clérigos y soldados
menester tantos criados,
hubiera más labradores. (Act III, 1203a)

This jaundiced mood of Lope's is frequently detectable in his correspondance, as we see from the following letter to the Duke of Sessa, written a few years later in May 1620:

> Mis priuanzas no lo serian, aunque fuessen del rey, sin Vex.ª, porque sólo estimo su amor, solas sus merzedes y sus fabores solos; que no se paga quien trata con el alma y con la verdad de intereses fingidos y de esperanzas necias, y creo que Vex.ª sabe que ningun ombre que oy viva tiene ni ha tenido tales desengaños de las cossas del mundo, y particularmente de las desta edad, a quien todas las historias antiguas rinden ventaja en suspension de sucessos, nouedad de esperanzas y monstruosidad de atreuimientos. Bien aya vn rincón sin obligaciones ni capillas, donde son los gustos gustos, y los daños no son daños. Los frenos se hizieron para los caballos. Quien se dexa gobernar de otro, con el herrador se calza. Vnos van donde los otros quieren, y otros no saben dónde los lleban los que los engañan, y al fin al fin se cansan todos, y el tiempo passa, que va siempre quitando la vida. Por lo menos no la dan los Reyes a los que la gastan en sus caminos. Servicio se les debe; pero más al del cielo, que no tiene quexosos ni se dexa gouernar de los que no saben, porque lo sabe todo, y es yndependiente.[36]

This vein of disaffection feeds the half of the play that argues for self-sufficiency, stoical detachment and the eternal verities supposedly encapsulated in rural life. The other half, that which appears to recognize change and the desire to improve oneself, and concedes the irresistible power and centrality of the court, corresponds to Lope's own ambitions for recognition and prosperity within the charmed circle of royalty. The play is in its way a paradigm for the struggle that had been taking place throughout Europe since the middle of the sixteenth century between an old order and a new – Juan Labrador the incarnation of the old, a portrait tinged with nostalgia and regret, Feliciano his son, the incarnation of the new, painted with a sneaking admiration; but neither entirely escaping mockery.

It is possible, just about, to read the play in diametrically opposed ways. A propagandist, pro-monarch and pro-court reading would present Juan Labrador getting his come-uppance for his pride, his curmudgeonly impertinence and his smug parochialness, whereas a fully ironical reading would interpret the play as showing how a world of great value is effectively destroyed in the name of a spurious mystique. But there are, as we have seen, too many elements which resist such readings to make either one of them entirely convincing. Most traditional readings have worked with the assumption that the play is ultimately an affirmation of social and political harmony, that it argues for the necessary compatibility of its two worlds under the benign patronage of monarchy, with the good of the individual rightly yielding to the good of the state in an ideal world.[37] But the play deals in enduring values as

36 *Epistolario de Lope de Vega Carpio*, vol.4, no.432, 54–5.

37 This approach has been most fully elaborated by J.E. Varey, 'Towards an

well as in political ideas and it does not suggest that the priorities are as resolutely uncomplicated as an 'ideal world' reading implies. The application to the play of that totalizing vision of a monarchist heaven to be found between the pages of contemporary political treatises overlooks not only the much grainier identity of the text, but the complexities of Spanish social and political life at the time and of Lope's own attitudes. At a surface level the resolution of the action ensures that the play fulfils its courtly task of flattering the monarch and the institution of monarchy, but the text in its entirety overflows that formal limit. The play's two worlds are in contention throughout and remain so at the end of the play, with little to suggest that boundaries have in any significant way been redrawn. Both value systems are fully present at the end, neither is privileged, but on the other hand the two are not shown to be synergistic. The play does not conclude with Juan Labrador retreating to his beloved rural existence once he has seen the King and conceded his mistake, nor is there anything to suggest that in embracing him the court itself is embracing what he stands for. Country ethos and court ethos are maintained in tension.

As they were, of course, in real life at the time, intellectually, at least, if not in practice. Lope de Vega himself was as disinclined to live in the country as were all those of his compatriots who fled both countryside and, in many cases, country itself to make a living elsewhere. Rural depopulation was a determining factor in the economic fortunes of seventeenth-century Spain, and since the publication of Noël Salomon's *Recherches sur le thème paysan* many commentators have accepted that the idealization of rural life in the theatre, Lope's above all, was part of a back-to-the-land movement, of an attempt to stem the tide of urbanization and social climbing and redirect attention back to what were thought to be the traditional values and attractions of the countryside.[38] But whereas there was indeed in Spanish thinking and writing at this time a strong vein of disillusionment, even disgust, with what was seen as the materialism of modern life, of nostalgia for an idealized past and of glorification of the peasant and rural life, it is difficult to believe

Interpretation of Lope de Vega's *El villano en su rincón*', *Studies in Spanish Literature of the Golden Age Presented to Edward M. Wilson*, ed. R.O. Jones (London: Tamesis, 1973), 315–37. P. Halkhoree in his 'Lope de Vega's *El villano en su rincón*: an emblematic play', *Romance Notes* (1972), XIV, no. 1, 141–5, suggested that the more knowing elements in Lope's audience would have recognized in Juan Labrador, his values and his elevation, an oblique criticism of the political career of Rodrigo Calderón, a man who had achieved political and social eminence without possessing the virtues of a man such as Juan. The inference might conceivably have been drawn by any who chose to draw it, but there is too much going on in the text for it to be convincingly seen as politically engaged in this narrowly specific way.

[38] Noël Salamon's *Recherches sur le thème paysan dans la 'comedia' au temps de Lope de Vega* (Bordeaux: Féret et fils, 1965) has been profoundly influential in the development of this idea.

that the theatre as an institution consciously espoused the political cause of those thinkers who saw that the government's economic policies had been a contributory cause in the process of rural depopulation and the decline of agriculture. And at whom was this propaganda supposed to be aimed? The *comedia* certainly makes heroes of peasants and in doing so contributes significantly to the redefinition of both peasants and heroes. But this would not have cut any ice with Spain's policy makers, and it is unlikely to have cut very much with the audience, not least because in practical terms it is extremely difficult to see how such a crude propagandist interpretation might be reconciled with the view of feudal oppression to which spectators are treated in plays like *Peribáñez*, *Fuenteovejuna* and *El mejor alcalde el rey*. Migrants from the countryside knew only too well what hardships they were seeking to escape, and urban dwellers could not have been entirely innocent of the realities of a rural existence. In any case, what impressions would they have taken away from these plays? For Peribáñez reward entails promotion to military captain, the rewards of honest toil in *Fuenteovejuna* (where peasants speak unrecognizably of platonic love) are scarcely lavish, while Sancho in *El mejor alcalde* achieves wealth and happiness in a manner that only a simpleton would regard as typical of the countryside. Where is the persuasive reinvestment of prestige in the farming life? The depiction of peasants with a justified sense of their own dignity could not in itself constitute effective demographic propaganda, and could not have been intended as such. *El villano en su rincón*, for its part, can hardly be seen as a call to ignore fame and fortune and stay in one's rural niche.[39] So what is Lope's apparently indeterminate text up to? Wolfgang Iser supplies part of an answer when he observes that 'in general literary texts constitute a reaction to contemporary situations, bringing attention to problems that are conditioned though not resolved by contemporary norms'.[40] But it is not a complete answer, for here the lack of resolution is central to the fashioning of the work itself. In the play Lope does not supply us with the orientation we traditionally expect even from complex works of art. *El castigo sin venganza* is an extremely ambiguous play which invites multiple readings, but there is little doubt as to what sort of world is being portrayed and as to where Lope intends us to position ourselves in relation to it. *El villano* is unusual amongst Lope's plays in that here he resists the pressure to authorize even implicitly any guiding ethical perspective and leaves us entirely to the issues and ourselves. The work is a

[39] The suggestion by R.O. Jones that the depiction of peasant heroes content with their lot was intended to counter urban aspiration for social advancement ignored Peribáñez's social ambition and the successes of Feliciano and Lisarda. See 'Poets and Peasants', in *Homenaje a William L. Fichter Estudios sobre el teatro antiguo hispánico y otros ensayos,* ed. A. David Kossof and José Amor y Vázquez (Madrid: Editorial Castalia, 1971), 341–56.

[40] *The Act of Reading*, 3.

sort of dramatized debate, an enactment of ideological positions, with the two sets of conflicting values personified in the appealingly polarized figures of peasant and king, and the dialectic left in suspension at the end. The idea of a conflict proper between a peasant and a king, of a challenge from below, is never really actualized, and it is left to Calderón, with Pedro Crespo in *El alcalde de Zalamea*, to show what can be done dramatically and theatrically with the character of the self-made peasant who remains his own man in the face of external pressure.

If we ask ourselves – as we have to – how the play's audience would have constituted the meaning of the work, the text seems to presuppose at least two categories of spectator – on the one hand the urban/ court lover (with a tendency perhaps to youth), and on the other the court critic or sceptic (with a tendency to age and experience). But the alignments, as we saw, are not quite as neat as that – youth versus age, raw ambition for betterment versus self-satisfied contentment, urban versus rural, national versus provincial, worldly versus parochial. Everybody is rewarded at the end, though in Juan's case reward may be construed as loss, and any final judgement is deferred. The King may through *force majeure* win the battle of wills, but what remains in the memory is the proud *villano* content with his lot rather than his enforced capitulation at the end – a perfect example of an ending not superseding or invalidating what has gone before. Court life brings with it a certain loss of values, but the parochial life of the peasant removes him from the heartbeat of the nation. This is not harmony but stand-off, and Lope refuses to adjudicate. The play offers not a unified but a double viewpoint, which, in denying the spectator a standpoint from which to construe the action of the play, seems to legitimize both.[41] I have used 'refuse' and 'deny' advisedly. All ways of communicating can fail, but what we have here is not a failure of communication but a wilful withholding of pronouncement.

Northrop Frye maintained that a literary text was something to which the author brought the words and the reader the meaning, but this is not entirely true.[42] Words have meanings which in sentences work together to create extensions of meaning, and in producing words the author is producing meaning, or a meaning at least. The meaning s(he) seeks to produce may not, of course, be the only one of which the text is susceptible. It may have more meaning(s) than the author realizes, and its meaning may be differently constructed by the reader, particularly by the reader in a different time or place. At the same time the author, since he is engaged upon an act of communication, presumably makes assumptions about the way it will/might be received and these assumptions determine what and how is written. This must be particularly true in the case of the commercial theatre where the playwright nec-

41 See Iser, *The Act of Reading*, 35.

42 Northrop Frye, *Fearful Symmetry: A Study of William Blake* (Boston: Beacon Press, 1967), 427ff.

essarily takes account of a known, or at least assumed, horizon of expectations. Even non-commercial theatre has traditionally adhered to the tacit bargain stuck between producer and receiver over dramatic forms – both comedy and tragedy in their different ways rely heavily on the expectations their audiences have of them. Lope was writing for a real rather than a hypothetical audience in so far as he knew its social profile, the various and varied circumstances of its historical existence, the range of its likes and dislikes. Mingling as he did with high and low, he had his finger squarely on the pulse of public opinion and taste, and on the evidence of his plays set out to cater for all, his broad pen strokes accommodating his more conventional and less demanding spectators, the finer tones and detail providing interest for those able and eager to put a different construction on what they saw and heard. As we try to envisage it now, that audience is necessarily more hypothetical than it was for Lope since it has to be reconstructed from historical knowledge of the time, but it can be substantially real provided any responses projected for it remain historically grounded. What meaning(s) would that substantially real audience have extracted from *El villano en su rincón*? There can be no doubt who wins the battle of wills between Juan and his king? But who wins the moral war?

Even seen in the play's historical context, however, the text remains stubbornly evasive, approbation and disapprobation being dispensed with even hand. Since the King has his way (how can a king not?) but Juan's integrity and values, if not his existence, remain intact and indeed in essence unchallenged, pro-court and pro-country factions might each read the play as they pleased. The allure of the court is conceded but the enduring values of rural life remain inscribed. The pastoral dream may be compromised but it is certainly not rejected.[43] Both men are shown to be in their different ways capricious, but both to be justified in the defence of their own kingdoms and ideologies – the mystique of Nature, the mystique of royalty. Both are highly glamourized, both are sent up, although the court comes off worse. The countryside is shown to be parochial, peopled by the smug, the simple and the socially ambitious, the court is denounced as materialistic and corrupt. A plague, perhaps, on both their houses? If the contest between the king in his corner and the king in his court is indeed a draw, which would seem to be the case, then we can only assume that Lope is being deliberately evasive; if we are somewhat baffled then it is because we are meant to be. Lope's text is thoroughly and carefully noncommital, even playfully so. He has taken two of the holy cows of the day, set them against each other, then stepped back and deferred to his audience – 'Well, what do you think?' It is an almost explicit recognition that a literary text does not have to be determinate, that the centre of interest even in a dramatic plot can be how effects are achieved

[43] See Frances Day Wardlaw, '*El villano en su rincón*: Lope's Rejection of the Pastoral Dream', *Bulletin of Hispanic Studies* 58 (1981), 113–19.

rather than what those effects are. It is certainly an exercising of reservations about both the mystiques with which the play engages – reservations containing the glint of ideas that do not sit entirely comfortably with the ideological orthodoxies of the day – and to some extent it is a picking of personal sores. But it is also, in its deployment of Lope's favourite double-handed 'give and take' technique, another, if extreme, example of the exquisite 'politeness' in his handling of contemporary issues that we see at work in the king-plays, a politeness which was by no means entirely due to the aesthetic concerns which motivated Laurence Sterne in *Tristram Shandy*: '. . .no author who understands the just boundaries of decorum and good breeding would presume to think all: the truest respect which you can pay the reader's understanding is to halve this matter amicably, and leave him something to imagine, in his turn, as well as yourself'.[44] Lope, when he chose, was certainly adept at flattering his audience by leaving something to their imagination, but he was equally adept at the practice of prudent double talk, a tactic, interestingly enough, not far removed from the political principle of dissemblance advocated by Machiavelli, denounced by Spain's traditionally minded theorists, but not disallowed by the proponents of Tacitism.

44 *Tristram Shandy* 2, II (London: Everyman's Library, 1956), 79.

8

CONCLUSIONS

As an outstanding literary figure and the confidant of the Duke of Sessa, Lope de Vega had an entrée to aristocratic circles where politics and affairs of court and state would have been a constant topic of conversation. It is hardly surprising, therefore, that these concerns find their way into his plays, and that he had views to express on them. Indeed, it would have been astonishing in a playwright with his interest in the passions and problems of man, particularly man in his social context, had he not been interested in a subject of such philosophical and practical concern at the time as kingship. That he was conversant with the ideas of the major Spanish political theorists of his time there can be no doubt, and with the constitutionalist Mariana he enjoyed something akin to a professional friendship. Mariana came to Lope's defence when he was attacked by his critics, only to be attacked in his turn, along with Lope, by Torres Rámila in his *Spongia* (1617). The fellow feeling this induced in Lope was intensified by his view of Mariana as another victim of the system, like himself honoured in other countries but unappreciated by an 'ingrata patria', as he points out in the prologue to his *Triunfo de la fe en los reinos de Japón* (1618) which is addressed 'Al Tito Libio Christiano, Luz de la Historia de España, el P.D. Juan de Mariana de la Compañía de Jesús'.[1] In 1620 Lope wrote to him on the Duke of Sessa's behalf to seek his advice on how a noble should behave to his prince, how he should conduct himself with his vassals and how he could meet his Christian obligations in dealing with the lay and ecclesiastical jurisdictions involved in the administration of his estates[2] – matters which might well have inspired the composition of a play such as *El mejor alcalde el rey* (1620–23). In the very nature of his duties and activities Lope was immersed in the social and political concerns of his age, and close reading of his plays makes it impossible any longer to believe in the view of Lope as an eternal adolescent whose feelings were exquisitely reliable but who did not have two thoughts of his own to rub together.

1 See the edition of *Triunfo de la fe* by J.S. Cummins (London: Tamesis, 1965), 7–10.

2 *Epistolario*, vol.4, no.730, 279–81. Lope refers in the letter to 'el amor con que he leydo sus libros y admirado sus acciones', clearly speaking on his own part rather than the Duke's for Sessa was certainly not given to intellectual pursuits. Mariana, by then in his eighties, pleaded old age and ill health in his refusal to underwrite Sessa's political ambitions.

This view was last developed at length by Francisco Márquez Villanueva in his book *Lope: vida y valores*[3] and in the light of the foregoing chapters its charges will serve very well as a springboard for my conclusions. The use of works of fiction or semi-fiction or even non-fiction as straightforward evidence for an author's life and world-view is an unreliable exercise at best, but it presents particular problems in the case of a writer answerable, as Lope was, to a complex range of official and unofficial pressures who did not see his fictions as obvious mouthpieces for any systematic personal philosophy. In his determination to see the arch-conformist in all Lope's writings Márquez Villanueva underestimates both the complexity of Lope's personality and the crucial relevance of the relationship between his work and its context. A glaring example discussed by Márquez Villanueva, is Lope's *Isidro*. This poem about San Isidro, the illiterate peasant who became Madrid's patron saint, was written at the suggestion of Fray Domingo de Mendoza to promote Isidro's chance of canonization and in the very nature of the undertaking promotes values which might well make Lope seem like some cosmic Tory – an unthinking, moralistic believer in God, king and cottage, anti-change, anti-intellectual, anti-individual. The poem was intended as a persuasive piece of propaganda, and Lope skilfully deployed the arguments and the rhetoric necessary to the task. He would undoubtedly not have been slow to see possible advantages in being associated with the values promoted in the work should the campaign prove successful, and indeed there subsequently came commissions for three plays and responsibility for the poetic jousts held to celebrate the canonization when it received papal approval in 1622. And elements of conservatism to a greater or lesser extent certainly did inform Lope's attitudes. Somewhere along the way, however, this conservatism has to be reconciled with the counter facts that he was an inveterate urban dweller who in his life and work openly flaunted rules and conventions – including in later life the requirements of his priestly calling – while he simultaneously clung to the coat tails of the nobility, entertaining social aspirations that brought mockery down on his head and hungering after an intellectual authority he did not fully possess and therefore sometimes affected to despise. It is simply not possible to base convincing categorical generalizations about Lope's life-time values from a hagiographical work written three-and-a-half decades before he died. Of Lope's autobiographical novel *La Dorotea*, Márquez Villanueva says 'En vano se buscará allí alguna idea que haga mínimo afrente a nada aceptado por la España oficial de su tiempo así en lo grande como en lo pequeño' (218). Even if this

[3] Francisco Márquez Villanueva, *Lope: vida y valores* (Puerto Rico: Editorial de la Universidad de Puerto Rico, 1988). It is with the general conclusions of this work that I take issue. It is otherwise a scholarly book packed with information, astute judgements and valuable insights. Its detail, however, is far more impressive than its generalizations – indeed it often contradicts them.

were entirely true (and taking that somewhat problematic phrase 'official Spain' for granted) it would not be very significant. The same could be said, and of course has been, of Shakespeare. Official Spain, like official England, had a system of censorship which did not concern itself overmuch with anything other than the principal bogey of the day, respectively heresy and sedition. But this left a world of values, rules and conventions which were more or less fair game. When Lope in *La Dorotea* explains that his characters wear prohibited materials because the action takes place before the new sumptuary laws of 1622 (219) he is not carefully covering himself, as Márquez Villanueva claims; he is poking fun at the widely ignored laws – as he does countless times in his plays. Again, to express surprise that the Inquisition did not clamp down upon the depiction of honour–vengeance in the theatre and to see this exemption as being due to the theatre's enshrining of old-Christian values (227) is not only to forget that the theatre was widely regarded as socially and morally subversive and that honour was in fact a controversial issue, but also that the Inquisition had different priorities, that theatre was fiction and that fiction usually gets away with murder, literally as well as metaphorically. Othello kills his wife but the play was not for that reason banned in a Christian society where the penalty for murder was death. Tragedies and tragicomedies for their very existence depend on the fact that terrible events take place within them. Márquez Villanueva's Lope is a man who did what he pleased, got all he wanted and saw life as being entirely unproblematical, who did not allow even the existence of alternative points of view, who was irremediably plebeian (how cross Lope would have been at that!), who knew only how to love or hate and was never motivated by base interests. It is a picture difficult to reconcile with the facts of his life as well as with his writing. He emerges from the book as a child-like, unthinking purveyor of bankrupt myths somehow redeemed by his ability to transform these myths into great art, but we are then left with the pressing question whether great art can ever be born of bankruptcy. If Lope purveys a blinkered, reactionary, out-dated view of the human condition, why do we, in our 'liberated' times, I wonder, respond so positively, in the theatre and in our armchairs, to the plays he wrote?

Lope was a jobbing playwright of genius with a living to earn and a reputation to keep and the pressures on him were varied and in some cases – the absolute need, for example, to reconcile his dramatic art with the imperatives of commerce – irresistible. In one direction, however, he was relatively if not entirely untrammelled. Through patronage the princely courts of Europe were able to make art serve their propaganda and their prestige,[4] and through patronage writers and artists were in turn able to make their way upward in

4 See, for example, Ronald G. Asch and Adolf M. Birke (eds), *Princes, Patronage and the Nobility: The Court at the Beginning of the Modern Age c.1450–1650* (Oxford: Oxford University Press, 1991).

the world – literary patronage was inseparable from systems of social and political patronage.[5] In Lope's case, however, the patronage was partial and to a significant extent peripheral. He never achieved the court appointment he longed for, which would have increased the flow of favour from other sources, as a dramatist he was not a particular royal favourite, though obviously given his reputation no court theatre could ignore him, and his long-term patron, the unruly, somewhat disreputable Duke of Sessa, was far from being an establishment stalwart. Lope – though not for want of trying – was no Hurtado de Mendoza (palace *guardadamas* and later Secretary of the Inquisition[6]), and his service to court propaganda and prestige was, as we have seen in his treatment of kingship, extremely unreliable for all that he took no foolhardy risks. Court theatre as performance, as ceremony, certainly fulfilled an important function in the symbolism of monarchy during the reign of Philip IV and in this Lope played his part, but he was predominantly a commercial playwright and subject therefore to wider requirements which in some sense provided him with a smokescreen to hide behind. As a playwright whose 'official' role was to entertain, Lope inhabited the political margin. The medium of his recreational art allowed him, as a reader of and commentator upon power, to articulate positions denied more centrally placed commentators, in much the way a court jester was allowed an irreverence denied everybody else. In other words, to be on the edge of power facilitated prudently negotiated dissent. If every play is in some sense a battle for the mind and imagination of its audience, then the cumulative impact of Lope's political plays has to be assessed against the facts that there is no evidence to suggest that Lope's aim was to augment the powers of the Crown and that what he has to say about kings could have done precious little to serve the cause of his own courtly ambitions.

For Hugh Trevor-Roper the period, notwithstanding the shaping power of patronage, was one 'when great art and powerful ideas were intimately connected. . .a period of ideological tension and excitement which for several reasons was directly expressed in art by some of the greatest European artists'.[7] Spanish literature is not exempt from this generalization and neither is that peculiar manifestation of it, the *comedia*. Lope's theatre, in fact, with its royal portraits, becomes the very embodiment of the shared schizophrenia of his time – of the disjunction between a profound need to believe in hereditary monarchy as the natural and logical way for man to govern himself and the

[5] See Arthur F. Marotti, 'John Donne and the Rewards of Patronage', *Patronage in the Renaissance*, ed. Guy Fitch Lytle and Stephen Orgel (Princeton: Princeton University Press, 1981), 207–35, p.201.

[6] See Ruth Lee Kennedy, *Studies in Tirso*, I, pp.77–150; also Gareth A. Davies, *A Poet at Court: Antonio Hurtado de Mendoza* (Oxford: Oxford University Press, 1971).

[7] *Princes and Artists: Patronage and Ideology at Four Hapsburg Courts 1517–1633* (London: Thames and Hudson 1991 [first pub.1976]), 8.

damaging challenge to this conviction offered by the contemporary realities of monarchical rule. Lope was the mouthpiece of an entire age's ambivalence on this matter. At first sight, his treatment of power consequently resists totalization. It follows rather a dialectic pattern in which contrary positions are dramatically explored. Nonetheless there is a consistency of approach and, beyond that, of vision. Individually and in unison the plays dwell on the mismatch between the real and the ideal: human nature militates decisively against the king's role as God's lieutenant in the realm of the secular. A popular, commercial theatre inevitably imposed conditions of its own upon the way such ideological tensions were expressed, subjecting them much, if not all, of the time to the imperatives of heroism and romance. But, for all that, a substantial proportion of Lope's kings-plays together constitute a sustained and serious critique of kingship which can also provide a reference point for the interpretation of those texts where kings play a more limited if still significant role. Thus it is possible in the light of other plays to return to the three peasant-honour plays and look at them in a more politically alert way, while avoiding the sort of revisionism that in recent years outside Spain has strained so hard to compromise the traditional perception of the works' heroes, both peasant and royal, that it has neglected the subtler political dynamism and reach of the plays. That Lope depicted kings with absolutist leanings and illusions there can be no doubt; the weakness in the argument of those who contend that Lope was thereby an absolutist propagandist is both evidential (as we have seen) and methodological – art does not necessarily promote what it depicts. The underlying assumptions of the Maravallian view of the *comedia* are that what a character says reflects the author's view, that representation is prescription, that endings are ideological statements rather than dramatic negotiations, that to portray a king dispensing justice is wilfully to produce state propaganda, that a plot is reliable evidence for a dramatist's relationship with authority, that the plays contain simple messages for dutiful consumption. Louis Montrose has observed that 'During the sixteenth and seventeenth centuries, the separation of literature and art from explicitly didactic and political discourses or from such disciplines as history or moral and natural philosophy was as yet incipient' and clearly the idea of literature as a historic formulation had scarcely begun to emerge during Lope's lifetime.[8] But this is not to say that Early Modern literary texts functioned like sermons or tracts, that they engaged with issues in an unproblematical or conventional way.

> Lope en *La estrella de Sevilla* o en *El Duque de Viseo* desarrolla la misma concepción de la cruel grandeza del absolutismo monárquico que, como

8 'Renaissance Literary Studies and the Subject of History', *English Literary Renaissance* 16 (1986), 12.

> observa Vossler, no permite ninguna rebeldía, ni la menor protesta de la libertad contra la injusta acción del rey. Añadiremos, como un comprobante más, que también Moreto hace suya tal doctrina.

Such is the statement made in an authoritative history of Spanish literature in a section ascribed to J.A. Maravall, Alberto Blecua and Noël Salomon.[9] Leaving aside Moreto's own views and the question of *La estrella de Sevilla*'s uncertain authorship, the doctrinaire assumptions evident in that revealing phrase '*también* Moreto *hace suya* tal doctrina' (my italics) are remarkable in their indifference to the ways in which literary texts work. These plays are two of the Golden-Age theatre's few self-professed tragedies and the tragic devastation and waste generated within them by monarchical authoritarianism constitutes in itself a powerful deconstruction of absolutism.

The textual juxtaposition of expressions of belief in monarchy with monarchical misbehaviour does not constitute advocacy of a cynical 'anything goes' philosophy, which is the logical inference to be drawn from the charge that Lope was the prophet of absolutism. On the contrary it constitutes the exact opposite, setting up as it does a powerful contradiction between the two which stimulates and guides audience response. In dramatic context, as we have seen, monarchical power of its very nature is seen to require constraints if it is not to escalate into tyranny. There can be no question on the evidence provided by the intermeshing of plots, characters, dialogue and imagery in his plays that for Lope royal sovereignty needed to be hedged around with qualifications and restrictions both desirable and necessary for just and effective rule. Even when he was writing to some sort of brief, this ingrained position of his affected the outcome. It is intriguing that whereas Spanish commentators from Menéndez y Pelayo to the present day have been unable or unwilling to acknowledge Lope's commitment to the principle of a restricted monarchy, a different, if undeveloped, perception has occasionally surfaced outside Spain. Guenter Levy in his book on Mariana (1960) says of the political philosopher: 'Mariana defends a limited and constitutional monarchy. . .as a Spaniard seriously concerned over the trend toward corrupt absolutism under Hapsburg rule. . .Mariana belongs to that generation of Spanish writers – men like Cervantes, Lope de Vega and Calderón – who were deeply worried about Spain's threatening decline'(162),[10] and in a note to these remarks points out that the similarity of the sentiments expressed, especially in many of the dramas of Lope de Vega, to the ideas of Mariana was

9 *Historia y crítica de la literatura española*, ed. Francisco Rico, vol.III, *Siglos de Oro: Barroco*, ed. Bruce W. Wardropper, 270.

10 *Constitutionalism and Statecraft during the Golden Age of Spain: A Study of the Political Philosopher Juan de Mariana S.J.*, C.N.R.S. Travaux d'Humanisme et Renaissance XXXV (Geneva: Librairie E. Droz, 1960).

stressed by the Italian historian Arturo Pasa in 1939.[11] Lionel Abel, in characterizing Racine as the great conformist to religious, classical and royal authority, exclaims, 'How different he was not only from his contemporaries Corneille and Moliére, but from Marlowe and Shakespeare, and also from the great Spaniards Lope de Vega and Calderón!'[12] The myth of Lope's royal idolatry dies hard, however. Even Stradling, who sees the *comedia* as a forum where political issues were debated, at one point unwittingly uses a form of words which lends some substance to it (4). In 1605 Lope was put in charge of the literary jousts held in Toledo to celebrate the birth of Philip III's heir, later Philip IV, in Valladolid on Good Friday of that year. The adjudication took place on 22 May before the Corregidor in the town hall with Lope seated as master of ceremonies on a raised chair of crimson velvet to one side of the table bearing the prizes, knowing full well, one suspects, that the first prize of a diamond ring for a *canción* in praise of the queen was shortly to go to none other but himself. In his opening address, Lope hails the divine origin of letters and then moves on to pay his tribute to the new-born prince: '¿Quién duda que naciendo humanos Príncipes/ será justo alabarlos con los versos?/ que los Reyes son Dioses de la tierra.'[13] The translation of this as given by Stradling is 'That princes are human, no-one may doubt/ But poetry must make their divinity shine out', a rendering which, yielding perhaps to the lure of a neat rhyming couplet, does not accurately reflect what Lope says. He does not suggest that princes partake of the divine, he states that they are Gods of the earth, a metaphor entirely consistent with the hierarchical patterns and associations by means of which the philosophy of divine order was conventionally expressed at the time. The distinction is an important one because the emphasis in Lope's own words is, if anything, on the humanity of princes.

The sort of doctrinaire interpretation propagated by Maravall utilizes an unacceptably blunt critical tool in its analysis of the plays' procedures in that its approach to the match between history and art is altogether too schematic and consequently reductive. At the same time, readings of fictional kings which harness historical detail too zealously to their purpose can also be misleading. Although in *Peribáñez*, *Fuenteovejuna* and *El mejor alcalde el rey* the characters of the kings – all three of them historical – are sufficiently

[11] *Un grande teorico della politica nella Spagna del secolo XVI: Il Gesuita Giovanni Mariana* (Naples: R. Alfredo, 1939), 110.

[12] *Metatheatre: A New View of Dramatic Form* (New York: Hill and Wang, 1963), 32.

[13] The account appears in L. Cortés Echanove, *Nacimiento y crianza de personas reales en la Corte de España 1566–1886* (Madrid: CSIC, 1958), pp.38–40. Interestingly a woman, doña Isabel de Figueroa, was amongst the winners who approached the platform to receive their prizes and another, doña Alfonsa Vázquez, was amongst those runners-up rewarded with perfumed gloves and the honour of having their verses published in the official *relación* of the festivities.

nuanced to lend interest and some solidity, in comparison with most of Lope's kings they are idealized in so far as at the end they fulfil a specific symbolic role as dispensers of justice or forgiveness without regard to class.[14] At that point they would have been seen by contemporary audiences as exemplary models of firm but just government, embodying the law in the face of nobles who ruled like monarchs over their vast estates and thought they were a law unto themselves. The plays, particularly *Fuenteovejuna* and *El mejor alcalde el rey*, contained in this sense a contemporary message about the appropriate way for nobles to conduct themselves vis-à-vis the Crown and the law, as well as being a celebration of the historical centralization of power in Spain in the monarch. But there are methodological problems inherent in a recent tendency to ground readings of entire plays upon the depiction of princes who until the dénouement occupy secondary or marginal roles. The strategy was first applied to the wife-murder plays of Calderón. It works well there because the texts themselves, by their characterization of the figures of authority or by references in the dialogue, invite the audience to assess those figures' words and actions at the end in relation to what else the plays have shown or suggested about them. It is not, however, a technique which can ever be convincingly applied independently of the text. It is not realistic to imagine that detailed comparisons between historical kings and their fictional incarnations in the plays would have been invited by Lope or supplied by the audience. Few of Spain's confusing cavalcade of medieval monarchs would have been familiar to the contemporary public. Lope of course did his homework and no doubt derived much satisfaction from manipulating for his purpose the accounts he found in the chronicles, but scarcely any one else would have been aware of the adjustments and changes he made.[15] Indeed in most plays Lope has to give the audience help in placing the monarch by briefly sketching in the historical background. Much of the time, as we saw in the cases of Pedro el Cruel and Alfonso VIII, he was singularly cavalier himself about historical identities, playing freely upon any historical ambiguity as to character and inventing relationships and escapades at will. Even with the help of the ballads, which themselves in any case blurred history and legend, few names other than Rodrigo, Pedro and Fernando *el católico* could have rung more than a distant bell and even in these cases the memory must have been very generalized and indistinct. The contribution made to the composite folk memory by the theatre itself was in most cases so inconsistent as only to deepen the confusion. The audience's view of

[14] Peribáñez, in becoming a captain, becomes a gentleman and Sancho in *El mejor alcalde el rey* claims the *hidalgo* origins consistent with his birthplace in the north of Spain, but of course they are still outranked by their opponents.

[15] Bernard Bentley makes the same point of *El mejor alcalde el rey* in 'El mejor alcalde el rey y la responsabilidad política', 417, n.8. Evidently it needs to go on being said.

a stage king would have been determined almost entirely by what it saw and heard in the *corral*, though this is not to say that occasionally it might not have left the playhouse slightly bemused at seeing Pedro portrayed as *cruel* when they had always thought he was *justiciero* (or vice versa as the case might be), or the revered Fernando *el católico* treating a woman less honourably than he ought. What it would never have done is meaningfully paint stage kings with chronicled colours that have no existence in the plays. Lope always provided the audience with the historical facts and indicators he wanted them to have.

A recent revisionist work on the *comedia*'s peasant protagonists supports its argument that Peribáñez is portrayed as another Iago – and would have been seen as an outright villain by contemporary audiences – partly by reassessing the characterization of the king who at the end not only pardons him for his crime but rewards him for his *valor.*[16] Enrique III *el justiciero*, we are told, is too sick and volatile to see to justice (176), therefore what is done is not justice but a travesty of it, for Peribáñez is in fact the villain of the piece and the Comendador the true hero (177). Now meaning may legitimately exist in the eye of the beholder, but if a reading is to convince anyone other than its own reader, or if it is to be offered as the likely contemporary reading, it presumably has to have some hermeneutical integrity. The fact that the historical Enrique was unstable and sickly, and died young before fulfilling his ambition to drive the Moors from Andalusia, illuminates Lope's procedures and his handling of source material; but it can have no direct relevance to the play and its reception, because none of this is anywhere mentioned and no member of the audience would have remembered it. Similarly, when Costanza claims to find the young king extremely handsome the audience was not expected to recall that Mariana, in his history of Spain published some eight years before, had claimed that his features were distorted by illness. As we know from Shakespeare's history plays, the Renaissance theatre created kings to suit its purposes and Lope was a master at the game – the liberties he took with Alfonso VIII are a striking example. In *Peribáñez* he took from the *Crónica de Don Juan II* the scrap that served the play in hand,[17] creating a king with a historical name, an idealized institutional role and a fictionalized persona – his usual recipe, for all that the balance of ingredients changes with the play. Enrique is more impetuous and more easily roused to righteous indignation by caste loyalties than a king ought to be, which serves to increase the audience's sense of danger at the crucial moment, but restrained by the Queen and persuaded to see Peribáñez's *valor* he then fulfils the function demanded of him by the play's action and its message: that justice requires that in a king the man must yield to the role.

[16] Dian Fox, *Refiguring the Hero*.

[17] The first scene of Act III, in which Leonardo lists the lords and prelates summoned by Enrique III to Toledo in 1406 is based on the chronicle's opening chapter.

The ironies that infuse *Peribáñez* and its ending are not supplied by the mismatch between fictional and historical Enriques.

As late as the early 1620s Lope could still, in one of the peasant honour plays, *El mayor alcalde el rey*, think dramatically in terms of an ideal ruler.[18] However, with the passage of time, personal disappointment and the general growth of disaffection in the reign of Philip IV seem to have worked their disillusioning effects on him. The irreproachable, or near-irreproachable, model king to all intents and purposes disappears from his theatre, and although his last play, *La mayor virtud de un rey*, depicts a righteous monarch, it is only in order publicly to reprimand a real one. To see Lope de Vega as a compliant purveyor of official views is to ignore the evidence of the plays themselves, which show not only that Lope in his own way was as locked into the contemporary debate on kingship and the Spanish Crown as any political philosopher, but that through his drama the debate reached a wider, theatre-going public. Within that debate the position he broadly occupies is that of the most influential Spanish political thinkers in his lifetime, who denounced absolutism and imposed upon royal power restrictions moral, tactical and legal. It would be pointless to expect of Lope's plays Mariana-like discussion of such issues as the role to be played in the limitation of royal authority by the nobility and the church (162–3); he was in the business of writing for the commercial theatre and the mechanics of political power would not have suited his brief. Difficult questions are therefore necessarily begged, and we have no means of knowing how Lope would have answered had he been asked them.

The language of court flattery was doubtless the rhetoric of absolutism that Mariana warned his young prince against when his courtiers advised him that he was the supreme civil authority and that 'todo el derecho y toda la justicia están subyugadas a su voluntad' (173–4). This rhetoric emerges frequently from the mouths of Lope's characters as they pursue their own interests and ends – he had no illusions whatsoever about the court he so much wanted to be part of – and Lope, too, turns it to his own account but in a very different way, deploying it as a dual-purpose weapon which protects

[18] It is not in this respect relevant, I think, that while the King pauses to eat lunch Elvira is probably being raped by don Tello (see P. Halkhoree, 'El arte de Lope de Vega en *El mejor alcalde el rey*', *Bulletin of Hispanic Studies* 56 (1979), 31–42; and Robin Carter, 'History and Poetry: A Re-examination of Lope de Vega's *El mejor alcalde el rey*', *Forum for Modern Language Studies* 16 (1980), 193–213. This is one of the play's poignant ironies, but the King can hardly be accused of dereliction of duty. His handling of the affair is scrupulous, he has come a long way and has to eat, and he cannot anyway anticipate that Tello will sink so low. More importantly, the rape is necessary to the story and its ending, as Dian Fox has pointed out (*Refiguring the Hero*, 89), and the scene is a highly effective generator of dramatic tension and anticipation: it delays the confrontation between king and noble, and the *gracioso* Pelayo teeters humorously on the edge of letting the cat out of the bag about the identity of the disguised monarch.

and attacks simultaneously. The blueprint provided by his plays is not a blueprint for absolutism. They do not enter a fictional world in order complacently to evade the larger anxieties and issues generated at the time by monarchy. They fashion a fictional world which confronts these anxieties and issues, in the process propagating – and deliberately propagating – a concept of kingship that has little in common with the blandishments of self-serving courtiers and of favourites eager to appropriate absolutism to themselves. To believe in monarchy, as the theorists and Lope and the rest of Spain along with them did, was not to espouse the cause of absolutism. To believe in the centralization of authority in the crown was not to believe in unrestricted royal power. Even when they argued the case for single rule, believing it be the most natural, rational and efficient, even when they invoked images of divine vicegerency, the theorists were categorical in their rejection of absolutism, seeing it as a form of government that was not only inefficient and counter-productive but virtually indistinguishable from tyranny. There can be nothing clearer or more trenchant or more insistent than their pronouncements on this subject:

> *Mariana*: No piensen, pues, los príncipes que están menos sujetos a sus leyes que lo están la nobleza y el pueblo a aquellas que hubiesen sancionado en virtud de su facultad; especialmente cuando hay muchas leyes que no han sido dadas por los príncipes, sino instituídas por toda la república, cuya autoridad e imperio es mayor que la del príncipe. . .el rey no sólo debe obedecer a estas leyes sino que ni le es permitido variarlas sin el asenso, y firme voluntad de la multitud. (I, chap.9, 172)

> *Rivadeneyra*: Ningún rey es absoluto ni independiente ni proprietario, sino teniente y ministro de Dios, por el cual reinan los reyes y tiene ser y firmeza cualquiera potestad. (475)

> *López Bravo*: Podráse, pues, decir varón justo el príncipe que se juzgare sujeto a las leyes y que aunque de poder absoluto lo pueda todo, sólo entienda que pueda lo que es loable y justo porque, en el sumo poder, ha de ser menos la licencia. Esta es voz de rey, y de tirano aquella. (*Del rey*, 112)

> *Saavedra Fajardo*: Ni ha de creer el príncipe que es absoluto su poder, sino sujeto al bien público y a los intereses de su estado; ni que es inmenso, sino limitado y expuesto a ligeros accidentes. Un soplo de viento desbarató los aparatos marítimos del rey Filipe II contra Inglaterra. (*Empresa* XX, 53b)[19]

Neither does Lope ever tire of portraying the dangers of absolutism – in *Lo fingido verdadero* (c.1608), a saint's play safely set in the Roman Empire, he

[19] This naturalistic interpretation of the disaster contrasts strongly with the view of many Spaniards at the time that it must have been a divine punishment for loose living.

is scathing in his denunciation of the ruler who does not privilege the public good and who neglects the execution of his duties.

Where the royal court was concerned, Lope, like the majority of Spaniards, was as deeply ambivalent as he was about Spain's monarchs. In the case of the court, however, the respect and awe inspired by the institution of monarchy, which exerted a tempering influence upon his perception and therefore his criticism of his kings, certainly did not operate and Lope reserved for it his bitterest and most outspoken complaints. The capital and the court – the use of the one word *corte* for both indicates how exact was the identification of one with the other – was the focus of so many ambitions and desires and possessed therefore such irresistible charisma that the reality inevitably fell far short of the illusion. One of the reasons for Lope's bitterness about the court was his dependence upon it. His view of it as a nest of corruption, injustice, treachery, hypocrisy, self-interest and deceit – charges itemized by Rugero in *El servir con mala estrella* and, in Lope's own voice, in his *Romance sobre lo que es la corte* – was the understandable conviction of all those who felt neglected and under-rewarded, as well as the predictable judgement of moralists. Yet Lope would not have lived away from the excitement, the glamour, the stimulation and the eternal lure of possible preferment and patronage it offered. The ambivalent feelings the court provoked probably go deeper than this, however. Its *raison d'être* and its very heartbeat was the institution of monarchy itself. And just as the concern caused by the rule of contemporary monarchs was fuelled by theories and notions of ideal kings and kingship, so criticism of the court was rooted in a betrayed vision of it as the seat of royal sovereignty, mystique and ceremonial, as a symbol of Spanish magnificence and power, and as an exemplary centre of manners, taste and service.[20]

The dilemma represented by the idea and the reality of the court is perfectly captured, as we saw, in *El villano en su rincón*, written years before personal disillusionment set hard. No man can cut himself off from the heartbeat of society and life, but the farmer has lost the life he loved for one which he is never given the chance to pronounce upon and is certainly not cut out for, while the king envies an existence he will not allow to continue. Juan's independence and contentment and his vision of a rural idyll (which in and through the children is also seen to be flawed), remain in perfect equipoise

[20] On the subject of seventeenth-century European courts see A.G. Dickens (ed.), *The Courts of Europe: Politics, Patronage and Royalty 1400–1800* (London: Thames and Hudson, 1977); Norbert Elias, *The Civilizing Process*, trans. Edmund Jephcott (Oxford: Blackwell, 1978) and *The Court Society*, trans. Edmund Jephcott (Oxford: Blackwell, 1983); J.H. Elliott, 'The Court of the Spanish Hapsburgs: A Peculiar Institution?', *Spain and its World 1500–1700*, 142–61; Jonathan Brown and J.H. Elliott, *A Palace for a King. The Buen Retiro and the Court of Philip IV* (New Haven/London: Yale University Press, 1980).

with the compelling centrality of monarchy. The route towards the one, positive conclusion (gain) necessarily produces the counter, negative conclusion (gain is loss). Lope was as capable as his fictional king of envying one dream while settling for another.

In *La sortija del olvido* the king's servant, in response to his master's irrational orders when he is under the influence of the poisoned ring, observes, 'no quiero replicar,/ sino vivir y callar,/ que es a quien sirve importante (Act III, 615b).[21] Unlike the servant, Lope could compensate for the dependence and sycophancy necessary in his life by exploiting the resources of his art. In the *corrales* he could deploy a range of manoeuvres to question, insinuate and probe, to explore with exactly measured diplomacy an adversarial position. The theatre was literally the stage where the contradictions in Lope's character – the yearning for respectability and success, the impulse to rebellion – could find free reign. In his art Lope refused to sell his soul to the academic establishment and by means of his art he managed to avoid selling it to the Crown as well. He is not compromised artistically by the accommodations he made, because his transgressive instincts so often make themselves felt in his writing, reflecting the dialectic of conformity and non-conformity that constituted his life. In the age in which he lived it was taken for granted that poetry could work on different levels, that books were often directed at different readerships and sported (sometimes seriously, sometimes sarcastically) double prologues, one written for the *vulgo*, the other for the *lector discreto*,[22] that mythological narratives worked allegorically, that the *autos* directed themselves at different levels of spectators, indeed that the scriptures themselves revealed to the faithful what they could comprehend. The assumption was that all these discourses possessed hidden levels of meaning legible by those equipped to read them. Such habits of mind, not least the philosophical conviction that appearances in general consistently deceive, that things are not as they appear to be, were not left behind at the entrance to the *corral* at the start of the performance of a play. Monarchy on stage and in life was a spectacle, but the relationship between stage kings and real ones went deeper than that. The court theatre was in the reign of Philip IV a consciously-wielded instrument of power and power was a central preoccupation of the theatre, at court and in the *corrales*. In *Lo fingido verdadero* theatrical display and the exercise of power become brilliantly one – a theatre-state that is also a microcosm of life and the universe. The semiotics of the performed text subjected power to a process of radical questioning, and although power where it is threatened is reinstated the perception of power does not remain unchanged.

21 *Obras*, Real Academia Española (nueva ed.), IX.

22 See Don Cruickshank, 'Literature and the Book Trade in Golden-Age Spain', *Modern Language Review* 73 (1978), 799–824.

The theatre possessed a special capacity for reacting to contemporary realities, however sensitive, and was the only 'literature' to which many of the audience would have been exposed. The fact that contemporary accounts of events often restrict their mention of the contribution made by the theatres to a terse 'hubo comedia' does not mean that their contribution was irrelevant. It emphasizes, on the contrary, the intense relevance of the theatre to the life of the capital while revealing at the same time that in the strict hierarchy of letters the theatre occupied a lowly place. It was in this low estimate of the theatre as mere entertainment that its freedom partly lay. Discerning commentators, however, recognized it for what it was, an outlet for anxieties, a source of warnings and advice, at best a restraining influence – Saavedra Fajardo was convinced that criticism, even gossip, played a crucial part in the republic in the control of vice (*Empresa* XIV is entirely devoted to the uses of *murmuración*). A play, of course, is a fiction, a construct of the imagination, not the bald expression of a view. But the only way in which we experience the past is through this and other forms of representation. Drama obscures the authorial voice because if the dramatic fiction is strictly observed the author is never able to speak to the audience direct. Views therefore become an elusive goal to be trapped, if at all, in the complex interaction of the work's parts. If a play without wilful or artificial misconstruction of the text can be read or performed as subversive, then it presumably possesses a subversive identity even if its traditionally perceived identity is not subversive. Systems of meaning are not just constituted by the reader/critic but inscribed in the work by the author with views he wants to convey and attitudes he cannot help conveying. In other words they are reconstituted as well as constituted. The approach to discourse pioneered by such as Bakhtin and Foucault removes the boundaries between individual texts. Transverse consideration of Lope's king-plays confirms the impression given by texts separately that they do not constitute a monologic body of writing but are largely dialogic. There is little glorification of princes in them and no endorsement of absolutism. There is no suggestion that pieties should be left unchallenged for all that pieties are shown to have a necessary place in the scheme of things. What there is, is a systematic campaign of demystification and a concerned and penetrating dialogue about the relationship between men and the institution of monarchy, between social and symbolic systems. In Lope's theatre art is by no means the servant of king. Kings, rather, serve art in order that art might engage with one of the great public issues of the day.

LIST OF WORKS CONSULTED

Texts: references for the texts of plays and of other primary sources referred to are given in the notes.

Abel, Lionel. *Metatheatre: A New View of Dramatic Form.* New York: Hill and Wang, 1963.

Abellán, José Luis. *Historia crítica del pensamiento español*, vol.2, *La Edad de Oro (Siglo XVI)*, and vol.3, *Del Barroco a la Ilustración (Siglos XVII y XVIII).* Madrid: Espasa-Calpe, 1979 and 1988.

Alborg Day, Cornelia. 'El teatro como propaganda en dos tragedias de Lope de Vega: *El Duque de Viseo* y *El castigo sin venganza*'. *Lope de Vega y los orígenes del teatro español. Actas del primer congreso internacional sobre Lope de Vega*, dir. Manuel Criado del Val. Madrid: Edi-6, 1981, 745–54.

Alonso, Amado. 'Lope de Vega y sus fuentes', *Thesaurus* (Bogotá) 8 (1952), 1–24.

Andrés, Fr. Alfonso, O.S.B. 'La mayor virtud de un rey, última comedia de Lope de Vega', *Ínsula*, 200–201 (1963), 10–23.

Anglo, Sydney. *Machiavelli: A Dissection.* London: Victor Gollancz, 1969.

Asch, Ronald G., and Adolf M. Birke (ed.). *Princes, Patronage and the Nobility: The Court at the Beginning of the Modern Age c.1450 –1650.* Oxford: Oxford University Press, 1991.

Aston, Margaret. *The King's Bedpost: Reformation and Iconography in a Tudor Group Portrait.* Cambridge: Cambridge University Press, 1993.

Austin, J.L. *How to Do Things with Words*, ed. J.O. Urmson. Oxford: Clarendon Press, 1962.

Bances Candamo, Francisco Antonio de. *Theatro de los theatros de los passados y presentes siglos.* Segunda versión, 1689–94, ed. Duncan W. Moir. London: Tamesis, 1970.

Barker, Francis. *The Tremulous Private Body: Essays on Subjection.* London/New York: Methuen, 1984.

Barreda, Francisco de. *El panegírico de Plinio en castellano.* Madrid, 1622.

Barroll, J. Leeds. 'A New History for Shakespeare and his Time', *Shakespeare Quarterly* 39 (1988), 441–64.

Barton, Anne. *Essays, Mainly Shakespearean.* Cambridge: Cambridge University Press, 1994.

Bastianutti, Diego. *La niñez del Padre Rojas. By Lope de Vega*, American University Studies. Series II: Romance Languages and Literature 54. New York/Bern/Frankfurt am Main/Paris: Peter Lang, 1988.

Bataillon, Marcel. 'El villano en su rincón', *Varia lección de clásicos españoles* (Madrid: Editorial Gredos, 1964), 329–72.

Bentley, Bernard. 'El mejor alcalde el rey y la responsabilidad política', *Lope de Vega y los orígenes del teatro español. Actas del Primer Congreso Internacional sobre Lope de Vega*, ed. Manuel Criado de Val. Madrid: Edi-6, S.A., 1981.

Blue, William R. 'The Politics of Lope's *Fuenteovejuna*', *Hispanic Review* 59 (1991), 293–313.

Bourdieu, Pierre. 'Censorship and the Imposition of Form', trans. Gino Raymond and Matthew Adamson, *Language and Symbolic Power*, ed. John B. Thompson. Cambridge: Polity Press, 1991, 137–59.

Bradman, Leicester, and Charles Arthur Lynch (ed.). *The Latin Epigrams of Thomas More*. Chicago: University of Chicago Press, 1953.

Brown, Jonathan, and J.H. Elliott. *A Palace for a King: The Buen Retiro and the Court of Philip IV*. New Haven/London: Yale University Press, 1980.

Brown, Penelope, and Stephen C. Levinson. *Some Universals in Language Usage*. Cambridge: Cambridge University Press, 1987.

Brownlee, Marina, and Hans Ulrich Gumbrecht (ed.). *Cultural Authority in Golden-Age Spain*. Baltimore/London: John Hopkins University Press, 1995.

Carter, Robin. '*Fuenteovejuna* and Tyranny: Some Problems of Linking Drama with Political Theory', *Forum for Modern Language Studies* 23 (1977), 313–36.

— 'History and Poetry: A Re-examination of Lope de Veg's *El mejor alcalde el rey*', *Forum for Modern Language Studies* 16 (1980), 193–213.

Cascales, Francisco de. *Cartas filológicas* (1634). Madrid: Espasa Calpe, 1961.

Casa, Frank P., and Berislav Primorac (ed.) 'El rey', *El mejor alcarde el rey: Lope de Vega*. Madrid: Cátedra, 1993, 13–20.

Cascardi, Anthony. *Ideologies of History in the Spanish Golden Age*. University Park, Pa: Pennsylvania State University Press, 1998.

Chadravorty, Swapan. *Society and Politics in the Plays of Thomas Middleton*. Oxford: Clarendon Press, 1995.

Clare, Janet. *Art Made Tongue-Tied by Authority: Elizabethan and Jacobean Dramatic Censorship*. Manchester/New York: Manchester University Press, 1990.

Clarke, Simon. *The Foundations of Structuralism: A Critique of Lévi-Strauss and the Structuralist Movement*. Brighton: Harvester Press, 1981.

Cohen, Walter, 'Political Criticism of Shakespeare', *Shakespeare Reproduced: The Text in History and Ideology*, ed. Jean E. Howard and Marion F. O'Connor. London: Methuen, 1987, 18–46.

Cortés Echanove, L. *Nacimiento y crianza de personas reales en la Corte de España 1566–1886*. Madrid: CSIC, 1958.

Cotarelo y Mori, E. *Bibliografía de las controversias sobre la licitud del teatro en España*. Madrid: Revista de Archivos, Bibliotecas y Museos, 1904, reissued 1933.

— *Ensayo sobre la vida y obras de don Pedro Calderón de la Barca*. Madrid: Revista de Archivos, Bibliotecas y Museos, 1924.

Cox, Jeffrey N., and Larry J. Reynolds. *New Historical Literary Study: Essays on*

Reproducing Texts, Representing History. Princeton: Princeton University Press, 1993.

Crapotta, James. *Kingship and Tyranny in the Theatre of Guillén de Castro*. London: Tamesis, 1984.

Crespo de Matellán, Salvador. *La parodia dramática en la literatura española*. Salamanca: Ediciones Universidad de Salamanca, 1979.

Cruickshank, Don. 'Literature and the Book Trade in Golden-Age Spain', *Modern Language Review* 73 (1978), 799–824.

Cummins, J.S. (ed.). *Lope de Vega: Triunfo de la fe en los reinos de Japón*. London: Tamesis, 1965.

Dansey Smith, Hilary. *Preaching in the Spanish Golden Age: A Study of Some Preachers of the Reign of Philip III*. Oxford: Oxford University Press, 1978.

Davies, Gareth A. *A Poet at Court: Antonio Hurtado de Mendoza*. Oxford: Oxford University Press, 1971.

de Armas, Frederick A. (ed.). *Heavenly Bodies: The Realms of 'La estrella de Sevilla'*. Lewisburg: Bucknell University Press, 1996.

— 'The Mysteries of Canonicity', *Heavenly Bodies: The Realms of 'La estrella de Sevilla'*, ed. de Armas, 15–28.

de Velasco, Recaredo F. *Referencias y transcripciones para la historia de la literatura política en España*. Madrid: Editorial Reus, 1925.

Dickens, A.G. (ed.). *The Courts of Europe: Politics, Patronage and Royalty 1400–1800*. London: Thames and Hudson, 1977.

Díez Borque, José Mª. 'Estructura social de la comedia de Lope: a propósito de *El mejor alcalde el rey*', *Arbor* 85 (1973), 453–66.

— *Sociología de la comedia española del siglo XVII*. Madrid: Cátedra, 1976.

Dollimore, Jonathan. *Radical Tragedy: Religion, Ideology and Power in the Drama of Shakespeare and his Contemporaries*. London: Harvester Wheatsheaf, 1989.

— *Sexual Dissidence: Augustine to Wilde, Freud to Foucault*. Oxford: Clarendon Press, 1991.

Dollimore, Jonathan, and Alan Sinfield (eds). *Political Shakespeare: Essays in Cultural Materialism*. Manchester: Manchester University Press, 1994; first edition 1985.

Dumont, Louis. *Homo hierarchicus: the Caste System and its Implications*. trans. Mark Sainsbury, Louis Dumont and Basia Gulati. Chicago: University of Chicago Press, 1980.

Eagleton, Terry. *Criticism and Ideology: A Study in Marxist Literary Theory*. London: New Left Books, 1976.

Egido, Teófanes. *Sátiras políticas de la España moderna*. Madrid: Alianza Editorial, 1973.

Elias, Norbert. *The Civilizing Process*, trans. Edmund Jephcott. Oxford: Blackwell, 1978.

— *The Court Society*, trans. Edmund Jephcott. Oxford: Blackwell, 1983.

Elliott, J.H. *Imperial Spain 1469–1716*. London: Edward Arnold, 1963.

— 'Philip IV of Spain: Prisoner of Ceremony', *The Courts of Europe: Politics, Patronage and Royalty, 1400–1800*, ed. A.G. Dickens. London: Thames and Hudson, 1977, 169–89.

— 'A Question of Reputation: Spanish Foreign Policy in the Seventeenth Century', *Journal of Modern History* 55 (1983), 475–83.
— *Poder y Sociedad en la España de los Austrias*. Barcelona: Edición Crítica, 1984.
— *The Count-Duke of Olivares. The Statesman in an Age of Decline*. New Haven/London: Yale University Press, 1986.
— Review of J.A. Maravall, *The Culture of the Baroque*, *New York Review of Books* 9 April 1987.
— *Spain and its World 1500–1700*. New Haven/London: Yale University Press, 1989.
— See also Brown, Jonathan, and J.H. Elliott.
Etreros, Mercedes. *La sátira política en el siglo XVII*. Madrid: Fundación Universitaria Española, 1983.
Exum, Frances. *The Metamorphosis of Lope de Vega's King Pedro*. Madrid: Colección Plaza Mayor Scholar, 1974.
Fernández-Santamaría, J.A. *Reason of State and Statecraft in Spanish Political Thought, 1595–1640*. Lanham, Md.: University Press of America, 1982.
Foucault, Michel. *Discipline and Punish: The Birth of the Prison*, trans. Alan Sheridan. New York: Vintage, 1979.
Fox, Dian. *Refiguring the Hero: From Peasant to Noble in Lope de Vega and Calderón*. University Park, Pa.: Pennsylvania State University Press, 1991.
Franklin, Julian H. *Jean Bodin and the Rise of Absolutist Theory*. London: Cambridge University Press, 1973.
Frye, Northrop. *Fearful Symmetry: A Study of William Blake*. Boston: Beacon Press, 1967.
García Aráez, Josefina. *Don Luis de Ulloa y Pereira*. Madrid: Consejo Superior de Investigaciones Científicas, 1952.
Geertz, Clifford. 'Centers, Kings and Charisma: Reflections on the Symbols of Power', *Culture and Its Creators: Essays in Honour of Edward Shils*, ed. Joseph Ben-David and Terry Nichols Clark. Chicago: University of Chicago Press, 1977.
Gilbert, Allan H. (ed.). *Literary Criticism from Plato to Dryden*. Detroit: Wayne State University Press, 1962.
Goffman, E. *Interaction Ritual: Essays on Face to Face Behaviour*. Harmondsworth: Penguin, 1972.
Gómez-Moriana, Antonio. *Derecho de resistencia y tiranicidio: Estudio de una temática en las 'comedias' de Lope de Vega*. Santiago de Compostela: Porto y Cía, 1968.
González de Amezúa, A. 'Un enigma descifrado: El raptor de la hija de Lope de Vega', *Boletín de la Real Academia Española*, XXI (1934), 357–404, 521–62.
— *Epistolario de Lope de Vega Carpio* (ed.), 4 vols. Madrid: Real Academia Española, 1935–43.
González Palencia, A. (ed.). *Noticias de Madrid, 1621–27*. Madrid: Ayuntamiento de Madrid, 1942.
Green, Otis H. 'La dignidad real en la literatura del siglo de oro: noticias de un estudioso', *Revista de Filología Española*, 48 (1965), 231–50.
Greenblatt, Stephen. *Renaissance Self-Fashioning: From More to Shakespeare*. Chicago/London: University of Chicago Press, 1980.

— Introduction, 'The Forms of Power and the Power of Forms', *Genre* 15 (1982), 3–6.
— *Shakespearean Negotiations, The Circulation of Social Energy in Renaissance England.* Oxford: Clarendon Press, 1988.
Greer, Margaret Rich. *The Play of Power: Mythological Court Dramas of Calderón de la Barca.* Princeton: Princeton University Press, 1991.
Grice, Paul. 'Logic and Conversation', *Studies in the Way of Words.* Cambridge, Mass./London: Harvard University Press, 1989.
Gumperz, John J. *Discourse Strategies.* Cambridge: Cambridge University Press, 1982.
Halkhoree, P. 'Lope de Vega's *El villano en su rincón*: an emblematic play', *Romance Notes* XIV, no. 1 (1972–73), 141–5.
—'El arte de Lope de Vega en *El mejor alcalde el rey*', *Bulletin of Hispanic Studies* 56 (1979), 31–42.
Halliday, M.A.K., and Ruqaiya Hasan. *Language, Context and Text: Aspects of Language in a Social-Semiotic Perspective.* Oxford: Oxford University Press, 1989.
Halpern, Cynthia Leone. *The Political Theater of Early Seventeenth-Century Spain, with Special Reference to Juan Ruiz de Alarcón.* New York: Peter Lang, 1993.
Hamilton, Bernice. *Political Thought in Sixteenth-Century Spain.* Oxford: Clarendon Press, 1963.
Harris, Wendell. *Interpretive Acts: In Search of Meaning.* Oxford: Oxford University Press, 1988.
Heineman, Margot. 'Political Drama', *The Cambridge Companion to English Renaissance Drama*, ed. A.R. Braunmuller and Michael Hattaway. Cambridge: Cambridge University Press, 1990.
— *Puritanism and Theatre: Thomas Middleton and Opposition Drama under the Early Stuarts.* Cambridge: Cambridge University Press, 1980.
Hermenegildo, Alfredo. 'Cristóbal de Virués y los signos teatrales del horror', *Horror y Tragedia en el Teatro del Siglo de Oro, Actas del IV Coloquio G.E.S.T.E., Toulouse 1983, Criticón* 23 (1983), 93.
Herrero, Javier. 'The New Monarchy: A Structural Interpretation of *Fuenteovejuna*', *Revista Hispánica Moderna* 36 (1970–71), 173–85.
Herrero García, Miguel. 'La monarquía teorética de Lope de Vega', *Fén*, I (1935), 179–224, 303–62.
Heywood, Thomas. *An Apology for Actors*, reprinted for the Shakespeare Society, London 1841.
Hirsch, E.D. *Validity in Interpretation.* New Haven: Yale University Press, 1967.
Holderness, Graham, Nick Potter and John Turner. *Shakespeare: The Play of History.* London: Macmillan, 1985.
— *Shakespeare Out of Court: Dramatizations of Court Society.* London: Macmillan 1990.
Hopkins, Lisa. *John Ford's Political Theatre.* Manchester: Manchester University Press, 1994.
Horn, Laurence R. 'Pragmatic Theory', *Linguistics: The Cambridge Survey.* Vol. 1, *Linguistic Theory: Foundations.* ed. Frederick J. Newmeyer. Cambridge: Cambridge University Press, 1988, 113–45.

Howard, Jean E., and Marion F. O'Connor (ed.). *Shakespeare Reproduced: The Text in History in and Ideology*. London: Methuen, 1987.

Iser, Wolfgang. *The Act of Reading: A Theory of Aesthetic Response*. Baltimore/London: John Hopkins University Press, 1978.

Jameson, Fredric. *The Political Unconscious: Narrative as a Socially Symbolic Act*. Ithaca: Cornell University Press, 1981.

Jones, R.O. 'Poets and Peasants', *Homenaje a William L. Fichter: Estudios sobre el teatro antiguo hispánico y otros ensayos*, ed. A. David Kossof and José Amor y Vázquez. Madrid: Editorial Castalia, 1971, 341–56.

Joucla-Ruau, André. *Le Tacitisme de Saavedra Fajardo*. Paris: Éditions Hispaniques, 1977.

Kamen, Henry. 'Toleration and Dissent in Sixteenth-Century Spain: The Alternative Tradition', *Crisis and Change in Early Modern Spain*. Aldershot: Variorum, 1993, first published in *The Sixteenth-Century Journal*, 19 (Spring 1988), 3–23.

Kamps, Ivo. *Historiography and Ideology in Stuart Drama*. Cambridge: Cambridge University Press, 1996.

Kantorowicz, Ernst H. *The King's Two Bodies*. Princeton: Princeton University Press, 1957.

Kennedy, Andrew. *Dramatic Dialogue: The Duologue of Personal Encounter*. Cambridge: Cambridge University Press, 1983.

Kennedy, Ruth Lee. *Studies in Tirso de Molina I. The Dramatist and His Competitors 1620–26*. Chapel Hill: North Carolina Studies in the Romance Languages and Literatures, U.N.C. Department of Romance Languages, 1974.

— '*La estrella de Sevilla*, Reinterpreted', *Revista de Archivos, Bibliotecas y Museos* 78 (1975), 385–408.

— 'La perspectiva política de Tirso en *Provar contra su gusto* y la de sus comedias posteriores', *Homenaje a Tirso*. Madrid: Revista Estudios, 1981, 199–238.

— 'La Estrella de Sevilla as a Mirror of the Courtly Scene and of its Anonymous Dramatist (Luis Vélez???)', *Bulletin of the Comediantes* 45 (1993), 104–43.

Kernan, Alvin. *Shakespeare, the King's Playwright: Theatre in the English Court 1603–1613*. New Haven/London: Yale University Press, 1995.

Kirschner, Teresa J. *El protagonista colectivo en 'Fuenteovejuna'*. Salamanca: Universidad de Salamanca, 1979.

La Barrera, Cayetano Alberto de. *Nueva Biografía de Lope de Vega*, 2 vols, Biblioteca de Autores Españoles, 262 and 263. Madrid: Atlas, 1974.

Labarve, Françoise, and Roland. 'Sobre la fecha de *Peribáñez y el Comendador de Ocaña*', *Criticón* (Toulouse) 54 (1992), 123–6.

Lacan, Jacques. *Écrits*. Paris: Éditions du Seuil, 1966.

Lafuente, Modesto. *Historia general de España*, 30 vols. Madrid, 1850–67.

Lamarque, Peter. 'The Death of the Author: An Analytical Autopsy', *British Journal of Aesthetics* 30 (1990), 319–31.

Lauer, A. Robert. *Tyrannicide and Drama*. Stuttgart: Steiner-Vel Wiesbaden 1987.

Levy, Guenter. *Constitutionalism and Statecraft during the Golden Age of Spain: A Study of the Political Philosopher Juan de Mariana S.J.* C.N.R.S. Travaux d'Humanisme et Renaissance, XXXV. Geneva: Librairie E. Droz, 1960.

Lewis, David. *Philosophical Papers* I. New York: Oxford University Press, 1983.

López Bravo, Mateo. *De rege et regendi ratione* (1627), trans. Antonio Pérez Rodríguez as *Del rey y de la raçón de governar*, in Mechoulan, *Mateo López Bravo: Un socialista español del siglo XVII.*

López-Vázquez, Alfredo Rodríguez. 'The Analysis of Authorship: A Methodology', *Heavenly Bodies. The Realms of 'La estrella de Sevilla'*, ed. de Armas, 195–205.

Lynch, John. *Spain Under the Habsburgs*, 2 vols. Oxford: Basil Blackwell, 1969.

Lyons, John. *Semantics*. Cambridge: Cambridge University Press, 1977.

Lytle, Guy Fitch, and Stephen Orgel (eds). *Patronage in the Renaissance*. Princeton: Princeton University Press, 1981.

MacKay, Angus, and Geraldine McKendrick, 'The Crowd in Theater and the Crowd in History: *Fuenteovejuna*', *Renaissance Drama* 17 (1988), 125–47.

McKendrick, Melveena. 'Calderón and the Politics of Honour', *The 'Comedia' in the Age of Calderón: Studies in Honour of Albert Sloman. Bulletin of Hispanic Studies* 70 (1993), 135–46.

— *The Revealing Image: Stage Portraits in the Theatre of the Golden Age.* London: Queen Mary and Westfield College, 1996.

— 'In the Wake of Machiavelli: *Razón de Estado*, Morality and the Individual', *Heavenly Bodies: The Realms of 'La estrella de Sevilla'*, ed. de Armas, 76–91.

Marañón, Gregorio, *El Conde-Duque de Olivares* [third edition]. Madrid: Espasa Calpe, 1952.

Maravall, J.A. *La teoría española del estado en el siglo XVII.* Madrid: Instituto de Estudios Políticos, 1944.

— 'Moral de acomodación y carácter conflictivo de la libertad (notas sobre Saavedra Fajardo)', *Cuadernos Hispanoamericanos*, nos. 257–8 (1971), 682.

— *Estado moderno y mentalidad social: Siglos XV a XVII*, 2 vols. Madrid: Revista de Occidente, 1972.

— *Teatro y literatura en la sociedad barroca*. Madrid: Benzal, 1972.

— 'Maquiavelo y maquiavelismo en España', *Estudios de historia del pensamiento español: Siglo XVII*. Madrid: Ediciones Cultura Hispánica, 1975.

Mariana, Padre Juan de. *De Rege et Regis Institutione* (1599), trans. E. Barriobero y Herrán as *Del rey y de la institución de la dignidad real*. Madrid: Mundo Latino, 1930.

— *Obras del Padre Juan de Mariana*, 2 vols. Biblioteca de Autores Españoles, 30–31. Madrid: M. Rivadeneyra, 1872.

Marotti, Arthur F. 'John Donne and the Rewards of Patronage', *Patronage in the Renaissance*, in Guy Fitch Lytle and Stephen Orgel ed. Princeton: Princeton University Press, 1981, 207–35.

Márquez Villanueva, Francisco. *Lope: vida y valores*. Río Piedras: Editorial de la Universidad de Puerto Rico, 1988.

Mauss, Marcel. *The Gift: Forms and Functions of Exchange in Archaic Societies*, trans. Jan Cunnison. London: W.W. Norton, 1967.

Mechoulan, Henry. *Mateo López Bravo: Un socialista español del siglo XVII.* Madrid: Editora Nacional, 1977.

Menéndez Pidal, R. (ed.). *Historia de España* (1975), vol. XXIV. Madrid: Espasa Calpe, 1979.

Menéndez y Pelayo, M. *Estudios sobre el teatro de Lope de Vega*. Madrid: Consejo Superior de Investigaciones Científicas, 1949.

Montero Díaz, Santiago. 'La doctrina de la Historia en los tratadistas del Siglo de Oro', in his edition of Luis Cabrera de Córdoba, *De Historia, para entenderla y escribirla* (1611). Madrid: Instituto de Estudios Políticos, 1948.

Montrose, Louis. 'Renaissance Literary Studies and the Subject of History', *English Literary Renaissance* 16 (1986), 12.

Mora, Fernández de la. 'Maquiavelo, visto por los tratadistas políticos españoles de la Contrarreforma', *Arbor* 13 (1949), 417–49.

Morley, S. Griswold, and Courtney Bruerton. *The Chronology of Lope de Vega's 'Comedias'*. New York: The Modern Language Association of America, 1940.

Mullaney, Steven. *The Place of the Stage: License, Play and Power in Renaissance England*. Chicago: University of Chicago Press, 1988.

Mulryne, J.R, and Margaret Shewring (eds). *Theatre and Government under the Early Stuarts*. Cambridge: Cambridge University Press, 1993.

Olsen, S.H. *The Structure of Literary Understanding*. Cambridge: Cambridge University Press, 1978.

Orgel, Stephen. *The Illusion of Power: Political Theater in the English Renaissance*. Cambridge: Cambridge University Press, 1975.

Orgel, Stephen and Guy Fitch Lytle (eds). *Patronage in the Renaissance*. Princeton: Princeton University Press, 1981.

Oriel, Charles. *Writing and Inscription in Golden-Age Drama*. West Lafayette, Ind: Purdue University Press, 1992.

Parker, Alexander A. 'The King as Centre of Political Life', *The Mind and Art of Calderón: Essays on the Comedias*. Cambridge: Cambridge University Press, 1988, 241–9.

Parr, James A. 'Method as Medium and Message: Technique and its Discontents', *After Its Kind: Approaches to the Comedia*, ed. Matthew Stroud, Anne Pasero and Amy Williamsen. Kassel: Reichenberger, 1991, 107–17.

— 'Criticism and the Comedia: Twenty Years Later', ibid., 137–59.

— *Don Quixote: An Anatomy of Subversive Discourse*. Newark, Del: Juan de la Cueva, 1988.

Pasa, Arturo. *Un grande teorico della politica nella Spagna del secolo XVI: Il Gesuita Giovanni Mariana*. Naples: R. Alfredo, 1939.

Patterson, Annabel. *Censorship and Interpretation: The Conditions of Writing and Reading in Early Modern England*. Madison, Wisc.: University of Wisconsin Press, 1984.

Pechter, Edward. 'The New Historicism and Its Discontents: Politicizing Renaissance Drama', *Publications of the Modern Language Association of America* 102 (1987), 292–303.

Perret, D. 'On Irony', *Pragmatics Microfiche* 1.7: D3, Dept of Linguistics, University of Cambridge.

Pitt-Rivers, Julian. *The Fate of Shechem or The Politics of Sex: Essays in the Anthropology of the Mediterranean*. Cambridge: Cambridge University Press, 1977.

Portocarrero y Guzmán, Pedro. *Theatro monárquico de España*. Madrid: García Infanzón, 1700.

Puigdomenech, Helena. *Maquiavelo en España*. Madrid: Fundación Universitaria Española, 1988.

Quevedo y Villegas, Francisco de. *Obras*. Biblioteca de Autores Españoles, 23. Madrid: M. Rivadeneyra, 1852.

— *Política de Dios y gobierno de Cristo*, Primera Parte (1617). *Obras completas*, ed. Felicidad Buendía, I, *Obras en Prosa*, chap.1. Madrid: Aguilar, 1958.

— *Política de Dios y gobierno de Cristo*, ed. J.O. Crosby. Madrid: Castalia, 1966.

— 'Del Rey don Fernando el Católico al Primer Virrey de Nápoles', *Obras completas I: Obras en prosa*. Madrid: Aguilar, 1958, 704a.

Rennert, H.A., and A. Castro. *Vida de Lope de Vega (1562–1635): Notas adicionales de F. Lázaro Carreter*. Salamanca: Ediciones Anaya, 1969.

Rico, Francisco (ed.). *Historia y crítica de la literatura española* III, *Siglos de Oro*: Barroco, ed. Bruce W. Wardropper. Barcelona: Editorial Crítica, 1983.

Rivadeneyra, Padre Pedro de. *Obras escogidas*. Biblioteca de Autores Españoles, 60. Madrid: M. Rivadeneyra, 1868.

Rodríguez, Leandro. 'La función del monarca en Lope de Vega', *Lope de Vega y los orígenes del teatro español: Actas del primer congreso internacional sobre Lope de Vega*, dir. Manuel Criado del Val. Madrid: Edi-6 (1981), 799–804.

Rodríguez de Lancina, Juan Alfonso. *Comentarios políticos a los anales de Cayo Vero Cornelio Tácito*. Madrid: Melchor Alvárez, 1687.

Rozas, Juan Manuel. *Lope de Vega y Felipe IV en el 'Ciclo de Senectute'*. Cáceres: Universidad de Extremadura, 1982.

Rupp, Stephen. *Allegories of Kingship: Calderón and the Anti-Machiavellian Tradition*. University Park, Pa.: Pennsylvania State University Press, 1996.

Saavedra Fajardo, Diego. *Idea de un príncipe político-cristiano. Obras de Don Diego Saavedra de Fajardo*. Biblioteca de Autores Españoles, 25. Madrid: Atlas, 1947.

Salomon, Noël. *Recherches sur le thème paysan dans la 'comedia' au temps de Lope de Vega*. Bordeaux: Féret et fils, 1965.

Sanmartín Boncompte, Francisco, *Tácito en España*. Barcelona: Consejo Superior de Investigaciones Científicas, 1951.

Searle, J. *Expression and Meaning.* Cambridge: Cambridge University Press, 1979.

Seco Serrano, Carlos, ed. *Cartas de Sor María de Jesús de Ágreda y de Felipe IV*, Biblioteca de Autores Españoles 109. Madrid: Atlas, 1958.

Shannon, Robert M. *Visions of the New World in the Drama of Lope de Vega.* American University Studies, Series II: Romance Languages and Literature, vol.67. New York/Bern/Frankfurt am Main/Paris: Peter Lang, 1989.

Sharpe, Kevin, and Stephen N. Zwicker (ed.). *The Politics of Discourse: The Literature and History of Seventeenth-Century England.* Berkeley: University of California Press, 1987.

Silverman, J.H. 'Lope de Vega's Last Years and His Final Play', *Texas Quarterly* (Spring 1963), 174–87.

Sinfield, Alan. *Literature in Protestant England 1560–1660*. London: Croom Helm, 1982.

Skinner, Quentin. *The Foundations of Modern Political Thought*. 2 vols. Cambridge: Cambridge University Press, 1978.

— *Meaning and Understanding: Quentin Skinner and his Critics*, ed. and introd. by James Tully. Cambridge: Polity Press, 1988.

— *Liberty Before Liberalism*. Cambridge: Cambridge University Press, 1997

Skinner, Quentin, and Russell Price. *The Prince: Machiavelli*. Cambridge: Cambridge University Press, 1988.

Soons, Alan. *Juan de Mariana*. Boston: Twayne, 1982.

Sperber, Dan, and Deirdre Wilson. *Relevance, Communication and Cognition*. Oxford: Basil Blackwell, 1986.

Stern, Charlotte. 'Lope de Vega Propagandist?', *Bulletin of the Comediantes* 34, 1 (1982), 1–36.

Sterne, Laurence. *Tristram Shandy*. London: Everyman's Library, 1956.

Stone, Lawrence. *The Family, Sex and Marriage in England, 1500–1800*. London: Weidenfeld and Nicolson, 1977.

Stradling, R.A. *Philip IV and the Government of Spain, 1621–1665*. Cambridge: Cambridge University Press, 1988.

Strong, Roy. *The Cult of Elizabeth: Elizabethan Portraiture and Pageantry*. London: Thames and Hudson, 1987.

Suárez de Figueroa, Cristóbal. *El pasajero*, ed. Mª López Bascuñana. Barcelona: Promociones y Publicaciones Universitarias, S.A., 1988.

Sullivan, Henry W. *Tirso de Molina and the Drama of the Counter–Reformation*. Amsterdam: Rodopi, 1976.

Swietlicki, Catherine. 'Lope's Dialogic Imagination: Writing Other Voices of "Monolithic Spain" ', *Bulletin of the Comediantes* 40 (1988), 205–26.

Szondi, Peter. *Theorie des modernen Dramas*. Frankfurt: Suhrkamp, 1959.

Tannenhouse, Leonard. *Power on Display: The Politics of Shakespeare's Genres*. New York and London: Methuen, 1986.

Thomas, Keith. *Religion and the Decline of Magic*. London: Weidenfeld and Nicolson, 1971.

Thompson, I.A.A. (ed.). *Crown and Cortes: Government, Institutions and Representation in Early Modern Castile*. Aldershot/Brookfield, Vt: Variorum, 1993.

Tierno Galván, E. 'El tacitismo en las doctrinas políticas del Siglo de Oro español', *Escritos 1950–1960*. Madrid: Editorial Tecnos, 1971.

Tillyard, E.M.W. *The Elizabethan World Picture*. London: Chatto and Windus, 1943.

Tompkins, Jane P. 'The Reader in History: the Changing Shape of Literary Response', *Reader-Response Criticism: From Formalism to Post Structuralism* ed. Jane P. Tompkins. Baltimore/London: Johns Hopkins University Press, 1980.

Trevor-Roper, H. *Princes and Artists: Patronage and Ideology at Four Hapsburg Courts 1517–1633*. London: Thames and Hudson 1991 [first pub.1976].

Valiente, Francisco Tomás. *Los validos en la monarquía española*. Madrid: Instituto de Estudios Políticos, 1963.

Varey, J.E. 'Towards an Interpretation of Lope de Vega's *El villano en su rincón*', *Studies in Spanish Literature of the Golden Age Presented to Edward M. Wilson*, ed. R.O. Jones. London: Tamesis, 1973, 315–37.

— 'The Audience and the Play at Court Spectacles: the Role of the King', *Bulletin of Hispanic Studies* 61 (1984), 399–406.

Velasco, Ricaredo F. de. *Referencias y transcripciones para la historia de la literatura política en España*. Madrid: Editorial Reus, 1925.

Vickers, Brian. *Appropriating Shakespeare: Contemporary Critical Quarrels*. New Haven/London: Yale University Press, 1993.

Vives, Juan Luis. *De Concordia et Discordia in Humano Genere*, trans. Laureano Sánchez Gallego, *Concordia y discordia*. Mexico D.F.: Editorial Séneca, 1940.

Walker, Greg. *Plays of Persuasion: Drama and Politics at the Court of Henry VIII*. Cambridge: Cambridge University Press, 1991.

Wardlaw, Frances Day. '*El villano en su rincón*: Lope's Rejection of the Pastoral Dream', *Bulletin of Hispanic Studies* 58 (1981), 113–19.

Wardropper, Bruce W. *La comedia española del Siglo de Oro*. Madrid: Ariel, 1978.

Willett, John (ed.). *Bertold Brecht: Brecht on Theatre*. London: Methuen, 1964.

Williams, Raymond. *Marxism and Literature*. Oxford: Oxford University Press, 1977

Wilson, Margaret. *Spanish Drama of the Golden Age*. Oxford/London: Pergamon Press, 1969.

Wilson, Richard, and Richard Dutton (eds). *New Historicism and Renaissance Drama*. London: Longman, 1992.

Wittgenstein, Ludwig. *Philosophical Investigation*, 1945. Oxford: Oxford University Press, 1969.

Worden, Blair. 'Shakespeare and Politics', *Shakespeare Survey* 44 (1992), 1–15.

Young, Richard A. *La figura del rey y la institución real en la comedia lopesca*. Madrid: Ediciones José Porrúa Turanzas, 1979.

INDEX